Communication in a Globalised World

Let's Speak Up

Communication in a Globalised World

Let's Speak Up

Binod Mishra
Gajendra S Chauhan

AUTHORSPRESS

Worldwide Circulation through Authorspress Global Network
First Published 2009
by
Authorspress
E-35/103, Jawahar Park
Laxmi Nagar, Delhi-110092
e-mail: authorspress@yahoo.com

Communication in a Globalised World: Let's Speak Up
ISBN 978-81-7273-477-0

Printed in India at Tarun Offset, Delhi.

Foreword

Communication is the manifestation of an intellectual process set in motion by a congregation of complex factors. To make it effective what is required is the ability for a judicious, goal-specific deployment of these factors within the framework of linguistic, social, political and cultural constraints. With the globalisation of human activity in almost all domains, this task has become all the more complicated. The increasing diversity in the strategies of communication is sometimes offset by the growing multiplicity of expectations and requirements. Hence communication in the global context poses a challenge and demands deep thinking. There are works galore in this area and several of these have tried to provide the answer. But there are many concerns which have yet to be pointedly explored.

The present collection is an attempt in this direction. Dr. Binod Mishra and Dr. Gajendra Singh Chauhan have been able to put together in a single volume well-argued viewpoints and innovative ideas of quite a number of scholars in this area. The first article by the editors provides an apt background and sets the tone, as it were, for a discussion in the articles that follow. A variety of issues and aspects related to the theme have been dealt with in depth by the contributors. The collection is thus rich in terms of variety as well as coverage.

I am sure those interested in communication as a field of study, or as an activity for advancement in career, and for enrichment of personality, would find this volume rewarding and thought-provoking.

Krishna Mohan
Formerly Professor of English
BITS, Pilani

Foreword

Preface

The world today has become a global family, thanks to the ever spreading wings of communication. We live in an age where things change fast and we also accommodate with the same pace. This once again has become possible because of the nitty-gritty of communication. But as we go global, we come across many issues which we are unaware of and often land ourselves in the midst of confrontation, chaos and conflict because of our unfamiliarity with various subjects making us sensitive at times. In a global world, we have to communicate globally to negotiate, to deal and to enable our discussion reach its desired destination. The communication lines continue to open and as corporate, we have to expand. As societies undergo transition, so does culture, both in its popular form and in its deepest fabric. The rapid changes of the post-technological, post-modern society on the infotech highway spawn new thoughts, new lingo, newer departments, and ever changing styles of day-to-day life and time. Societies, too, grope to annex and reconcile with its ancient and new cultural identities.

As independent India went on to make rapid strides in all spheres, socialistic-mixed economy gave way to reforms and the current state of liberalisation and privatisation. Changes are fast and inevitable. The need to communicate and communicate effectively is the challenge before all of us. Today, it has become mandatory for the academicians, writers, thinkers, mediamen, advertisers and film-makers to rethink and revamp their communication strategies with the changing times.

The anthology in your hand is the outcome of our endeavours to cater to the growing needs of all concerned whose experiences and well-researched articles can address and come out with possible solutions to the challenges being posed in a globalised world of today. This book has been aimed at providing a platform for scholars and experts from various regions to share, and exchange their views and try to unearth the most 'politically correct' way to express themselves in the present global society and mitigate various critical, sensitive and touchy issues crippling many deals signed and unsigned. The anthology has 19 papers drawn from teachers and researches spread out both in and outside India.

The book opens with an introductory chapter on global communication. Binod Mishra and Gajendra Singh Chauhan have tried to give a comprehensive view of all the chapters relating to the theme of the book. An effort has been made to trace the challenges and suggest the remedies arising in the present day world. The duo is of the view that nothing in the world can strengthen the idea of global citizenship better than breaking all barriers of land, language and identity to foster the foundation of vasudaive kutumbakam (the world is one family) by merging the history and geography of the world causing more harm than good. They warn the communicators of the world not to ignore small issues which often debunk bigger realities.

Kumar Neeraj Sachdeva in his well researched paper raises many philosophical enquiries and suggests that it is only a normative stance that could lead to a meaningful global communication. He argues that a sympathetic, humanistic approach based on the notions of moral standards plays a key role in resolving the crisis that challenges global communication.

José Carlos Redondo Olmedilla in his exhaustive and well researched paper raises the issues of many globalisations. He is of the view that English will always stand as the force that galvanises globalisation. Quoting generously from different sources, Jose believes that the true essence of globalisation, in effect, can be realised by free flow of other languages too with English as a lingua franca. Globalisation encompasses agreement amid disagreement with a plausible amount of self-sufficiency lest the powerful dominate over the powerless in matters of culture, literature or set of values.

G. A. Ghanshyam & Devasree Chakravarti in their incisive paper present a historical account of how English, a language of the colonisers, has become an acceptable worldwide phenomenon. The role of English in ensuring globalisation has been so instrumental that though it has been some powerful nations' inheritance but it is everyone's possession in the present-day world.

Syed Nadeem Fatmi argues in his scholarly paper that the role of gender and culture cannot be ignored while extracting the meaning from a particular discourse. Examining language use, taking into consideration the user's background and gender also helps in unveiling significant discoveries since language use stems not only from nature but also from nurture. Such a measure will, as Nadeem proposes, eliminate the biases and make communication a global weapon in overcoming misunderstandings of all kinds.

Shubha Mukherjee in her incisive paper believes that the use of language in a global context can be realised only when it takes into consideration the various speech acts offering a universal acceptance. She accentuates that though the proliferation of mass media has brought a rapid change yet the sociocultural and linguistic capabilities of users often create the gaps between the intended and received messages.

Sangeeta Sharma in her incisive paper emphasizes the role of advertising in ensuring the spirit of globalisation. Though a commercial ploy, it has brought the entire world under one umbrella where all differences of language and culture sink making way for common vested interests. Dr. Sharma emphasizes that in addition to growing consumerism, advertising disseminates varied cultures and strengthens ties in the most effective way by adapting to the subtleties of products, people and paradigms.

Chandra Shekhar Sharma in his brilliant paper makes a historical analysis of communication in Bhutan. He is of the view that the communication scenario in Bhutan has to face the natural barriers but that doesn't dampen people's spirit to join the process of globalisation through various ways of communication.

Ashok Kumar in his short paper examines how the impact of information and technology has revolutionalised the lifestyle of people at local and global level. He emphasizes that the various forms and tools of communication have led to a newer level of consciousness to compete with the challenges that merit global concerns.

Tarika Singh in her scholarly paper underlines the importance of team communication in the success of organisations in today's world. A successful team communication, according to her, requires an open atmosphere in addition to the members' collective responsibility to ensure cooperation with an inquisitive and encouraging approach.

Vijay Kumar Pandey in his paper shows the role that gender plays in communication. His case study suggests that the fundamental gender differences contribute to the moderating role for attitudes and after sales service communications. According to him, organisations can accommodate customers' attitudinal change and keep pace with the changing need of the customer in order to cater to their demands.

Roopa Shinde & Anurag Joshi in their brilliant paper focus on the importance of corporate communication in establishing a global outlook. They consider corporate communication as an attitude towards communication or a set of mental habits that employees internalise. Corporate communication results in creating excellent communication practices that permeate an organisation and pave the way for globalisation which has become a worldwide phenmenon.

Priyanka Tripathi in her concise paper stresses the importance of technology in enhancing and ensuring the effectiveness of global communication. She is of the view that only an open mind and a positive approach instead of an ethnocentric vision may help in achieving this global outlook.

Anupama Kaushal in her paper discusses the problem of identity created by cyberspace. Taking a cue from Hari Kunjru's book, *Transmission,* she opines that the craze for cyberspace distances humans from their roots and it is again the same cyberspace that consoles them. Technological advancements might have brought mankind to a crossroad of challenges but to ensure order in a globalised world, we have to take the road taken by everyone.

R.C. Parida & D.P. Panda argue that corporate communication plays a significant role in combating the challenges of global world. They opine that corporate communication is a strategic management function which enables sharing of information and knowledge exchange with both internal and external groups. The duo emphasizes that effective communication with partners, prospects, customers, channels, employees, investors, shareholders and other stakeholders can contribute to the success of marketing plan and survival of the business in a globalised world.

Koyel Chakrabarty in her detailed paper on developmental communication traces how it has bridged the gap between the haves and the have-nots. The interpersonal communications of Indian visionaries with the rural masses have revolutionised the living conditions of the common masses bringing them to the mainstream of globalisation. She underlines the need of striking a balance to poise both labour-oriented and capital-oriented technologies to bring about a comprehensive development in India.

Prof. A.A.Khan & Dr. Qamar Talat in their joint paper emphasise the interference of technology in information processing. This right to privacy, according to them, is directly linked to the right to freedom and human autonomy. They are of the view that the information professionals who deal with private and personal information have to follow practical guidelines in the handling of these problems keeping into consideration the norms of freedom, truth and human rights.

B. Utpal makes a historical study of advertising in India and states how it has unified the rural and the urban divide. He also argues that Indian advertising has not only ameliorated the quality of life but it has also created an opportunity to abandon taboos and accommodate the challenges of globalisation through language, culture and beliefs. Despite the huge amount spent on advertising, it has created employment opportunities and increased consumerism and cultural proliferation both among the old and the young resulting in knowledge expansion as well.

Sunil K. Rai in his paper emphasizes that excellence in communication is the stepping stone of leadership the world over. He brings in various theories and refers to the contestations made by many celebrated philosophers who examine the concept of communication in their own ways.

The anthology could not have been possible without the co-operation of our scholar contributors who kept egging us on our dream project. We thank them from the core of our heart for their scholarship and also for their patience. We place on record our profound respect to our teachers, Prof. Pashupati Jha (IIT, Roorkee), Prof. Pratap Narayan Jha (LNMU, Darbhanga)., Prof. M.R Verma (Gurukul Kangri, Hardwar) Prof. Charusheel Singh (Kashi Vidyapeeth, Varanasi), Prof. B.K. Khan (BRCM, Bahal, Haryana), Prof. B.Y. Lalithaba (Bangalore), Dr. Shoeb Adil (Indore), and Dr Sumpam Tangjang (Arunachal Pradesh), who have always exhorted us in our ventures. We extend our indebtedness to Prof. Krishna Mohan (BITS, Pilani) who despite his illness read the manuscript patiently and wrote a foreword to the anthology. We also register our gratitude to our friends Dr. S.K Pandey (NDA, Khadagwasla), Shri Shiva Shanker Jha (J.M. College, Assam), Dr. G.S. Jha (Arunachal Pradesh) and Dr. Rahul Banerjee (BITS, Pilani) who have always given us sane suggestions and applauded our efforts. We shall be failing in our duties if we do not mention a word of appreciation for our colleagues both at IIT Roorkee & BITS Pilani, for their suitable advice and timely suggestions in the preparation of the manuscript of this anthology. We are also thankful to Prerna Priyadarshini and Abhyudaya Anand who typed the manuscript patiently.

Our sincerest thanks are also due to Sudarshan Kcherry, the M.D. of Authorspress, New Delhi, for reposing faith in us and bringing this volume out in time. The staff members of Authorspress also deserve mention for their active help and cooperation. We do hope that the book will successfully address the issues raised in the anthology and suggest remedies for the communication challenges being faced around the globe. The responses of the readers will act as the feedback in ensuring the relevance of the anthology.

May, 2008

Binod Mishra
Gajendra Singh Chauhan

List of Contributors

Anupama Kaushal, Lecturer in English, Govt. P.G.College, Tonk, Rajasthan.

Anurag Joshi, Lecturer, Humanities, Shri Vaishnav Institute of Technology & Science, Indore, Madhya Pradesh.

A.A. Khan, Professor of English, Govt. College, Utai, Durg Chattisgarh.

Ashok Kumar, Government College, Agaspur P.O., Jayanteshwar Dist. Almura, Uttarakhand.

Binod Mishra, Assistant Professor of English, Department of Humanities & Social Sciences, IIT Roorkee, Uttarakhand.

B. Utpal, Lecturer, M.P. Christian College of Engineering & Technology, Bhilai Chattisgarh.

Chandra Shekhar Sharma, Lecturer, College of Science and Technology, Phuentsholing. Post Box: 450 Bhutan.

Devasree Chakravarti, Research Scholar, Pt. Ravi Shankar Shukla University, Raipur (C.G.) India.

D. P. Panda, Sr. Lecturer, Department of Commerce, J. N. (Govt.) College, Pasighat, Arunachal Pradesh-791103.

Gajendra Singh Chauhan, Assistant Professor of English, Languages Group, BITS Pilani, Rajasthan.

G. A. Ghanshyam, Assistant Professor of English, Govt. Arts College, Seepat, Bilaspur, Chattisgarh.

José Carlos Redondo Olmedilla, University of Almería (SPAIN).

Koyel Ckakrabarty, Lecturer in English, BRCM College of Engineering and Technology, Bahal, Bhiwani, Haryana.

Kumar Neeraj Sachdev, Assistant Professor, Humanistic Studies Group, Birla Institute of Technology and Science, Pilani - 333 031, Rajasthan.

Syed Nadeem Fatmi, Lecturer, Humanistic Studies Group, BITS, Pilani – 333 031 (Rajasthan).

Priyanka Tripathi, Research Scholar, Dept. of Hum & Social Sciences, Indian Institute of Technology, Kharagpur, West Bengal.

Qamar Talat, Professor of English, Govt. V.Y.T. PG Autonomous College, Durg.

R.C. Parida, Reader & Head, Department of Commerce, Rajiv Gandhi (Central) University, Rono Hills, Itanagar-791112, Arunachal Pradesh.

Roopa Shinde, Lecturer, Humanities, Shri Vaishnav Inst. of Tech. & Science Indore, Madhya Pradesh.

Shubha Mukherjee, Senior Lecturer, Department of English, Sathyabama University, Chennai.

Sunil K. Rai, Salwan Public School, Gurgaon.

Sangeeta Sharma, Assistant Professor, Languages Group, Birla Institute of Technology and Science, Pilani - 333 031, Rajasthan.

Tarika Singh, Lecturer, Prestige Institute of Management, Airport Road, Gwalior-474020, Madhya Pradesh.

Vijay Kumar Pandey, Lecturer, Prestige Institute of Management, Airport Road, Near Deendayal Nagar, Gwalior-474020, Madhya Pradesh.

Contents

1

Global Communication : Challenges and Remedies

—*Binod Mishra* and *Gajendra Singh Chauhan*

Broadly, communication can be defined as a process which helps in the dissemination of information for greater common good. In an age of information and technology, communication has become an essential ingredient much like our food and clothing. The communication revolution has brought a drastic change in the living standard of the masses. The effects of this revolution are visible in the way of people's dress, speech and disposition. Moreover, a majority of organisations the world over have provided computers in their offices and people find it easier to gather information the moment they want, than glossing over files and registers eaten away by worms. Educational institutes, too, have put important information on their websites and have eased the toils of travel.

It may today appear ridiculous to think of the past when the pigeons used to carry messages and telegrams used to be the only way to send urgent information whether of joy or of sorrow. A child of today will outrightly reject the cumbersome procedure of the collection and distribution of news much before Reuter's innovation. The postman's job, too, nowadays has become questionable. The helplessness has come to such a pass that the postmen, instead of distributing letters and parcels, have been put to distribute telephone bills. No wonder if their services are also utilised to distribute electricity bills etc. But then, of course, in a country like ours, the postman's role is being confined to rural areas and that too where telephonic facilities are not available. But one cannot deny that the postman's bag is becoming thinner day by day.

Communication has globalised the world today and there is no exaggeration to say that the world has shrunk into a global village—a worldwide interconnected and interdependent community. The Internet has become a panacea to all queries. The telephone, which used to be a luxury, has become a need. Land-lines have become redundant even in government offices. Many organisations have provided cell phones to their employees and they see to it that no information escapes them. In many companies intercom facilities are used adequately. This has minimised the disturbances caused by employee's arrival for every piece of information/ advice. No doubt, the frequent ringing of phones, though irritating at times, has become a part of workplace. The open atmosphere of communication has mythicised the olden decorum of who should talk to whom and when. The focus today is mainly on being connected to the office, home and to one's kinsmen.

Infocentric Society

In today's world people have become wildly information crazy. It has grown to such an extent that calls during meeting hours too are not unwelcome though careful people take the caution of keeping their cells on silent mode. In the recent years we have noticed a sea-change even in the usage of cell phones. The idea of switching off their cells during journey too has become obsolete since the roaming charges have been slashed. I do remember an acquaintance of mine who told me that he had never switched off his cell since the day he bought it.

Communication has led to a new consciousness among all classes of people. The STD booths of the past have been substituted by Internet cafes. People carry their cell phones much like their handkerchiefs and pens. They book their tickets (bus, trains and flights) from their houses and pay through credit cards. Another milestone is the introduction of ATM counters throughout the nation. Travellers do not need to carry travellers' cheque, rather an ATM or a credit card. It is the blessing of communication that you have the home in the form of your cell and happiness in the form of your ATM card.

People can make their transaction online, write their exams online, arrange and participate in their meeting through teleconferencing. Online tests are soon going to substitute the pen and paper exams. In fact, many institutes have already started computer-based online tests. This has not only minimised the excessive use of papers but has helped in prompt publication of results. The idea of a paperless office will soon become a reality. For young impressionable minds, the Internet is a tool to be handled with care and supervision. We don't know if they are chatting with a kidding pervert, seeing pornography, downloading illegal files or viruses and other bad software. Well, the Internet comes with Jekyll and Hyde character. We love the fact that we can find any information within a few minutes, and we love the fact we can make a good living via the Internet but we also hate all the bad things out there, which can hurt us, our children and our property (Chauhan, 2007).

Global Forces

The world scenario after September 11 has changed dramatically. It has revealed the gaps in communication and also the other side of various means of communication. A handful of people showed the world the ugly face of how modern means of communication could be misused. The incident brought death and devastation in America but shocked the citizens of the world too.

Globalisation has affected the world in many ways. Ethnicity in the present world has its limited connotation and world citizenship is on the rise. The signing of many new pacts and exchange of ideas on the issues of non-alignment, CTBT, nuclear deals symbolize a welcome sign. The echoes of globalisation can be felt in the world of marketing where both Indian and foreign products are getting momentum. The most common examples are Samsung, Nokia, L.G. etc. The dissemination of culture worldwide is a case in point. The holding of beauty contests, international conferences and symposiums not only helps in the exchange of information but also the exchange of lifestyle and culture. The recent move of IPL is an innovation to familiarise the cricketers of the world with the techniques and ploys of cricketers from all the corners of the world. The cricketers not only get lucrative offers but are also made to understand each other's cultural and climatic conditioning. The advertisers and traders make a lot of money and the spectators in addition to extracting entertainment also get to watch the tricks and intrigues of cricketers all around the world. To a greater extent, the idea of harmonising foreign players with adverse conditions in order to develop tolerance and accommodating with the unaccommodating is born of nothing but globalisation.

Internet Lingo

Globalisation has also affected the use of English in people's everyday life. The Internet's most favoured language, English, is also redefining and reshaping itself with the changing times. While communicating via the Internet, we find it as a lingo of youngsters—a distinct variety that is young, vibrant and enough to mention generation gap. It is the youngsters who make it fanciful and love to play with its basic structure. They write as they speak and make it more 'cool and 'off beat' than actually it is. The "Netlish" is very infectious and it is catching up with standard language. There is no formal set of instructions to guide how to use English in Internet communication but we tend to use the way our youngsters do it. For them, it is a new media to explore their imagination and innovative skills to coin new usages for different expressions. Let it be an SMS, email, or chats, it works on acronyms and abbreviations. English on the Net mainly consists of letters of the alphabet, numbers, smiley, etc. We doubt, if we keep on using the language with its pervasive volatile character, perhaps one day we'll be having our primitive language system where our forefathers had expressed themselves through gestures and body movements. Thanks to the Internet, the world is going to be the same again (Chauhan, 2007).

Socio-global Consciousness

Effective communication is at the heart of every activity. Effective communication builds a healthy learning environment, where we all are receptive and ready to share and learn. Let it be a professional world with boss, peers and subordinates or a company of our own friends and relatives; we communicate to make sense In fact, poor communication or no communication is at the bottom of every problem we are facing today. Effective communication is all about reaching out and reaching convincingly. There has never been a pertinent time to recognise Al Gore for the Nobel Prize for Peace. It is Al Gore who made climate change a part of family dinner table conversation. The reason why his achievement is in many ways outstanding is simply because he has been able to reach out to people across cultures and continents even if they don't understand the science behind the issue. To be able to communicate to a large number of people from different persuasions, to be able to get across a complicated message to the common citizen, is a more onerous task than, say, sophisticated technology transfer between countries or even planning a space mission (Ganesh, 2007).

A Fragmented Society

Times have changed. Technology has brought offices into homes, but has life changed for the better? In recent decades, the processes of social change – modernisation, urbanisation and technological change leading to urban migration, employment of women outside the home, nuclear families – have created an increasingly aloof and fragmented society (Sujatha C 2007). We are becoming more and more insensitive, insecure and irresponsible. A similar concern is echoed by IIT Mumbai. It has restricted daytime Internet access from hostel blocks as it was leading to a drop in attendance, poor sleep patterns and an environment in the hostels where students were unaware who was living next door.

Express Yourself

Although we are always connected in the 24x7 virtual world, it is more important we are connected by heart-a-heart that is full of grace and soul filled with openness. It is not the hotline but the communication between open hearts which may put an end to all the worries globally. We feel that the whole world would be a nice place to dwell in when we all believe and practise the Airtel's brand message "Express Yourself". It doesn't mean that people don't express themselves but they fail to express meaningfully. When Osama's men expressed their frustration by demolishing the WTC, Mr. Bush and his allies immediately retaliated by attacking a neutral nation like Afghanistan. In both actions, the communication took place but it yielded no constructive outcome. It is a grim situation that prevails globally and disturbs the humanity in the absence of effective communication. Ironically the world order is changing fast in a borderless world where peace talks and negotiation deals fail with each side claiming its respective rights to territorial sovereignty, economic parity and cultural autonomy (James Leigh 2004). Let it be India or Pakistan, Bush or Laden, it is the writing clearly on the wall appealing to its honourable citizens of the world to be more caring, sensitive and adaptive to each other's nature and needs in order to live happily and peacefully ever.

Conclusion

The world is getting smaller, as people like to say, but it is not coming together. Indeed as economies are drawn closer, nations, cities and neighbourhoods are being pulled apart. The processes of global economic integration are stimulating political and social disintegration (Barnet and Cavanagh 1995). There is no upright solution to what should we do and how should we live to overcome the culture of conflict in this world. It is the responsibility of every nation and individual to channelise the efforts to help each other and communicate to build a strong bond of trust, mutual understanding and communal harmony. Globalisation has given an important term—'networking'. We should all strive to network people and institutions at some common platform where we all are mature and sensible to appreciate each other's cultural, political and social differences.

In the course of recognising and dealing with global-scale problems, we tend to look for 'big' solutions, forgetting how little things can make a big difference. We live in a global village. Let our global village be free from fear, greed, violence and terror. Let us keep the human and physical environment clean and healthy. Let us protect it from sheer technocentric activity and capricious consumerism. Let us learn to be human first and follow the ancient Indian philosophy of 'vasudhaiva kutumbakam', that is, 'the whole world is but one family', which promotes global citizenship and a culture of peace. Let us speak up for a more uniform and homogeneous world, with a global culture uniting all mankind into a single universal community, unfettered by war, ethnic conflict and inequality, and live life peacefully, purposefully and prosperously.

Cited Works

Barnet, R. and Cavanagh, J. 1995. *Global Dreams: Imperial Corporations and the New World Order*. New York, Touchstone.

Mishra, Binod. 2007. Technology & Communication: Myth or Reality. Paper presented in International Seminar on Contemporary Trends in Language, Discourse and Cultural Studies, January 20-21, 2007, Gurunanakdev University, Amritsar.

Chauhan, Gajendra S. 2007. Empowering Education through New Technology: Let Learning be Simple, Human and Valuable. Paper presented at Sixth Asia CALL International Conference on "Computers and Language Learning Technologies in and for the Developing Economies" organised by IIM Indore, November 17-19, 2007.

Ganesh, Narayani. A Great Communicator. *Times of India,* 16 October 2007, New Delhi ed.:14.

James Leigh. 2004, *Reflections of Babylon: Intercultural Communication and Globalisation in the New World Order.*

Sujata, C. The Shrinking Social Space of a Digital Child, *The Hindu,* 4 March 2007.

2

The Need for a Normative Stance of Global Communication

—*Kumar Neeraj Sachdeva*

INTRODUCTION

Communication is a partnership that begins from a willingness to convey, listen and understand an idea. The idea as such is an act of mind that occurs in the mind of a person who makes an effort to respond to the changing conditions in the world, and feels naturally disposed to communicate his response to others in the world. The sharing and understanding of an idea begins from a mutual exchange of symbols and signs.

The making of an idea implies the dynamic presence of attitudes and belief systems. And the effective communication of an idea does involve resourcefulness and skilfulness that reflect in regular components of communication such as speaking, writing, and listening. The non-verbal accompaniments of oral communication, for example: gestures, voice, pitch, and facial contact, play an equally important role (Sen, 3). The uniform and intelligible style of written communication contributes to the effective communication of an idea. Be the case as it may, I wish to maintain that one ought to cultivate a normative stance to build a foundation from which mindful and meaningful communication may spring. And in this direction one is expected to go an extra mile to meet the requirements of global communication as it requires cross-cultural connectivity.

In view of the above, I touch upon and argue for in the paper the need for a normative stance of global communication. The term 'global' refers to something that operates all around the world, for example trade, technology or even terror. We happen to witness such an operation in terms of a continuous expansion of human activity whether economic, political or cultural. The expansion of human activity, is mediated through compression of space. And the means of compression of space are transport, communication and information technologies. Thus, global communication is a very important means to enable the expansion of human activity. The nature of human activity and its expansion, of course, determine the corresponding contours of global communication. In any case, one has to go beyond cultural boundaries for information resolution because one cannot achieve the target of information resolution in the comfort of one's cultural cocoon.

Global communication, as such, is an attempt among humans, despite their mutually remote geographical location or political divides, to connect with each other to achieve information resolution. The purpose of global communication may vary. Humans may want to connect for sharing and finding solutions to economic, religious or political problems. The examples given are general but still do not exhaust the list of purposes. Whatever the purpose of global communication may be, we are witness to enormous difficulties attached to the idea of global communication itself. Since humans find it difficult to connect in their own local communities because of varied beliefs, attitudes and goals, it becomes all the more difficult to imagine a smooth transaction of global communication. This is why, the issue before hand is to touch upon a normative stance of global communication, which may be meaningful and justifiable for information resolution.

Specifically, I argue that the recognition of a normative stance of global communication may strengthen the means of expansion of human activity; the reason being such means generally work on amoral assumptions, which are primarily meant to secure the regional or national interests. And the recognition of a normative stance, namely Hume's conception of natural human sentiment of "sympathy", may bring in the requisite elements in a given means like concern for good human life, freedom and impartiality, which are required to have equal regard for all affected stakeholders such as individuals, groups or nations.

Global Communication and Good Life

Global communication as a means for information resolution is an ideal. It assumes a space and time where conflict-free interaction among all humans occurs. This is anyway highly improbable since there is a wide range of behaviour and personal circumstances that mark the life of all human beings. This implies that either there can be a conflict free situation or there is no individuality that characterises us as human beings. And if individuality holds the grain of truth, then one may accept the inevitable occurrence of conflict especially with regard to conflicting beliefs, judgments and desires. Bernard Mayor contends that "... conflict is natural, inevitable, necessary, and normal, and that the problem is not the existence of conflict but how we handle it" (Mayor 3).

Anyhow, whatever the contours of global communication may be, the striving for information resolution remains a worthwhile exercise. It resembles and in a way supports the idea of a good human life. The majority of humans directly or indirectly make attempts to realise the ideal of global communication much like they strive to live a good human life. A human being, for example, in a reflective stance decides to speak the truth as a part of his desire to live a good human life. He strives to speak the truth in the given situation and thereby retains the associated tendency to repeat the act of speaking the truth, which is an equivalent of cultivating the virtue of truth. Similarly, making attempts to bring in step-by-step improvement in the existing situation of communication is, thus, considered to be a situation of progress. And global communication is nothing but a sum total of such improvements in particular existing situations.

It is a well-known fact that humans do not resolve information related issues in the first attempt. They get into conflicts to secure their needs, interests and identities (Mayor 17). And conflict, if pertaining to cross-border disputes, at times, metamorphoses into irreconcilable issues. Indo-Pak border or Israel-Palestine border disputes on the one hand and war-like conflicts among various religious groups on the other indicate the complexities involved in global communication. The listing of such problematic issues does not imply that we humans do not want information resolution for peace in our region or elsewhere. In fact, many terrorist groups in the event of border disputes claim to create terror in order to compel the people of ruling class to agree with their social or political design and restore peace. They do not realise, however, that the attack on innocent civilians or the state infrastructure has never offered a solution for peace.

On the other hand, many stakeholders and facilitators opt for various routes of communication to bring in peace. They approximate the ideal through various processes such as social, political or religious. It is noteworthy to observe, however, that decision-makers or policy makers work through such processes on a set of assumptions, which are generally amoral in nature. They seldom pay attention to the need for a normative stance of global communication. They talk of adopting a practical approach – an approach based upon calculation of consequences that are geared to protect regional or national interests (McMahan 384).

I propose to look for a normative stance of such processes namely Hume's conception of the natural human sentiment of "sympathy". A normative stance of global communication is a pervasive and crucial ingredient. It is pervasive because it forms the basis of value-oriented communication – compassionate, truthful, honest and trustworthy. And it is crucial because it allows a communicator to cultivate inner transparency at an individual level and establish an ethically comprehensive link with others at a group level. But first a brief look at the nature of ethics will help to connect the idea of sympathy as a normative stance of global communication.

Nature of Ethics

Ethics is a study of values, virtues, rules or principles to live a good human life. How should one live a good human life, or, what ought one to do in a particular situation, is a fundamental question of ethics that every one of us faces sometime or the other and we try to answer in someway. We happen to face this question on our own because it is a natural human inclination to improve upon the way we live. Living a good human life, thus, is a goal that we all strive to attain.

However, we stumble many a times on the way to achieve the goal of living a good human life because we find it difficult to discover the correct path. But it is possible for a human being at any given moment of his life to reflect upon what he thinks or does. This is exactly where the role of ethics assumes vital dimension. The role of ethics is to enable us to be reflective – to reflect upon and understand the nature of good human life.

David Hume on Sympathy

I propose that the source of reflective understanding of good human life may align with David Hume's conception of 'sympathy', or 'humanity', or 'fellow-feeling'. He suggests that the sentiment of sympathy is universal because it is natural to be human and to have the sentiment of sympathy. It is, of course, not to be understood in the narrow sense in which it is now commonly used, to mean something like 'compassion' or 'pity'. Richard Norman informs:

> He means by it a capacity to be moved or affected by the happiness and suffering of others – to be pleased when others prosper, and distressed when others suffer. He insists that sympathy, thus understood, is an independent human tendency which exists in its own right (Norman 53).

Everyone, thus understood, is to some extent affected by the happiness or suffering of others. It is not about an impractical claim that everyone is always motivated by feelings of kindness and concern for others or we have nobody who acts inconsiderately or cruelly towards others. Hume simply asks us to envisage a situation where someone is incapable of responding to people as human beings. He behaves as if other human beings are toys or chairs. This cannot be true in case of a normal human being. He does possess the feeling of sympathy for humanity (Norman 60).

We may note, however, that the sentiment of sympathy itself is not a morally admirable quality but the source of all morally admirable qualities. For the sentiment of sympathy denotes not an object of approval but the source of moral approval. And this may further imply that since we have this capacity we are inclined to morally praise or blame people in so far as they exhibit morally admirable or deplorable qualities. We respond favourably to personal qualities like benevolence, justice, cheerfulness, modesty, decency and politeness because they are either useful or agreeable to their possessor or to others. In other words, they are directly or indirectly advantageous to the possessor or others. The possession of such qualities promotes happiness and it is through sympathy with happiness, whether of the individual possessor or of general sort, that we admire such qualities. And, through the same mechanism, it is natural again that we blame people so far as they bring in suffering, the opposite of happiness.

The sentiment of sympathy, Hume goes on to add, denotes a fellow-feeling. It takes one out of one's language of self-love. He maintains:

> When a man denominates another his enemy, his rival, his antagonist, his adversary, he is understood to speak the language of self-love, and to express sentiments peculiar to himself and arising from his particular circumstances and situation. But when he bestows on any man the epithets of vicious or odious or depraved, he then speaks another language, and expresses sentiments in which he expects all his audience are to concur with him. He must here, therefore, depart from his private and particular situation and must choose a point of view common to him with others; he must move some universal principle of the human frame (Hume Section IX, Paragraph 6)

This universal principle is the natural human sentiment of sympathy that Hume wants us to invoke.

Sympathy as a Normative Stance of Global Communication

We may adopt the universal principle of sympathy to bring in the ideal of global communication for information resolution. It may be noted that no aspect of human life is exclusive in itself or value neutral. All aspects of life, social or personal, are interconnected. We cannot, for instance, say that a person's life has no bearing upon his relations with his family members or members of society in general. Or anybody may do anything in his life and claim that it would have no bearing upon the social fabric or the way he should live a good human life. The point being made here is that we must come out of value neutral stance that we may adopt in a communication process for protecting sectarian interests and recognise the need for admitting a normative stance of any such process that we as a group may undertake.

The recognition of natural sentiment of sympathy as a normative stance may strengthen other processes such as social, political, or religious to attain the ideal of global communication for information resolution. The front page headline of *Sunday Times of India,* New Delhi on November 19, 2006 quotes Afghan president Hamid Karzai, "Karzai Pushes Pakistan to Do More Against Taliban" and as reported in *The Week,* May 13, 2007 Pakistan president Pervez Musharraf reacts, "The ones who do nothing against terrorism, like Karzai, are those who criticise the ones who fight, like us." This example shows a small part of ongoing global communication as a means of finding a solution to a socio-political problem, which rests on the calculation of consequences to secure national or group interests – explicit interests of Afghanistan, Pakistan and Taliban and implicit interests of India, USA, and of course the newspaper and the weekly news magazine. And if the utility of a normative stance of global communication in the above-mentioned context is recognised, the headline could be, "Karzai and Musharraf Resolve to Contain Taliban". Such a collective human response would accommodate a greater degree of uniformity. It is not easy though. Hume maintains:

> Sympathy, we shall allow, is much fainter than our concern for ourselves, and sympathy with persons remote from us much fainter than that with persons near and contiguous; but for this very reason it is necessary for us, in our calm judgments and discourse concerning the characters of men, to neglect all these differences and render our sentiments more public and social (Hume Section V, Paragraph 42)

Hume suggests here the adoption of criteria such as freedom, impartiality, conceptual clarity, and information about all possible relevant facts to correct the operation of sympathy, so that we may attach equal moral importance to the happiness or suffering of ourselves and others.

The recognition of sympathy and its correct application, therefore, may bring in the requisite elements in global communication like concern for human life, freedom and impartiality, which in turn gets translated into equal regard for all affected stakeholders such as individuals, groups or nations in the given political spectrum. It is equally true of other processes such as religious process – if it is sectarian and ritualistic and social process – if it is sectarian and partial to bring in the requisite changes in the recognition of a normative stance that is sympathy or humanity.

Conclusion

We may conclude that the recognition of a normative stance of global communication is necessary. And second, the recognition of a normative stance in the form of sympathy or humanity may definitely be an answer to a morally meaningful and justifiable global communication because it helps in strengthening the processes such as political, social or religious. The strengthening of processes may figure in impartial fellow-feeling that reflects in having an equal regard for all affected parties such as individuals, groups or nations. Such an impartial fellow feeling, therefore, is not a mere cosmetic requirement but a life-thread of global communication.

Cited Works

Hume, David. *Enquiry Concerning the Principles of Morals*, first published 1751.

Mayor, Bernard. *The Dynamics of Conflict Resolution*, San Francisco: Wiley Company, 2000.

McMahan, Jeff. "War and Peace", in *A Companion to Ethics*. Oxford, edited by Peter Singer, UK: Blackwell Publishers, 1993.

Norman, Richard. *The Moral Philosophers: An Introduction to Ethics*, Oxford: Oxford University Press, Second Edition, 1998.

Sen, Leena. *Communication Skills*, New Delhi: Prentice-Hall of India, 2004.

3

Nuances on the Paradoxes of Language, Culture and Society in a Globalised World

—José Carlos Redondo Olmedilla

To tell any story that implies any analysis on globalisation in a measured but engaging way is a hard task. It is an analysis torn between admiration and fear. Globalisation can be analysed by itemising it into different aspects, elements involving the intensity, speed and degree of change or any other patterns of interchange. At the same time, this observable fact can also be understood as multiple, i.e., there is not one, but different globalisations.

Grant Kien affirmed that exploring globalisation requires reconciliation "between the traditionally binary contests of materialism versus idealism."[1] Whichever the stand one takes, common elements are to be regarded within globalisation. Some important remarkable features associated to this phenomenon that one cannot ignore are the significance of mass culture in contemporary societies, the spread of the English language and the expansion of North American culture and the new information and technology society together with its implications on the new mass-media. These elements are powerful homogenising agents that go beyond language, region or nation barriers and that contribute to a new system of common values. When we speak of globalisation, we speak of interconnections in all the fields and in the different regions of the world and about the way they transform through time.

For many globalisation is a wrong concept or at least one that is rather unsatisfactory in its scope. Paul Hirst, David Held and Anthony McGrew[2] wondered how is it possible that the term 'global'—literally meaning a universal phenomenon—is, in fact, nowadays a synonym of 'Westernisation' or 'Americanisation'. It is also about which side you are. We can even use Harold Bloom's terminology and white or black it. Are you an apocalyptic or are you an integrate? Stan Smith said, when referring to the phenomenon, that 'for some it is a secular version of the Fall; for others the promise of Redemption'.[3] It is also true that no accurate interpretation of globalisation has reached the status of orthodoxy in the academia, though it is also clear that there are challenging theories fighting for the supremacy. The idea of globalisation itself seems to alter the patterns and the settled political orthodoxies. It is an idea that creates new political alignments and continuous repositionings. It is also about recognising and, in this sense Kien stated that "Recognising the pluralism of motivations behind the state and globalisation suggest a need to accommodate a pluralistic analytical approach."[4]

We find today a panorama in which the old local self-sufficiency and isolationism have been replaced for all-directions traffic. There is a new general interdependence in the nations. But it also happens in the intellectual field. The intellectual products of the different countries become an international wealth. The limitations and the national exclusivisms turn more unworkable every day, and a new universal literature grows and takes shape from the multiple national literatures. The interpretation of globalisation and its multiple positioning have left a plethora of new terms and concepts: 'globalisation', 'overlapping fields of global-local linkages,' 'offshoring', 'overarching umbrella', 'ethnocentrism', 'acculturation', 'coca-colonisation', 'globalised panlocality', 'transnationality of commodity chains', 'cultural miscegenation'... Everyone is able to see how the nature of work is changing around the world; modern technologies and anti-capitalist protest have thrust globalisation into the spotlight. Sharon Ouditt[5] referred to a speech delivered by Tony Blair to Members of the European Parliament in Brussels on the eve of Britain's six-month presidency of the European Union. He remembers Tony Blair's warning: "If European nations... decide to huddle together, hoping we can avoid globalisation... then we risk failure on a grand, strategic scale."[6] The same kind of not, but yes or vice versa can be applied to the present state of globalisation. For many it is a positive idea, eroding frontiers means suppressing barriers and we know that it makes communication and any kind of exchange much easier. For them, these are the glorious days of global capitalism. The mix of technology and economic integration transforming the world has created unparalleled prosperity. In the rich world labour's share of GDP has fallen to historic lows, while profits are soaring. Apparently everything is good, but not everything is so rosy. On economic and marketing terms obvious perks are going to be obtained, but what are we going to obtain if we derived a scientific analysis?

As we know, the Swiss Ferdinand de Saussure (1857-1913) was the starting point of structuralism and one of the linguists who laid the foundation for much of the progress of the linguistic sciences of our time. Among the many relevant ideas that he put forward was the principle that a language is a self-contained relational structure, the elements of which originate their existence and importance from their distribution and oppositions in the discourse. The idea of opposition is crucial to understand the relational world within language, and it is the distinctive feature that makes one linguistic sign different from another. As we know, Saussure stated that distinctive features are essential to language, in fact, they are the quintessence of it, and we can add that they are the tools of communication. They have a rich operational environment and can be determined through absence or presence.

Language homogenisation and language globalisation contradict the basic principles of language and communication in some terms, as in many ways the global linguistic ergonomics tends to one language. If language and communication are sustained upon the values of distinction, any suppression of distinctiveness is going to curb communication. Today's situation can also be understood as a cultural paradox made of two coalescing forces tending to suppress each other. If we become apocalyptic for a while, we can pay attention to Will Durant (1885-1981) when he affirmed that "a great civilisation is not conquered from without until it has destroyed itself within."[7] But what is the big civilisation? Is it the West of our age? Is this opening the gates of globalisation the clearest manifestation that the West is definitely disappearing from the inside? Is it that things are falling apart because the centre cannot hold?

Jean François Lyotard, Roland Barthes, Michael Foucault and Jacques Derrida were all from the far left, and referred affectionately by adherents as 'the pomos'–post-modern–. They wanted to destroy capitalism and the bourgeois society. We know that all these critics wrote about many aspects of society—literature, sociology, psychology, architecture—and scarcely about economics, but most of them sought to unfetter the individual from authority and state power, and that is why, in one way or another, they surreptitiously supported globalisation. What apparently was a confrontation of principles between the Marxist guided credos and the neo-liberalist ones is, in fact, now a corporative society that is working well. It is all about giving the impression of totality but keeping the principle of niches. And that in terms of market is market liberalisation with the success of globalisation. It is based upon the idea of totality that retails individually according to the individual liking. In this sense the 'pomos' ideas are successful. An insightful article in *The Economist* (December 23rd, 2006) referred to Chris Anderson's description of the "shattering of the mainstream into a sillion different cultural shards" and how the post-modern 'fragment' becomes a 'niche' and the mass market is "turning into a mass of niches". Chris Rollason, in an insightful study about the Nobel Prize winner for Literature in 1998 José Saramago and his work *A Caverna* (2001), analyses the way the shopping mall looms over the whole of the novel. He traces the origins of the shopping centres in the arcades and links them to an unfinished study by Walter Benjamin, but what strikes us even more is the mention made by Benjamin to the 'dream and wish-image of the collective':

> Today shopping-centres have their origins in the arcades, or "passages", of nineteenth-century Paris. As socio-historical phenomenon the arcades need no introduction, having been immortalised by Walter Benjamin in his immense unfinished study Das Passagen-werk (The Arcades Project), which occupied his attention across the 1930s and is today seen as one of the key books of the twentieth century.... Viewing the arcades as constituting "the most important architecture of the nineteenth century" (834), Benjamin reads them as a historically ambiguous, Janus-faced phenomenon, a "dream and wish image of the collective.[8]

Although, basically the symbolism of the Shopping-Mall in *A Caverna* makes the reader see the work as an icon of resistance to globalisation's cultural homogeneity, other nuances can be inferred and positive routes, such as human communication, can be found in the work.

The discourse of modernity and the phenomenon of globalisation tune magnificently among each other and what initially was intended as a weapon to destroy capitalism is paradoxically its best ally. We find that the new marketing uses the tools of the diversified post-modern discourse. Microcultures in globalisation, that is the paradox. It is the fallacy of the world as a big cultural department store with and endless retailing system. It is an 'unimaginable wonder' where you can even have your own fantasies and pretend that you are buying old style at the local grocer. Obviously, at first gaze, people in Bolivia don't feel the same degree of globalisation as people in France, but let's take time. Capitalism and globalisation are using the same language to discuss the same ideas and evidently the most important language of globalisation is economy through capitalism. It is the language that allows you to watch the Fox news, eat MacDonald's food, drive a Toyota, smoke Marlboro or buy clothes at Zara in different locations of the planet. It makes the intellectuals and people feel good because they are sharing an eclectic principle, which, in same way, presupposes a psychological and physical balance. In addition, the apparent benefits are incredible, because the percentage of the 'niches' included in the new 'eclectic' and globalised behaviour can be expanded according to the individual preferences. The niche spirit works so well within globalisation that "In the mode of irony, it relativises all local events and allegiances by bringing them into unprecedented conjunction, but simultaneously provokes as reaction the heterogeneous fundamentalisms that it then progressively incorporates. Under its rubric, eschatologies diverging from centuries begin to reconverge, exposing kinship."[9]

For others it is a disabled globalisation, as it is only an economic one and the erroneously called anti-globalisation movement bets on a proper 'global globalisation'. It may be that the much criticised anti-globalisers are after all the true globalisers. On the other hand, one thing is clear and that is that globalisation clearly defies isolationism. The old cultures and the defenders of cultural differences and national cultural traditions can no longer offer solutions to the new situation. The new world situation demands material, conceptual and intellectual solutions that must be dealt globally, as many national or regional cultures are totally unable to face them. The question is if we are prepared to celebrate national diversity while being conscious that we are unable to sustain it without the help and assistance of global entities and organisations.

Language Paradoxes and Globalisation, Globish and the Unifying Languages

The advantage of a global language is specially valued by the business and academic communities. In addition, the adoption of a lingua franca for communication in most of the environments seems to evidence that people are more mobile, both physically and electronically. The benefits of a global language are considerable, but there are commentators that have pointed out different risks, for example, that a global language will make people apathetic about learning other languages, and so reduce their nuances and opportunities; that there will appear a monolingual linguistic class, indifferent towards the other languages; that there will be a kind of linguistic death as a global language hastens the disappearance of minority languages and widespread language death.

One of the recent attempts to create a global language has been 'globish', the name is a portmanteau neologism of the words 'global' and 'English'. It was the creation of Jean-Paul Nerriere, a Frenchman who retired as vice-president of IBM. He wrote two books: *Découvres le globish* (2005) and *Parlez globish. Don't speak English* (2006) about this artificial language, a kind of planet language in which all the letters are pronounceable and pronounced in the same way and the grammar is logical and presents very few exceptions. Among other important features is a vocabulary of just 1,500 words, and no idioms, abbreviations or humour. It centres on the basics and abandons everything that makes cross-cultural communication arduous or complicated. As a result the English word 'nephew' is transformed into 'the son of my brother' and 'surfboard' becomes 'a board that allows you to walk over water'. This apparent make-it-easier language has received some criticisms that indirectly affect the phenomenon of globalisation. Laura Cerrato, a lecturer from the University of Buenos Aires in *The Argentine,* dared to state that: "If languages are nowadays impoverished it is because the speakers are in the same state too. We cannot live in determined ways, owing obedience to some values and try, at the same time, that the language does not reflect them."[10] But this decaffeinated English had its predecessors: 'Basic English', 'Simplified English' and 'International English'. That without accounting for Esperanto, Volapück.... languages that reveal the paradoxical fact that "the different attempts to create a unilingual world through artificial languages have eventually meant an enrichment of the panorama of the diversity of languages."[11] But there have been and there will always be attempts to create languages and panlinguae. It is a dream that has obsessed mankind for ages. Umberto Eco[12] reminded us in a lecture how in the seventh century Irish grammarians, in a work titled *The precepts of the poets,* stated that the Gaelic language was created after the confusion of tongues by the seventy-two wise men of the school of Fenius, through a peculiar 'cut and paste' manoeuvre on all the languages born after the dispersion, so that the best of every language was picked and maintained in Irish. Dante Alligheri, too, tried to do the same and in his work *De vulgari eloquentia* tried to create a noble vulgar language and aimed to follow the trail left from the hypothetical first perfect language: Adam's one.

It is clear that different people need some shared language to understand each other, but that doesn't involve eliminating minority languages; it only requires bilingualism. J. Diamond admitted that "monolingualism is no safeguard of peace. Even if the suppression of differences of language, religion and ethnicity did promote peace (which I doubt), it would exact a huge price in human suffering."[13] For others this loss of linguistic diversity that globalisation and its attachés imply represents a problem analogous to the loss of species in Biology. However, David Crystal thought otherwise: "A world containing only one species is impossible. But a world containing only one language is by no means impossible, and may not be so very far."[14] Other linguists, like J. A. Laponce, add some nuances and for him, what applies to languages applies to other plant and animal species, but "unlike the latter, languages in contact cannot ignore one another. If they meet, they form hierarchies, and in the long run, with exceptions to which we shall turn our attention later, the strong reduce the effectiveness of the weak and eventually eliminate them."[15]

The situation of globalisation is well-reflected in the microcosm of the European Union. On January the 1st, 2007, the register of official languages in the European Union rose from 20 to 23 with the addition of Romanian, Bulgarian and Irish. It apparently is good as European politicians manifest that it is an expression of the European Union's convergence while being diverse at the same time, but these politicians are unwilling to admit that too many languages is an economic and linguistic headache. To make the national governments pay for the bill of regional languages can reduce the European Union's costs down, but what about the non-regional languages? A solution seems to be partially appearing since there has been a change from the foundational times. In a truce twenty years ago it was agreed that English, French and German were the main working languages of the European Commission and experience demonstrated that most of the documents were elaborated in English. Today with the enlargement of the European Union to Eastern Europe and Scandinavia there is a bigger group of people that present English as their first choice for second language.

If we analyse it world-scale we can see that almost a quarter of the world population speak some English. In this figure around 400 m have English as their mother tongue and about the same number speak this language fluently. The situation today is one in which "English is the global language of academic research, and perhaps 1,500 master's degrees are taught in English countries where the language has no official status. It provides the vocabulary for some specialised fields, such as air-traffic control. And is the growing number of international companies—a big reason why so many of them choose London for their headquarters."[16] The situation is even more expansive and we find examples of it all around the world. Last year English was added to the curriculum of Mexican primary schools. Mongolia and Chile have declared their purpose to become bilingual in two decades. In China 180 m students are learning English with voracity and Japan, an old ahead of his age, allows the luxury of teaching their five-year-olds English conversation. All that without paying attention to other facts like McLuhan's, medium is message, where we could account, for example, that a newspaper made by Indians for Indians, but published in English, transmits, through the linguistic medium, a message in favour of the British contents and culture.

So, according to this panorama, the dominance of the English language is clear, but is it going to be so for long? If we link Ferdinand de Saussure's dictates about the distinctive features of the linguistic sign to languages in a general sense, we realise that difference is inherent to communication, though apparently hinders it. J.A. Laponce stated that all languages have two functions: "to communicate and to exclude", so any language can thus be used as a mask and "This wall effect can be used in- from out-groups, notably when the out-group uses the dominant language."[17] It seems that many communities of the world are moving towards unilingualism by way of bilingualism involving a lingua franca. In other words, the most suitable way for a lingua franca to operate and be successful resides upon the existence of many different languages. What would happen in the hypothetical case that there was only one language? Fragmentation? Surely, and that is the paradox. This, at the same time, points to an unsettling conclusion for advocates of multilingualism: in a union of many languages, increasingly there is but one language.

In the situation of the 'big natural languages', the road is and has been similar. In the case of the big languages of our time: English, Chinese, Spanish, their unifying power will start to split into different languages—as it occurred with Latin and the Romance languages. However, it will not happen through regions or geographical areas, but through social classes and social, cultural and economic differences. Another incidental and meaningful fact that we referred is the so-called 'artificial languages': Esperanto, Volapück. They started as attempts to create a unilingual world, but in fact contributed to increase the list of world languages, demonstrating by this way a linguistic paradox.

There are many of our contemporaries who have the sensation that modernisation and its 'special correspondent': globalisation will progressively make all the cultures in our world converge into a unique model. But this is not a new feeling, and in the sixties of the last century many sociologists, like Samuel Einsestadt, spoke about inevitable convergence thanks to modernisation.

However, Jean- Pierre Warnier[18] has put it clear that forty years later, the expected modernisation has not fulfilled the long-awaited convergence. In his work the author makes it clear that mankind is constitutively bound to produce social stratifications, particularities, cultural distinctions, different ways of life, different ways of consume. It is as if there was a powerful machinery of producing cultural differentiation in spite of all the processes acting in the opposite direction.

The conclusión that we can reach is that the myth of Babel is not a failure. It is just the opposite, a triumph of diversity. The semiologist Umberto Eco[19] admits that this undertaking is a previous condition for the beginning of the social, political and scientific History of mankind. It is like a Jacobin drum-roll before beheading the irritating Adam and his Linguistic Ancient regime. Everything points out that diversity is an inborn fact in language and that is very positive for the human species.

Relocating Globalisation Beyond the Paradoxes

The question we can make involves the difference between present globalisation and previous globalising times. Examples of globalisation are omnipresent throughout history. We can account for recent ones and mention, for example, 1944, a year of Allied advances on all the fronts in the Second World War, and how the Normandy landings achieved the participation of countless English-speaking people from the four quarters of the globe. Roy Jenkins in his biography of Winston Churchill refers to Churchill's work *A History of English-Speaking Peoples* and to the fact that the British Empire was the biggest Muslim nation of the twentieth century. The great French historian Fernand Braudel devoted a great deal of intellectual effort in the sixties of the last century to analyse the 'mondialisation'. In that time the term 'globalisation' did not exist, but according to Joaquín Estefanía, Braudel wrote in one of his works that "the History of the world economy is the history of the world, but viewed from only one observatory: the economic observatory. To choose this observatory beforehand is a way of explaining that is both unilateral and dangerous."[20] It was Braudel too who referred that the historic 'mondialisatons' were Phoenicia, Carthage, Rome, Christian Europe, Islam, Muscovy, China and India. The problem is precisely to think that we are facing a new phenomenon and to try to turn it into an expression of self-admired local fat cats. Smith refers to it: "Globalisation, then, is neither a new nor a unitary process."[21] Globalisation always existed and, though some critics could claim that its extension and dimension is bigger today, they should also think through a diachronic conscience to place this happening in the right temporal coordinate.

Another statement that we can make in a general sense is that globalisation expands when things go well, basically, periods of economic expansion, without wars or important conflicts. In the same way it undergoes difficulties when the different societies and economies close, get more self-sufficient and more nationalistic. This phenomenon coincides with recession. The implication also applies to the international system as Henry Kissinger stated:

> International systems live precariously. Every 'world order' expresses an aspiration to permanence; the very term has a ring of eternity about it. Yet the elements which comprise it are in constant flux, indeed, with each century; the duration of international systems have been shrinking.... Whenever the entities constituting the international system change their character, a period of turmoil inevitably follows.... In each transition, what had been taken for granted suddenly becomes anachronistic: multinational states in the nineteenth century, colonialism in the twentieth.[22]

All in all it is a phenomenon that has more to do with a curious interplay of political and economic forces, more to do with the imperialism of capitalism and with its cultural tools and legacy. For the moment it follows the blueprint that the British Empire received from liberalism and subsequently transmitted to America. It permeates well to the rest of world because it presents plasticity. Kissinger stated that "Since the American tradition emphasizes universal truths rather than national characteristics, American policy makers have generally preferred multilateral approaches to national ones... the American refusal to be bound by history and the insistence on the perpetual possibility for renewal confer a great dignity, even beauty, on the American way of life." This continuity between the British Empire and America's 'New World Order' was, according to Smith "neatly summed up in Ferguson's coinage, 'Anglobalisation'."[23]

The two trends—in favour of and against globalisation—are and will be there. Nial Ferguson referred to the way Leftist opponents consider it as a manifestation of "a damnably resilient international capitalism while, by contrast the liberal economists show clear consensus on this 'increasing economic openness raises living standards even if there will always be some net losers' as hitherto privileged or protected social groups are exposed to international competition."[24] Nicolas Baverez, the French historian and essayist, author of *La France qui Tombe* (2003), admits that there is often a recoil for identity as it is the manifestation of a fear for a new planet reality. This recoiling is clear in the case of nationalisms, but also in other grounds such as the religious or cultural. On cultural grounds it is almost the same and David Crystal referred to it: "Arguments about the need for national or cultural identity are often been seen as being opposed to those about the need for mutual intelligibility. But this is misleading. It is perfectly possible to develop a situation in which intelligibility and identity happily co-exist."[25] It may be that globalisation is simply an abstraction, a generalisation. It might be so because it cannot assert any authority over this jumbled world, and it might be the only means to bring it under regulation.

There are more gaps associated with globalisation, what about health and school system globalisation, what about food distribution globalisation, social protection globalisation, solidarity globalisation, labour standards globalisation... the list could be extended almost limitless, we simply have to follow studies like Bernard G. Gunter and Rolph van der Hoeven's on the social dimension of globalisation to realise the full extension of the phenomenon. We certainly do not know—though we are tempted to think self-sufficiently on the contrary—if globalisation is a 'forcing forward'. It is a forcing forward of economic liberalism, but not a real intellectual or cultural forcing forward one, one that promotes clear big steps for humanity. George Steiner applied this idea of the 'forcing forward' to art. For him, it made Western arts metaphoric and symbolic of "The Achieve, the mastery of the thing."[26] If opposing globalisation is a minimalist exercise of impotence or a righteous and daring battle for identity, it is an ineffectual scrutiny. Globalisation today is, above all, an icon, it is true fiction and everything is circumscribed to it.

Mankind today, as it was in the ancient times, is a machine of manufacturing differences. It produces stratifications, specificities, clan distinctions, dialects, residences, classes, countries, religions, ideologies... Globalisation is neither a several-head Hydra nor a medieval brotherhood, nor both. Globalisation is an almost biological impulse in the human species and so in its different manifestations. It has more to do with an inborn, 'phylogenetic' wish to spread, to proliferate, to expand, to communicate. It is more about the biology of the human species and its ethology and less about the deceitful consideration of being at a special time under particular conditions. Our self-sufficiency misguides us in the consideration of globalisation. If we simply think of literature we can see important milestones that have given testimony of this global human attitude and their attempt to encompass the world before our age: *The Odyssey, the Bible, the Mahabharata,* the *Ramayana, Romance of the Three Kingdoms, Shahnameh, The Book of One Thousand and One Nights, the Divine Comedy, Don Quixote, the Human Comedy, Moby Dick, Ulysses*... they were not just masterpieces of literature, but an essential part of the Weltanschauung of people which were written down by either a single author or several writers. Globalisation is not a particular phenomenon happening in our times. It is history transvestited and ours is a world where the elements that differentiate us are as important as our elements in common.

Works Cited

Baverez, Nicolas. *La France qui tombe.* Paris: Perrin, 2003.

"Babelling on. English v the English Language". *The Economist,* 16-12-2006.

Benjamin, Walter. *The Arcades Project.* Trans. Howard Eiland and Kevin McLauglin. Cambridge (Mass.): Harvard UP. 1999.

Blair, Tony. "Address to the European Parliament, 23 June". *Guardian,* 24 June-2005, p. 12. http:// www.number-10.gov.uk/output/Page7714.asp.

Bourgon, Jacques, Nerrière, Jean-Paul, and Dufresne, Philippe. 2005 *Découvrez le globish.* Paris: Eyrolles.

Churchill, Winston. 1956-58. *A History of English-Speaking Peoples.* Volume IV: *The Great Democracies.* London: Cassell & Company, Ltd., 1956-58.

Crystal, David, *English as a Global Language.* Cambridge. Cambridge University Press, 2003.

"Vanishing Languages", *Civilisation,* March (1997): 40-45.

Diamond, J.. "Speaking with a Single Tone", *Discover,* February (1993): 78-81.

Durant, Will. *Caesar and Christ.* New York: Simon and Schuster, 1944.

Eco, Umberto. *La Ricerca della lingua perfetta nella cultura europea.* Roma: Laterza, 1993.

"The Dream of a Perfect Language. A Lecture presented by Umberto Eco". The Italian Academy for Advanced Studies in America, 26-11-1996.

Einsestadt, Samuel. *Modernisation: Growth and Diversity.* Bloomington: Indiana University Press, 1963.

Estefanía, Joaquín, Hij@, *¿qué es la globalisación.* Madrid: Madrid: Santillana Edicones Generales, S.L, 2002.

Ferguson, Nial, Empire: *How Britain Made the Modern World.* London: Penguin, 2003.

Jenkins, Roy, *Churchill: a Biography.* London: MacMillan, 2001.

Kissinger, Henry, *Diplomacy.* New York: Simon & Schuster, 1994.

Laponce, J.A. "Minority Languages and Globalisation." *Nationalism and Ethnic Politics* 10, no. 1 (2004). 15-24.

Laube, Natalia, "Globish, ¿el aliado de Babel?", *Clarín.* com (18-7-2006).

Miloss, Czeslaw. "On Hope" in *Literature in the Modern World,* Ed. Dennis Walder. Oxford: Oxford University Press, 1990.

Nerrière, Jean-Paul. *Parlez globish. Don´t speak English.* Paris: Eyrolles, 2006.

Oudit, Sharon, "Lost Worlds: Shouthern Italy and the Resistance to Globalisation", in *Globalisation and its Discontents.* Ed. Stan Smith. Cambridge: D.S. Brewer, 2006.

Redondo Olmedilla, José Carlos. "James Fenimore Cooper: La desaparición de lenguas y la necesidad de Babel", *Revista A Distancia,* Universidad Nacional de Educación a Distancia, vol. 21, nº 1 febrero (2003): 201-205.

Rollason, Christopher. "Globalisation and Particularism in the Work of José Saramago: The Symbolism of the Shopping-Mall in A Caverna" in *Global Neo-Imperialism and National Resistance: Approaches from Postcolonial Studies.* Ed. Belen Martinez Lucas & Ana Bringas López. Vigo: Universidade de Vigo, Servicio de Publicaciones, 2004.

Sharpe, Tony. "The Planet on the Table: Some Modernist Perspectives on Globalism" in *Globalisation and its Discontents.* Ed. Stan Smith. Cambridge: D.S. Brewer, 2006.

Steiner, George, *Grammars of Creation.* London: Faber and Faber, 2001.

"Post-modernism is the new black", *The Economist,* 23-12-2006.

Warnier, Jean- Pierre. *La mondialisation de la culture.* Paris: Éditions La Découverte et Syros, 1999.

Gunter, Bernard G & van der Hoeven's, Rolph "The Social Dimension of Globalisation: a Review of the Literature". Working Paper No. 24, World Commission on the Social Dimension of Globalisation, International Labour Office: Geneva: ILo Publications, (2004)

References

1. Grant Kien, "Culture, State, Globalisation: The Articulation of Global Capitalism". *Cultural Studies & Critical Methodologies,* Volume 4, Number 4 (2004), 472-500.
2. Paul Hirst "The Global Economy: Myths And Realities", *International Affaires,* Vol. 73, Nº 3, July, (1997). David Held and Anthony McGrew, *Globalisation/ Anti-Globalisation.* (Oxford: Blackwell Publishing Company, 2002) 15.
3. Stan Smith, "Introduction: Globalisation and its Discontents" in *Globalisation and its Discontents,* ed. S. Smith (Cambridge: D. S. Brewer, 2006) 1.
4. Grant Kien, "Culture, State, Globalisation: The Articulation of Global Capitalism". *Cultural Studies & Critical Methodologies,* Volume 4, Number 4 (2004), 477.
5. Sharon Ouditt, "Lost Worlds: Southern Italy and the Resistance of Globalisation" in *Globalisation and its Discontents,* ed. Stan Smith, (Cambridge: D. S. Brewer, 2006) 89.
6. Tony Blair, "Address to the European Parliament, 23 June". *Guardian,* 24 June 24, p. 12, 2005. http:// www.number-10.gov.uk/output/Page7714.asp.
7. Will Durant, *Caesar and Christ* (New York: Simon and Schuster, 1944) 605.
8. Christopher Rollason,. "Globalisation and Particularism in the Work of José Saramago: The Symbolism of the Shopping-Mall in *A Caverna*" in *Global Neo-Imperialism and National Resistance: Approaches from Postcolonial Studies,* eds. Belen Martinez Lucas and Ana Bringas López (Vigo: Universidade de Vigo, Servicio de Publicaciones, 2004) 210.
9. Stan Smith, "Introduction: Globalisation and its Discontents" in *Globalisation and its Discontents,* ed. S. Smith (Cambridge: D. S. Brewer, 2006) 1.
10. Translation by the author, in the original it appears: "Si los idiomas están hoy en día pauperizados, es porque los que los hablan también lo están. No podemos vivir de determinadas

maneras, obedeciendo a determinadas tablas de valores, y pretender que la lengua no los refleje." Natalia Laube, "Globish, ¿el aliado de Babel?", *Clarín.* com ,18-7-2006.

11. José Carlos Redondo Olmedilla, "James Fenimore Cooper: La desaparición de lenguas y la necesidad de Babel", *A Distancia,* Universidad Nacional de Educación a Distancia, vol. 21, nº 1 febrero (2003) 205.
12. Umberto Eco, "The Dream of a Perfect Language. A Lecture presented by Umberto Eco". The Italian Academy for Advanced Studies in America, 26-11-1996.
13. J. Diamond, "Speaking with a Single Tone", *Discover* (February 1993) 78-81.
14. David Crystal, "Vanishing Languages", *Civilisation* (March 1997) 40-45.
15. J. A. Laponce, "Minority Languages and Globalisation.", *Nationalism and Ethnic Politics* 10, no. 1 (2004) 15-24.
16. "Monolingual Britain. They all speak English". *The Economist* (16-12-2007).
17. J. A. Laponce, "Minority Languages and Globalisation.", *Nationalism and Ethnic Politics* 10, no. 1 (2004) 20.
18. Warnier, Jean- Pierre Warnier, *La mondialisation de la culture* (Paris: Éditions La Découverte et Syros, 1999) 27.
19. Umberto Eco, *La Ricerca della lingua perfetta nella cultura europea* (Roma: Laterza, 1993) 286.
20. The translation is from the author. The original is as follows: "la historia económica del mundo es la historia entera del mundo, pero vista desde un solo observatorio: el observatorio económico. Elegir este observatorio es privilegiar de antemano una forma de explicación unilateral y peligrosa." Joaquín Estefanía, *Hij@, ¿qué es la globalisación* (Madrid: Santillana Ediciones Generales S.L, 2002) 28.
21. Stan Smith, "Introduction: Globalisation and its Discontents" in *Globalisation and its Discontents,* ed. S. Smith (Cambridge: D. S. Brewer, 2006) 5.
22. Henry Kissinger, *Diplomacy* (New York: Simon & Schuster, 1994) 806.
23. Nial Ferguson, *Empire: How Britain Made the Modern World* (London: Penguin, 2003) xiii.
24. Nial Ferguson, *Empire: How Britain Made the Modern World* (London: Penguin, 2003) xx.
25. David Crystal, *English as a Global Language* (Cambridge: Cambridge University Press, 2003) 22.
26. Steiner, George, *Grammars of Creation* (London: Faber and Faber, 2001) 63.

4

Colonial to Global: Changing Perspectives of English

—*G.A. Ghanshyam* and *Devasree Chakravarti*

I have crossed an ocean
I have lost my tongue
From the root of the old one
A new one has sprung.
—*Grace Nichols*

Cross-cultural encounter, multiculturalism, hybridity are all phenomena closely associated with the concept of globalisation, or in other words, the shrinking of the distances that had separated men and culture from others. Today globalisation has broken down the walls that were constructed as barriers, segmenting the world into sharp divisions. Contemporary society is a 'Global Society' and this phenomenon of globalisation has touched and transformed not only the world community but also its very culture and psyche. The process of globalisation has invariably made its mark on the languages of the world. "The globalisation of languages can be viewed as a process by which some languages are increasingly used in international communication while others lose their prominence and even disappear for lack of speakers"[1]

Language is the basis of civilisation. Evolving from the earliest spoken word, it has developed to symbolise the culture, society, people and their ethos. It is the signifier of identity, the 'self' which when asserted corelates to the assertion of one's individuality. Language is power, the feature that proclaims supremacy for the human race. Closely linked with culture and society, it has been used as a weapon by the conquerors to subdue and strengthen their authority on the conquered; to silence them into submission. "Colonialism, whether as indirect rule or the exploration and settlement of continents, brought with it the English language, English literary forms, and English cultural assumptions."[2]

English is the language of preference in this globalised world. The process of globalisation has endowed the English language with an eminence that has eclipsed many other languages with time. The history of globalisation of languages that led to English being given the top slot among the various world languages is quite old. Starting from the sixteenth century, British colonialism reigned over almost the entire Third World. It was but natural that wherever they went, they took their language with them, and used it as a medium of cementing their colonial rule. And so English "...came to represent the British Empire and symbolised the hegemony of the colonisers....."[3]

English was the language used by the Britishers to stamp their rule on the countries they had colonised not only geographically but also culturally and psychologically. Introduced in India with the advent of the East India Company in the 1600, the language started taking roots in the Indian soil with Macaulay's minute of 1835, the purpose of which was the creation of "...a class who may be interpreters between us and the millions whom we govern-a class of persons, Indian in blood and colour, but English in taste, in opinion, in morals and in intellect."[4]

With the spread of colonialism, English language spread across the globe. The language gained currency in all the colonies proving to be the windows to the world for the native people, first intellectually and later literally. Being associated with the colonisers who brought the language with them, it became synonymous with power and prestige. Long after their rule ended, this association of the language with power stayed on in the psyche of the people.

English became the language of the world. The language of the British nation, in conformity with the British rule was followed and considered to be the pure and correct form of the language throughout the colonies. Like in India and other colonies of Britain, English was introduced in America by the Britishers after Columbus first set foot on the new land. But in the last 400 years or so, the language of both the nations have diverged in various ways, basically because of the need to internalise the language as their own by the Americans in a bid to assert their independence and distinct identity.

After the Second World War, the position of Britain as a world power was lost to the emerging power of America. With time, America made tremendous advancement in science, technology and military affairs. Gradually it gained in power and importance becoming the new super power of the world. And today, covertly or overtly, American influence can be felt in every nook and corner of the world, in every sphere of life, and language is no different.

The American way of life, culture and ethos invaded the whole world. Even the most conservative of societies have come under its influence. With the growing influence and intrusion of science and technology, computers and the Internet, American English or 'Amerilish' has defined and transformed the lingua franca of the world. Today evidence of the wide use of English or more precisely American English can be seen in each and every aspect of our life, in media, movies, literature, etc. In the present global scenario, English or Amerilish is gradually colonising the entire world. "Global English speaks with two voices: British and American. The differences are essentially differences of accent, inflection, spelling an above all, vocabulary."[5] Contemporary world being a fast-paced world, people have little or no time for formalities and long, complicated rules. Everything today is preferred simplified and easy, the American way, even the language.

So the Standard English language used across the world is either British or American. In India like in other former colonies of Britain, British English is considered the standard form, followed in all academic and formal occasions. However, with time and increasing influence of America, the preference is steadily getting tilted in its favour, especially in technical fields and in oral communication. To quote the British linguist, J.R. Firth: To begin with English is an international language in the Commonwealth, the colonies and in America. International in the sense that English serves the American way of life and might be called American."[6]

The hegemony of English over the world, particularly Asia and Africa, was imperialistic in nature in its primary form which has been presently transformed by the forces of globalisation. The economic boom, opening up of markets, inclusion of computers in every sphere of life, etc., has altered the imperialistic, tradition-bound image of Queen's English into a more liberalised, open and hybrid form of 'Global English'. Rendered an international character first by the Britishers as a part of their colonial rule, the dominance of English has further gained in strength and usage due to the neo-colonial power of America. But as Salman Rushdie says, English, no longer an English language, grows from many roots; and those whom it once colonised are carving out large territories within the language for themselves."[7] And so with time, English has absorbed many influences taking roots in alien soil.

An Anglo-Frisian language that was brought to the British isles by the Germanic settlers, its diverse and multi-cultural borrowings from Greek (Telephone, Psychology), Latin (War, Household), French (Haute Couture), Scandinavian (Bank, Skin), Italian (Prima Donna, Teracotta), etc. have rendered to the language a very liberal and flexible character. This distinctive feature of evolution is largely responsible for its wide acceptance throughout the world and its longevity when many local dialects are on their way to extinction.

Being a highly flexible and fluid language, English adapts itself and also adopts the native environment, contributing and also borrowing in return. The vast repertoire of the English vocabulary is continuously being enriched and enhanced by the varied languages of the world. This unique 'hybrid' quality of the language sustains as well as helps in its global acceptance.

Apart from the borrowings from other European languages, English has also acquired some distinctive regional colours wherever in the world it is in use. In India, for instance, English has developed its unique Indian character of 'Indian English' or 'Indlish' wherein words like 'prepone', pronunciation like /dais/ instead of /'deiis/, frequent use of adding *–ing* form to the words or difference of interpretation in the meaning of the words like 'childlike' and 'childish' are very common.

Language is power. Aristotle remarked, "The ability to speak is a shortcut to distinction".[8] And English is the language of today that promises new vistas of success and opportunities for its users. It is the global language linking the whole world together in one single thread, and providing its speakers with the power to excel, to progress and transcend barriers of nation and culture.

A major factor that has made a huge contribution to the phenomenon of globalisation is the communication revolution. Computers and Internet have literally thrown open the windows to the world. To interconnect and correspond globally, English is essential. The increasing importance of these new technological advancements has further strengthened the stronghold of English on India as well as the whole world. India is a forerunner in the field of software development, and a strong hold on the English language has provided millions of Indians to excel in the field.

In this globalised world, the Third-World or developing countries of the world have realised the importance and power of gaining proficiency in the global language to stay ahead in the competitive global market. New business opportunities and openings provided by the free economy like the emergence of the BPO companies, outsourcing of jobs, increasing number of multinationals making their foray into the world market, growing demand in the IT sector, have awakened the people everywhere to the growing demand for proficiency and skill in the communication of English. In this regard India has an advantage. English has been given the status of authority and prominence by the Indian government's decision to keep English as the second official language of the nation along with Hindi. Today English has a predominance in India in administration, education, media and so on.

Media is a major player in imparting a distinctly global image to English and also in making the masses familiar with the language. Even regional channels use English mixed with their native tongue. The exposure to English language channels, films and music have also largely contributed in making English popular and colloquial throughout the world. Circulation of English newspapers has increased considerably and so has the popularity of English language channels and websites. "By 2005, the number of publishing houses and Indian registered newspapers/periodicals in English alone has risen to almost 8000, of which 750 regularly reach the newsstand."[9]

Education has also played a vital role in the spread of English and in its increasing importance. Starting from the teachings of missionaries, to the establishment of the Hindu College

(Presidency College) in Kolkata, and the contribution of individuals like Raja Rammohan Roy and David Hare it has come a long way. English language is the chosen language of higher education in India. Hence it has been recommended that "English be studied in high schools and universities in order that we keep in touch with the living stream of ever-growing knowledge".[10]

A significant field in media is that of marketing and advertisements. This field has made its impact in the globalisation of language tremendously. Today the global language has been given a local colouring and feels by coining such phrases that reflect the global and hybrid character of English. This also gives English a wider and easy acceptability among the masses thus breaking its earlier elitist image.

The availability of opportunities to the skilled and efficient candidates having the right educational qualification has suddenly given an elevation to the status of the urban, educated middle-class society. The familiarity of the masses in the country with the English language has given an edge to their expertise. With increasing income and increasing exposure to a wider world panorama due to greater mobility, the general Indian public has emerged from its segregation. This has largely been influenced by the changing global trends, including in the preference and predominance of the English language.

From attire to etiquettes, to language we are witnessing a gradual shift towards a liberal, free and global transformation. The exchange of cultures, ethos and language is no longer lop-sided but mutual and complementary. English, having taken 'many roots', is moulding the native languages, and is also being moulded by them.

Globalised English is the language of the new age. Its use is also rampant in traditional sectors like banks, army, administration as well. Any criticism that the language had attracted earlier from purists has long risen above such debates and arguments by gaining popular acceptance among the global speakers of the language. Today, English is no longer the legacy of the colonial rulers but the language of the people in its new image that has transcended the barriers of nation, culture, race and even language to embrace all in itself.

The language that had approximately 7 million users in the sixteenth century grew to over 3,500 millions in 1990, and in the present age almost about half of the world speaks English. In India, English has acquired a prominent position. The language that was largely criticised for its association with the imperialistic rulers has stayed on in the country long after the Britishers have left. English is the language that has, in fact, unified this diverse country, and also given its inhabitants a global mobility.

In the present scenario English is no longer a foreign language but one of our own, its presence being felt in each and every sphere of our lives. Even the illiterate person, the street vendors, domestic workers, etc. have a capability of approximately 100 English words of everyday common usage like, Thank you, Welcome, etc. Words, like these have, in fact, been assimilated into the regional languages, and are being used extensively in everyday speech. So now the languages, whatever they be, Hindi, Bengali, Tamil or any other language, it has acquired a new form which is a blend of the regional language with English like 'Hinglish' (Hindi and English). This trend is reflected in the colloquial language, in movies, media, in advertisements like 'Go Fida', 'Ye Mummy Made hai', 'Taste Main best, Mummy aur Everest', etc.

If the regional languages have borrowed from English like the blend of languages mentioned above or in the borrowings of words like Time, Table, Police, etc., it's also not surprising that English language has also been influenced by them in turn. Many of the words from the regional languages have found their way into English, and this trend is increasing by the years. Every year the new edition of the *Oxford English Dictionary* comes out with new words adapted or borrowed from the regional languages, starting from bungalow, thug, jungle, chapatti to many words and coinages like 'doosra' (related to Cricket), 'half-widow' (originating from Kashmir for a woman whose husband is missing), 'patel-shot' (related to photography) or 'swalpa adjust maadi' (just adjust a little), etc. The latest edition of *Oxford English Dictionary* includes such Indian words as bindas (cool), tamasha (create a scene), mehndi (hair colour), desi (local), and lehnga (a type of skirt)."[11] Catherine Soannes, editor of the dictionary, commenting on such inclusion of Indian words, defends the decision by saying, "We are merely reflecting the language as it is today. Indian English is one of the growing areas of language, which is contributing to the language as a whole."[12]

English is referred to as a 'living language', a language that is organic in form and content, growing and transforming with changing times. It is no longer the legacy of Britishers. In fact, today English is a language which cannot be claimed by any one nation. It has transcended geographical, social and cultural barriers. It is a language signifying mobility and uniformity. A truly global language, it is the language of the new global world, not only confined to British or American influence but absorbing and assimilating the various diverse world influences in itself. From being a 'vehicle of spiritual subjugation' as remarked by Ngugi Wa Thiong'O, it has come to represent a free, unified world, a genuine transformation from imposition to liberation. This truly democratic character and spirit of the language has given a new perspective to English, reflecting its journey from colonial history to its present global image.

References

1. Manfred B. Steger. "The Cultural Dimension of Globalisation". *Globalisation: A Very Short Introduction.* (New Delhi: Oxford University Press, 2003) p. 82.
2. Bruce King. *Literatures of the World in English* (Routledge & Kegan Paul, 1974) p. 2.
3. Sudhakar Pandey. "From 'Angrezi Hatao' to 'English Badhao': English in the Republic of India". *IJES,* Vol. XLIII, (2005-2006), p.15.
4. Bruce King, op.cit., p. 2.
5. Sudhakar Pandey, op.cit., p. 16.
6. J.R. Firth (1956). "Descriptive Linguistics and the Study of English", Ed. F.R. Palmer, *Selected Papers of J.R. Firth,* 1952-59 (Bloomington: Indiana University Press, 1968)
7. Salman Rudhdie. "The Empire Writes Back with the Vengeance", *The Times,* July 3rd, 1982.
8. Vandana Sharma. "The Art of Communication", *JELT,* Vol. 44/5, 2006. Sept-Oct. p.41.
9. Seemita Mohanty. "English in India: A Global Language with an Indian Identity". *Diviner,* Vol. 3. No. 2. Sept. 2006. p.112.
10. Braj B., Kachru (1994), 'South Asian English', Robert Burchfield (Ed. 1994), *The Cambridge History of the English Language.* (Cambridge: Cambridge University Press) p. 545.
11. Seemita Mohanty. p.113.
12. Ibid.

5

Perspectives on Communication and Gender

—*Syed Nadeem Fatmi*

The difference in styles of communication in men and women is constant and overwhelming. Men and women sometimes perceive the same messages with different meanings. Much of the research conducted on gender differences attempts to discover areas of similarity and difference in communication habits and styles of men and women. Researchers in this area often ask questions such as, "Are men and women fundamentally different?" or "Are men and women socialised differently and therefore employ different communication strategies?"

Gender communication is also viewed as a form of intercultural communication. Communication practices by and about women clearly fit definitions of both subcultures and co-cultures. Furthermore, communication between the sub or co-culture and the dominant culture represents a form of intercultural communication. The communication perspective allows us to examine gender communication as a form of intercultural communication. Differences in the amount of space given to and taken by men and women reflect societal gender roles.

Language is another significant element of intercultural communication. The importance of language in intercultural communication becomes most obvious when cultures speak different languages. Language also reflects differences in social status between genders. This paper attempts to offer an overview of the language use pattern and gender differences.

A lot of discussion focuses on the idea that men and women communicate differently. This difference in styles of communication in women and men is constant and overwhelming. Women and men sometimes perceive the same messages with different meanings. All of us have different styles of communicating with other people. Our style depends on a lot of things: where we're from, how and where we were brought up, our educational background, our age, and our gender. Generally speaking, men and women talk differently although there are varying degrees of masculine and feminine speech characteristics in each of us. But men and women speak in particular ways mostly because those ways are associated with their gender.

Gender and Communication

In the lay population, the terms *gender* and *sex* often are used interchangeably. In academia, however, there is presumably a distinction between that which is biologically male or female (sex) and that which is socially constructed as masculine or feminine (gender). In the field of communication, the term gender difference typically is used because the researchers want to acknowledge that differences are based not solely on discrete biology but on a continuum of psychological, social and interactive characteristics. Reflection on the methods and interpretations in communication reports, however, suggests that there is little indication that the socially constructed aspects of men and women are taken into account.

Gender (sociological) is often studied as sex (biological), a pattern that perpetuates misinformation about the meaning of male-female differences. In addition, the results of many of the studies are generalised, leaving crucial within-group differences relatively ignored. Researchers, too, often study gender as a predictor variable, paying less attention to how communication creates gender. Much of the research conducted on gender differences attempts to discover areas of similarity and difference in communication habits and styles of men and women. Researchers in this area often ask questions such as, "Are men and women fundamentally different?" or "Are men and women socialised differently and therefore employ different communication strategies?" Recently, however, this research has begun to be criticised for a number of reasons. One primary criticism is that once differences are found, the significance of the data is unclear. Reporting statistically significant gender differences is very different from providing theoretical frameworks in order to understand those differences. By focusing on the former practice, gender-difference researchers may perpetuate a misunderstanding of the meaning of gender and difference as organising principles in society. Despite this criticism, however, this line of research is alive and well in communication research.

The styles that men and women use to communicate have been described as "debate vs. relate", "report vs. rapport", or "competitive vs. cooperative". Men often seek straightforward solutions to problems and useful advice whereas women tend to try and establish intimacy by discussing problems and showing concern and empathy in order to reinforce relationships. Ivy and Backlund, while arguing from a psychological perspective, state that "female identity revolves around interconnectedness and relationship." Conversely, they argue that male identity "stresses separation and independence" (Ivy and Backlund, 1994: 57).

Coates studied men-only and women-only discussion groups and found that when women talk to each other they reveal a lot about their private lives. They also stick to one topic for a long time, let all speakers finish their sentences and try to have everyone participate. Men, on the other hand, rarely talked about their personal relationships and feelings but "competed to prove themselves better informed about current affairs, travel, sport, etc." The topics changed often and men tried to "over time, establish a reasonably stable hierarchy, with some men dominating conversation and others talking very little" (Coates, 1986). Glass also details her findings on many differences in the way men and women communicate, both verbally and non-verbally (Glass, 1992).

Studies reveal that women are more sensitive to the interpersonal meanings that lie "between the lines" in the messages they exchange with their partners. That is, social expectations often make women responsible for regulating intimacy, or the closeness they allow others to come. For that reason, it is argued that women pay more attention than men to the underlying meanings about intimacy that messages imply. Men on the other hand, to a greater extent than women, are more sensitive to "between the lines meanings" about status. For men, social expectations are that they must negotiate hierarchy, or "who's the captain and who's the crew" (Tannen, 1990; Wood, 2001).

These differences in emphasis on interpersonal vs. status implications of messages lead women to expect relationships to be based on interdependence and cooperation. Women more frequently emphasize the similarities amongst themselves and others, and try to make decisions that make everyone happy. In contrast, it is more typical for men to expect relationships to be based on independence and competition. Men more frequently emphasize the differences between themselves and others, and often make decisions based on their personal needs or desires.

These differences between men and women can be felt in the ways they communicate. Women tend to be relationship-oriented and men tend to be task-oriented. Women are typically the experts in "rapport talk" which refers to the types of communication that build, maintain and strengthen relationships. Rapport talk reflects skills of talking, nurturing, emotional expression, empathy and support. Men are typically the experts in task accomplishment and addressing questions about facts. They are experts in "report talk", which refers to the types of communication that analyses issues and solves problems. Report talk reflects skills of being competitive, lacking sentimentality, analysing and focusing on task accomplishment.

Gender Communication and Culture

Women, like so many other groups, have gained legal rights only to face less institutional, perhaps more subtle but insidious forms of discrimination. In today's age when political, educational and social discussions centre on issues of diversity and of creating a constructive, multi-cultural society, it may be helpful to examine problems in communication between the genders as a cultural issue. This is not the only, the right, or the best way of examining gender and communication, but it does offer an alternative framework for analysis, one that perhaps diffuses the potential for offensive and/or defensive posturing when discussing gender

(Reeder, 1996). Gender is both an influence on and a product of communication. Gender communication, is viewed as a form of intercultural communication. Intercultural communication, which is defined as occurring "whenever a message producer is a member of one culture and a message receiver is a member of another," has been of interest to communication scholars since 1960s (Porter and Samovar, 1985: 15).

Literature on intercultural communication often includes discussion of subcultures ("a racial, ethnic, regional, economic, or social community exhibiting characteristic patterns of behaviour sufficient to distinguish it from others within an embracing culture or society") or co-cultures (an alternative term for subcultures adopted by Pearson so as not to imply inferiority in relation to the dominant society). Pearson defines co-cultures as "groups of persons united by a common element who live in a culture operating within a dominant culture" (Pearson, 1994: 192).

Communication practices by and about women clearly fit definitions of both subcultures and co-cultures. Furthermore, communication between the sub or co-culture and the dominant culture represents a form of intercultural communication. Scholars in this area often begin their discussions by identifying the main characteristics of intercultural communication. For example, Samovar and Porter identify what they call the "constituent parts of intercultural communication". These constituent parts are perception including beliefs, values, attitudes, worldview, and social organisation, verbal processes including verbal language and patterns of thought, and non-verbal processes including non-verbal behaviour in general as well as concepts of time and use of space (Porter and Samovar, 1985: 20-24).

Penington calls such elements "significant cultural components." She includes in her list of components the existential worldview, cosmology, ontology, language, symbol systems, schemes, beliefs, attitudes, values, temporality, space, religion, myths, expressive forms, social relationships, communication networks and interpolative patterns (Penington, 1985: 31-36).

Elements of Intercultural Communication

For the purposes of illustration, it is important to describe three elements of intercultural communication common to most discussions. Worldview, language and non-verbal communication (particularly the use of space and/or time) are often identified as important elements of intercultural communication. Differences in these three elements suggest that gender communication is a form of intercultural communication. Worldview refers to a culture's orientation toward such things as God, humanity, nature, the universe, and the other philosophical issues that are concerned with the concept of being. Differences between female and male worldviews, like differences between Indian and American worldviews or European and Asian worldviews, may significantly affect communication. In fact, it is difficult to discuss differences in worldviews without talking about language, since our view of the world is expressed through language and other symbol systems.

Language is another significant element of intercultural communication. Language is the medium through which a culture expresses its world view. Like culture in general, language is learned and it serves to convey thoughts; in addition it transmits values, beliefs, perceptions, norms and so on. The importance of language to intercultural communication becomes most obvious when cultures speak different languages. Yet, differences in meaning across culture can be just as significant when each culture uses the same language. If an Indian tells his American friend to put the bags in the boot, the American may not know to place them in the trunk of the car. While this is an obvious example, it is important to point out that objects, events, experiences and feelings have a particular label or name solely because a community of people have arbitrarily decided to so name them. Language serves both as a mechanism for communication and as a guide to social reality.

A major issue in sociolinguistics has been the close affinity between language and sex. More specifically, a question germane to this paper is, "Why does women's speech differ from men's speech?" In other words, the concern is with some of the factors that induce women to use standard language more often than men do, thus appearing more linguistically polite.

In order to attempt an answer to this question, language should be treated as social, value-loaded practice, which reflects an intricate network of social, political, cultural and age relationships within a society. For instance, in a society where men are socially superior to women, linguistic differences between men and women are only one example of more extensive differences having to do with the social structure of the society itself. There is no denying that linguistic behaviour is not to be kept separate from society and its values. The slightest difference in the language of the two sexes reveals that women are not on the same footing as men.

Some linguists believe that women are aware of their low status in society and as a result use more standard speech forms, in their attempt to claim equality and achieve high social status. Women in our society are more closely involved with child-rearing and the transmission of culture, thus are therefore more aware of the importance, for their children; of the acquisition of (prestige) norms. Men in our society have traditionally been rated socially by their occupation, their earning power, and perhaps by their abilities, other words, by what they do. It may be, therefore, that they (women) have had to be rated instead, to a greater extent than men, on how they appear.

This line of thinking implies that women in paid employment should have the tendency to use fewer standard forms than unemployed women, in so far as the former have, to a greater or lesser extent, achieved some kind of status. Nevertheless, this is hardly the case. In fact, it is the other way around. An American study revealed that women in paid employment used more standard forms than those working in the home. This stands to reason as the first group spent most of their time talking to people they were unfamiliar with, while the second group interacted with members of their own families. Obviously, this evidence throws some doubt on the contention that women are more formal with a view to achieving high social status or appearing smart and polite.

A second plausible explanation for the fact that women use more standard forms than men relates to the ways in which society treats women. For example, people usually tolerate boys' behaviour, while little girls' misconduct is very often frowned upon and punished on the spot. According to Janet Holmes (1992: 173), women "are designated the role of modelling correct behaviour in the community." In view of this, women are *expected* to speak more correctly. However, this is not always true. We are well aware that interactions between a mother and her child or a husband and wife are usually informal, interspersed with colloquial or vernacular speech forms. Moreover, it is inconceivable for a woman to use "strong" expletives, such as *damn* or *shit;* she can only say *oh dear* or *fudge.*

A third explanation is that, by using standard or polite forms, a woman claims more status in society. Her greater use of standard forms may also imply that she does not attend solely to her own face needs but also to those of the people she is interacting with, thus avoiding disagreement and seeking agreement and rapport. Women experience linguistic discrimination in two ways: in the way they are taught to use language, and in the general way language use treats them. For example, 'Man has unfortunately made inroads into *his* environment', 'The spaceship was *manned* by experienced scientists,' 'This discovery will benefit all *man*kind.' (Fasold, 1990:111).

Apart from the problem regarding generic use of masculine forms, there are various sex-paired words that carry negative overtones with respect to women, while the corresponding man's term has considerably positive connotations. An oft-quoted example is the pair *bachelor-spinster,* whereby a bachelor is seen as a happy man, while a spinster always evokes an image of an ugly, scrawny woman plunging into self-pity in consequence of her being "on the shelf"!

Finally, non-verbal communicative behaviour, such as concepts of time or the use of space, differs widely from culture to culture. For example, proxemics, the study of "the way in which people use space as a part of interpersonal communication," recognises that people of different cultures do have different ways in which they relate to one another spatially. Furthermore, the use of space helps define social relationships and social hierarchies. A father traditionally sits at the head of the table in Western cultures, thus signifying his primary role in patriarchal societies. Similarly, we all know that a supervisor will exhibit a more relaxed posture than a subordinate, or that Arabs stand very close when conversing.

The ways in which concepts of social relationships (and their accompanying communication patterns) differ between genders are parallel to gender differences in worldview. Language also reflects differences in social status between genders. Research on gender and language reveals that female language strategies invariably emulate the subordinate, non-aggressive role of women in Western society. Differences in language usage and worldview are woven together and difficult to separate. And, non-verbal behaviour is another form of "language" which demonstrates differences between men and women. Earlier example of proxemics offers considerable evidence that gender communication is a form of intercultural communication. Thus, worldview, language usage, and proxemics are three constituents of intercultural communication which can be easily applied to communication between the genders.

Communication between men and women appear like cross cultural communication and is a prey to a clash of conversational styles (Tannen, 1990: 42). This is due, at least in part, to differences in the way men and women generally look at the world. Therefore, it is no coincidence that women see talk as the essence of a relationship while men use talk to exert control, preserve independence and enhance status (Wood, 1994: 141-143).

Space is a primary means by which a culture designates who is important, who has privilege. Differences in the amount of space given to and taken by women and men reflect societal gender roles. So, women are less likely to have their own private space than men within the family and home. And, in the workplace, employees in the traditionally female role, secretary, generally have a smaller space than the employee in the traditionally male role, executive. Responses to invasion of space also differ between men and women. While men may respond aggressively, women tend to yield space rather than challenge the intruder (Wood, 1994: 160-162).

These are but a few examples of the ways in which differences in communication between the genders fit categories of primary elements in intercultural communication. The point is that these differences can create problems in communication. Wood describes the ways in which these problems are manifest in the educational system. It may be assumed that the same problems are likely to be there at the university level as well. Wood's discussion includes issues familiar to us all: lack of female role models, curricular content which misrepresents men as standard and renders women invisible, biased communication in the classroom (in both student-faculty and student-counsellor communication, women are not taken seriously (Wood, 1994: 206-229). Wood, at the end of her chapter on gender and communication in the school setting, calls for programmes which would increase sensitivity to gender (Wood, 1994: 227-228). But she fails to provide specific advice.

Challenges to Intercultural Communication

By looking at these problems through intercultural communication perspectives, some specific behaviours can be outlined which may improve communication between genders. In intercultural communication, identifying problem areas can also help us learn to avoid them. These problem areas can be applied to gender communication as well. Laray identifies six stumbling blocks in intercultural communication: (i) assumed similarity, (ii) language, (iii) non-verbal misinterpretations, (iv) preconceptions and stereotypes, (v) tendency to evaluate, and (vi) high anxiety (Laray M. B. 1985: 330-338).

This last stumbling block, high anxiety, occurs when people are completely separated from their own culture, and usually does not apply to gender communication (except, perhaps, in overtly abusive situations or highly sex-segregated societies). Awareness of the other five stumbling blocks, however, can be useful in improving our gender communication.

By learning not to assume that men and women are the same, we can become more sensitive to the fact that men and women's values and goals may differ, and generally their verbal and non-verbal language will vary as well. Conversely, awareness of societal preconceptions and stereotypes which portray the other sex as "different", or "opposite", can help us avoid such stereotypes. The tendency to evaluate another's culture as inferior to our own is perhaps the most difficult stumbling block to avoid, especially when applying it to gender communication. So, instead of being annoyed with a male's aggressive communication style, we should recognise that it is a style which, is, as much a part of his identity as an ethnic cuisine or a religious tradition is part of a culture. The onus, thus in improving intercultural communication is to create awareness and to respect rather than to evaluate.

Conclusion

Communication, no doubt, plays a significant role in contemporary gender issues. The communication perspective allows us to examine gender communication as a form of intercultural communication. It can be said that examining language use may lead to significant discoveries as to the structure of society or a specific community and the values and determine the ways in which individuals are viewed and treated. Interestingly, language always implies more than what is literally meant. This paper has highlighted some of the factors responsible for the differences in gender's linguistic behaviour.

From the social inter-actionist perspective, it may be said that differences in language between women and men result from a misunderstanding of the intent of the other sex, and not (necessarily) from the dominant position of men in society. It may also be argued that the socialisation process undergone by males and females sets various types of preferential cognitive networks and that gender-specific psyche ultimately stem from nurture rather than nature. Differences in language use between males and females do not stem exclusively from inherently natural and neuro-linguistic preferences: the socialisation process undergone by males and females, whether at home or at school, past or present, play a big role on shaping of communication styles. It can be said that nurturing affects and shapes nature to the point where males and females end up developing different communication styles imposed by society. The self is shaped by socio-cultural processes life history, and social ideology. Gender-specific patterns of behaviour will always be the important social variables to be analysed through the most common cultural codes of society, that is, its language. For all its deficiencies and shortcomings, it is hoped that it will not fall short of its main goal to make people think.

Works Cited

Coates, Jennifer. 1986. *Women, Men and Language,* New York: Longman Inc.

Fasold, R. W. 1990. *The Sociolinguistics of Language.* Oxford: Blackwell. p. 111.

Glass, Lillian, 1992. *He Says, She Says: Closing the Communication Gap Between the Sexes.* New York: Perigree Books.

Holmes, J. 1992. *An Introduction to Sociolinguistics.* London: Longman. p.173.

Ivy, Diana K. and Backlund, Phil . 1994. *Exploring GenderSpeak: Personal Effectiveness in Gender Communication,* New York: McGraw-Hill, p. 57.

Laray M. Barna, 1985. "Stumbling Blocks in Intercultural Communication," in Larry A. Samovar & Richard E. Porter (eds.) *Intercultural Communication: A Reader,* 4th ed., Belmont, CA: Wadsworth, pp. 330-338.

Pearson, J. C. and Nelson, P. E. 1994. *Understanding and Sharing: An Introduction to Speech Communication,* 6th ed. WCB Brown & Benchmark, p. 192.

Penington, Dorothy L. 1985. "Intercultural Communication," in Larry A. Samovar and Richard E. Porter (eds.), *Intercultural Communication: A Reader,* op.cit., 31-36.

Porter, Richard and Samovar, Larry (ed). 1985. *'Intercultural Communication: A Reader,* 4th ed. Belmont, CA: Wadsworth, p. 15. Porter and Samovar, Ibid, p. 20, p. 24.

Reeder, H. M. 1996. *Communication Studies,* Winter.

Tannen, Deborah. 1990. *You Just Don't Understand: Women and Men in communication,* New York: William Morrow, Tannen, D. Ibid., p. 42.

Wood, Julia T. 1994. *Gendered Lives: Communication, Gender and Culture,* Belmont,CA: Wadsworth, Ibid., pp. 141-143, 160 -162, 206-229, 227-228.

6

Impact of Social Communication Transition in a Globalised World

—Shubha Mukherjee

The word 'communication' is derived from the Latin term 'communicare' or 'communico' both of which mean 'to share'. But communication is not merely transmission of meaning from one person to another through symbols. It implies that the system of communication is commonly possessed, acknowledged and documented by the members of a community. It enables them to acquire, substitute, accumulate, reclaim and process information. Communication is thus essentially a social affair.

Though human society has progressed with remarkable speed, the use of language for communication is still not free from ignorance, prejudice and superstition. As communication is a network of interactions and naturally the sender and receiver keep on changing their roles, it is very natural that the ways of communication differ from one place to another. A person belonging to a particular area may not follow the speech of another person from a different locality though the language used by both of them is a common one. Therefore, it is seen that society plays a very vital role in framing the communication of the place. Social advancement has to be matched with the development of efficient techniques of communication to sustain the tempo of growth. Society influences communication and in its turn communication set the standards of a society. The impact is from both the sides: it is society that generates the emblem and accepts a communication standard and it is communication that proves the escalation of the society.

The rapid changes in the ways of communication across the globe have continuously altered the many facets of society. In this globalised world today, an analogous system of communication is the desperate cry of all. Efforts have been made and are still on, and researchers are trying their best to minimise the communication gap by giving communication a global touch. Both interdisciplinary and intercultural in its approach, global communication in transition scrutinises the human dimensions and technological urgencies of international communication. Hamid Mowlana, the foremost tracker and analyser of global communication, provides a comprehensive analysis beginning with the rise of modern political systems and the interactions of various cultures, through the expansion of social organisations and the growing global infrastructure.

Media has at all times been used as a means to conquer the hearts and minds of the people to further strengthen and sustain the dominance of the powers that are in society. The different social movements must recognise and provide support to the efforts that are made by media and communication recourses for public as well as non-market interests. Community radio, other community-based media and communication activists' work towards expanding and maintaining what little space exists for non-commercial and community based alternatives. It is the social duty and responsibility of every individual to accept media as one of the most dominant communication aid and thus handle it with utmost care. Television has become one of the most commonly used mass media of the present age and so it has become the most challenging media of the time. Vaclav Havel (*Sunrise Magazine*, 1995) has rightly said:

> Those who have the mass media in their hands ... bear responsibility for the world and for the future of humanity. Just as the splitting of the atom can immensely enrich humanity in a thousand and one ways and, at the same time, can also threaten it with destruction, so television can have both good and evil consequences. Quickly, suggestively, and to an unprecedented degree, it can disseminate the spirit of understanding, humanity, human solidarity and spirituality, or it can stupefy whole nations and continents. And just as our use of atomic energy depends solely on our sense of

> responsibility, so the proper use of television depends on our sense of responsibility as well.

The powerful role that communication can play is often overlooked and individuals are more concerned about other efforts rather than shaping the communication skills and competence. The 1999 position paper from the US-based Rockefeller Foundation warns: "in the current hyper-commercialised media landscape, development groups must redouble their efforts to help 'shape communication environments that can work for people, not against them".

Computers also play an important role in determining the communicative trends in today's globalised world. Computer based communication system demonstrates a fundamental function on the organisation and development of even scientific specialty. It is through computer communication that, at times, individuals in a scientific community become aware of one another and develop ties of mutual acquaintanceship. The whole of scientific endeavour depends on effective communication among people working in the same vicinity. To be effective, scientists require talking to one another, writing to each other and reading each other's works.

Science is essentially a collaborative expression that is based entirely on communication. Particularly at the premature phases of the materialisation of a new concept, progress demands communication in order to ascertain the varieties of standards and agreements that define both predicament and advancement. Not only in the area of science or scientific truths is communication essential but in every other specific as well as academic purposes the necessity of communication is felt to the core.

Computers can solve the problem to a large extent and satisfy the desired needs of the learners and users who feel the necessity of communication to the extreme core. The computer, researchers have found, can perhaps take the place of protracted face-to-face interaction and provide the sort of social structure out of which a scientific specialty can grow. Spindel rightly says: "Not only did I need to know the right words. I needed to know the appropriate situations in which blessings were given and the appropriate moments at which to give them" (Spindel 1989:215).

The view Spindel presents is that language learners need to know more about the target language rather than the phonological, morphological and the syntactic rules. Due to the works of Canale and Swain (1980), Hymns (1972 & 1974) and Wolfson (1981) all have become aware of the concepts of communicative competence, that language must not only be linguistically accurate, but socially appropriate and sociolinguistic rules must at times be unambiguously taught.

The term 'speech act' has been defined as a minimal unit of discourse, a basic unit of communication. (Searle 1969). Speech act is another effective means that can handle the challenges of communication in the globalised world with efficient remedies in the social prospective today. Examples of speech act include giving compliments, making statements, asking questions, apologising, leave taking, making introductions, making requests, expressing gratitude, making refusals, giving blessings, etc. Speech acts are comprehended from culture to culture in different ways and these disparities may result in communication complexities that range from the hilarious to the serious. Not only does the linguistic recognition of the same speech act differ, but the force of a speech act might also vary. For example, in some cultures to refuse an offer of something may call for much 'beating around the bush' before an actual rejection might be made whereas in other cultures, a refusal may not necessitate as much alleviation. The problem is that, in some cases, a misrepresentation may lead to complete misunderstanding. Olshtain and Cohen cite the following example of a misunderstanding due to the apprehension of speech act of apology:

> One morning, Mrs. G, a native speaker of English now living in Israel, was doing her daily shopping at the local supermarket. As she was pushing her shopping cart she unintentionally bumped into Mr. Y, a native Israeli. Her natural reaction was to say "I'm sorry" (in Hebrew). Mr. Y turned to her and said, "Lady, you could at least apologise." On another occasion the very same Mr. Y arrived late for a meeting conducted by Mr. W (a native speaker in English) in English. As he walked into the room he said, "The bus was late", and sat down. Mr. W obviously annoyed, muttered to himself, "These Israelis, why don't they ever apologise!" (Olshtain–Cohen 1989: 53).

Speech acts have been scrutinised and illustrated from a variety of perspectives: philosophical, social linguistic and cultural. An attempt has also been made to identify universal standards of speech performances and to discriminate them from explicit norms in order to better understand and assess inter-language behaviour. From different studies it has been found out that successful scheduling and fabrication of speech act expressions depend on socio-cultural and socio-linguistic capabilities of the speaker. Socio-cultural ability refers to the respondents' dexterity at selecting speech act strategies which include the culture concerned, the age and sex of the speakers, their social category and profession and their responsibility and position in the interaction. Socio-linguistic ability, on the other hand, is the speakers' control over the actual language structures used to recognise the speech act as well as their control over record or regulation of the utterance from most intimate to most formal language. To come out with solution researchers should start with the generation of preliminary assumptions based on ethnographic data collection of natural speech. Then they should continue to stimulate speech such as role-plays which can serve to test the primary hypothesis. From there they can go to the paper and pencil written completion test in order to focus on specific recognition and manoeuvre the social and situational capriciousness.

Wolfson (1981) and Manmor & Jones (1989) have argued that ethnographic data collection is the most consistent means of learning about social and linguistic constraints on a particular speech act. This methodology permits for surveillance of naturally happening speech events with accurate recording about the social surroundings, location and the participants, thereby providing information about the linguistic and social constrictions on the application of a given speech act (cf. Watson–Gegeo 1988 for a discussion of methodological issues). Focusing on production data, Kasper and Dahl illustrate two major data elicitation evaluations – discourse completion and role play.

Researchers have suggested and are still on the verge of diverse solutions about different means and ways to tackle the universal speech differences. To bring in uniformity a global language is a necessity. Diverse challenges attack and counterattack the language in different ways and remedies come up to tackle the situation. From the primitive time man has tried his best to make the best use of language so that communication gap is minimised. It started on a small scale first – the society that each community belonged to. Gradually they moved out and the societies became larger. The language of one society was affected by the language of other and as a consequence a third language came into existence. Gradually language affected the society and was in turn affected throughout. Now it is a global demand for it is not the societies but it is now the countries that have come closer. Language faces a new challenge of universality and efforts are made to confront the state of affairs with dexterity and fortitude.

Works Cited

Cohen, Andrew, *Investigating the Production of Speech Act Sets, Speech Act Across Cultures,* www. deGruyter.com.

Ebsworth, Miriam Eisenstein, Jean W.Bodman, Mary Carpenter, *Cross-Cultural Realisation of Greetings in American Englishv, Speech Act Across Cultures,* www. deGruyter.com.

Freeman, Linton C., The Impact of Computer Based Communication on the Social Structure of an Emerging Scientific Specialty, *Social Network 6* (1984) 201-221, North Holland.

Gass, Susan M. Joyce Neu, *Speech Act Across Cultures: Challenges to Communication in a Second Language, Speech Act Across Cultures,* www. deGruyter.com.

Houck, Noel, Susan M. Gass, Non-Native Refusals: *A Methodological Perspective, Speech Act Across Cultures,* www. deGruyter.com.

Moulana, Hamid, *Global Communication in Transition: The End of Diversity?,* Thousand Oaks: Sage, 1996.

Nelson, Gayle.L., Waguida El Bakary, Mahmoud Al Batal, *Egyptian and American Complements: Focus on Second Language Learners, Speech Act Across Cultures,* www. deGruyter.com.

7

Advertising: A Global Phenomenon

—Sangeeta Sharma

Advertising is everywhere and it has penetrated in society through all the possible media. From the cosmetics you use to the car you drive, everything is advertised. Advertising leaves an indelible mark on you as it plays a major role in your decisions while purchasing. Advertising is prevalent from the grassroots level to the international level. International advertising entails dissemination of a commercial message to target audiences in more than one country. It can be viewed as a communication process that promotes the same product in multiple cultures which differ in terms of values, communication styles and consumption patterns. It is also a business activity involving advertisers and advertising agencies that create ads and buy media in different countries.

INTRODUCTION

The world is becoming a common marketplace where people have the same basic needs, wants, desires and tastes no matter where they live. Twenty-five years ago global village was a concept; today it is a reality. We have come a long way since the days of centrally produced, locally translated, one-ad-fits-all approach to global advertising. Advertising on worldwide scale is a major element in the growth of this global village. It has become a primary tool to gain brand awareness in both developed and emerging countries. Brand ideas that can literally come from anywhere and travel anywhere have a new power-primarily because many so-called developing markets around the world have become as sophisticated and complex as the countries that had produced the goods.

International advertising is advertising that reaches across national and cultural boundaries. Advertising in the past was mere translation according to domestic needs which were ineffective and sometimes even offensive. But today the real issue is not nations but culture. International advertisers have started paying greater attention to local cultures.

Advertising and marketing are truly worldwide, no longer dominated by American companies. A number of consumer-product companies such as PepsiCo, Coca-Cola, Procter and Gamble, and Nestle have been successful in turning many of their products into global brands. The importance of international market can also be seen in the advertising budget of domestic firms.

With the development of communication, transportation, and financial transactions, time and distance are no longer barriers to global marketing. Products and services developed in one country quickly find their way into other countries where they are finding enthusiastic acceptance. Consumers around the world wear Adidas shoes and Levis jeans, eat at McDonald's, shave with Gillette razors, use Apple and Dell computers, drink Coca-cola and Pepsi cola soft drinks, talk on cellular phones made by Nokia and Motorola, and drive cars made by global automakers such as BMW, Honda, etc.

Global Marketing and Advertising

The term, Global Marketing, attributed to Theodore Levitt of Harvard University, suggests that companies can develop worldwide advertising and marketing strategies for their products. At the heart of this concept is the assumption that consumers are basically alike all over the world and will respond to similar appeals regardless of their apparent differences. As one advertising executive observed, "the most difficult thing about international advertising is attaining relevance for your target audience while remaining faithful to the single message goal of the campaign." Talking specifically to differing cultures runs contradictory to this.

To accommodate the demands of global marketing, multinational companies have started to combine two marketing strategies which seem very contradictory but in fact work very well.

Centralised management: For global marketing to work it must be coordinated at the very top management levels. A number of companies have initiated very sophisticated control centres to market worldwide. For example, Nestle has long been viewed as a master of multinational marketing. From its headquarters in Vevey, Switzerland, it manages 10 worldwide corporate brands and approximately 7,000 local brands.

Two-way flow of information: Regardless of the approach used by the company for its international strategy, a key element is to maintain brand identity. The less standardisation of the product quality, advertising themes, and marketing tactics, the more difficult it is to establish a global personality. For example, Pizza Hut.

When considering global marketing and advertising the companies are faced with three options as to how to proceed. It is important to realise that each has a number of variations, and most companies will use some aspects of each in one or more countries or for particular products. There are a few absolutes in the emerging field of international business.

Standardisation: The strategy and execution of campaigns are handled globally with copy translated but no changes in creative or other elements of a campaign. Under this plan, one advertising agency is retained with centralised responsibility to interface with client counterparts at the central office. The strongest supporters take the view that "globalisation will only be possible for companies that exploit a very specific and clearly-defined market sector, with practically no international differences."

Pattern standardisation: Under this plan, a global advertising agency controls over all strategy, general creative and general campaign approaches; the execution is handled locally or regionally. Each country handles its own media selection and tailoring of campaigns.

Localisation: At the other end of the management spectrum from standardisation is localisation. Under this management philosophy, each country manages strategy and execution of campaigns with a local focus. Local advertising agencies tailor campaigns to each area's culture and needs. Organisational control is decidedly decentralised.

In fact, a few companies would contemplate adopting a plan of full standardisation or full localisation. Marketers know that, with the exception of relatively small companies operating in only a few countries, a strict adherence to standardisation will not work. Companies have to be flexible enough to deal with culture, language, the political system, and economic dissimilarities from one country to another. Each has a number of variations, and most of them will use some aspects of each in one or more countries for particular products.

Most companies have two primary objectives. One is a single brand image and the second, related to the use of single brand, is to exploit cost efficiencies inherent in a single marketing and advertising strategy worldwide. As one international advertising executive pointed out, "standardisation seems to work best when the product is pragmatic or utilitarian and when it satisfies a universal physical need such as shaving or diapering habits. In such cases the message is often informational..."

It is clear that technology is becoming more readily available to make the idea of international advertising and global marketing a reality. However, it is impossible to accommodate all the cultural and national differences in any single marketing strategy. Global marketing is such an appealing concept from a cost and efficiency standpoint that companies are tempted to adopt it even when it has obvious pitfalls. It can be argued that misapplication of global marketing places the well-being of the firm ahead of the customer.

The idea of continuum of strategies is more common than an either-or notion of choosing between a strict interpretation of global marketing and the consumer orientation of the marketing concept. In most cases, companies develop a broad marketing and advertising plan. From this plan they then make necessary adaptations that consider the special cultural, economic and language differences present in each country they enter.

Regardless of how much the international companies would like to adopt a global strategy for their brands, the local market dictates that local brands will continue to be a major force. E.g.: Coca-Cola sells a host of local soft-drink brands including Thumbs Up, an Indian distributed cola; fruit-flavoured Splash in Germany and Spain; and Beverly, a herbal drink sold in Italy.

The Importance of International Markets

Companies are focusing on international markets for a number of reasons. Many companies in the U.S. and Western Europe recognise that their domestic markets offer them limited opportunities for expansion because of slow population growth, saturated markets, intense competition, and/or an unfavourable marketing environment. For example, many U.S. tobacco companies and brewers face declining domestic consumption as a result of restrictions on their marketing and advertising efforts and the growing anti-smoking sentiment in this country.

Many companies must focus on foreign markets to survive. Most European nations are relatively small in size and without foreign markets would not have the economies of scale to compete against larger U.S. and Japanese companies. For example, Swiss-based Nestle and Netherlands-based Unilever are two of the world's largest consumer-product companies because they have learned how to market their brands to consumers in countries around the world. Two of the world's major marketers of cellular phones are from Scandinavian countries. Nokia is based in Finland and Ericsson is located in Sweden.

Companies are also pursuing international markets because of the opportunities they offer for growth and profits. The dramatic economic, social, and political changes around the world in recent years have opened markets in Eastern Europe and China. The growing markets of Far East, Latin America and other parts of the world present tremendous opportunities to marketers of consumer products and services as well as business-to-business marketers.

While many U.S. companies are becoming more aggressive in tier pursuit of international markets, they face stiff competition from large multinational corporations from other countries. Some of the world's most formidable marketers are European companies such as Unilever, Nestle, Siemens, Philips and Renault, as well as the various Japanese car and electronic manufacturers and packaged-goods companies such as Suntory, Shiseido, and Kao.

The International Environment

Just as with the domestic marketing, companies engaging in

international marketing must carefully analyse the major environmental factors of each market in which they compete, including economic, demographic, cultural and political/legal variables. These factors are important in evaluating the potential of each country as well as designing and implementing a marketing and promotional programme.

Cultural variables marketers must consider language, customs, tastes, attitudes, lifestyles, values and ethical/moral standards. Nearly every country exhibits cultural traits that influence not just the needs and wants of consumers but how they go about satisfying them. Although the basic functions of advertising are similar in all parts of the world, the specific execution and methods of operation vary widely. As firms introduce products of on a worldwide basis, their problems range from something as familiar as product category competition to the much more difficult problem of convincing buyers to change established habits or even reject previously held cultural taboos.

Marketers must be sensitive not only in determining what products and services they can sell in foreign cultures but also in communicating with them. Advertising is often the most effective way to communicate with potential buyers and create markets in other countries. But it can also be one of the most difficult aspects of the international marketing programme because of problems in developing messages that will be understood in various countries.

International advertisers often have problems with language. The advertiser must know not only the native tongue of the country but also its nuances, idioms, and subtleties. International advertisers must also be aware of the connotations of the words and symbols used in their messages and understand how advertising copy and slogans are translated. Advertisers mostly have problems in translating their advertising messages and brand names into various languages. The Heineken ad is one example. Though this ad worked well in the U.S. and other English-speaking countries, the line "you don't have to make a great fuss" could not be translated in a meaningful way into other languages. A list of some funny translations is as follows:

1. In Taiwan, the translation of the Pepsi slogan *Come alive with the Pepsi Generation* came out in Chinese as Pepsi will bring your ancestors back from the grave.

2. When Parker Pen marketed a ballpoint pen in Mexico, its ads were supposed to say *It won't leak in your pocket and embarrass you*. However, the company mistakenly thought the Spanish word *embarazar* meant embarrass. Instead the ads said: It won't leak in your pocket and make you pregnant.
3. Frank Perdue's slogan *It takes a tough man to make a tender chicken* sounds much more interesting in Spanish. A photo of Perdue with one of his chickens appeared on billboards all over Mexico with a caption that explained: *It takes a hard man to make a chicken aroused (or) It takes a sexually stimulated man to make a chicken affectionate.*
4. Coors translated its slogan; *Turn it loose,* into Spanish, where it was read as *Suffer from diarrhoea.*
5. Scandinavian vacuum manufacturer Electrolux used the following in an American campaign "Nothing sucks like an Electrolux".
6. When Braniff translated a slogan touting its upholstery, *"Fly in leather,* it came out in Spanish as Fly naked".
7. The Microsoft ad slogan, as translated into Japanese: *If you don't know where you want to go, we'll make sure you get taken.*
8. Clairol introduced the Mist Stick, a curling iron, into German only to find out that Mist is slang for (to put it delicately) manure. Not too many people had use for the Manure Stick. This is the reason why Rolls Royce decided not to call one of its models the Silver Mist - for fear of lost sales in the German-speaking world.
9. When Chevrolet developed the Chevy Nova, they decided to market it heavily in Mexico, where the name translates as *Doesn't go*. The car was later renamed Caribe.
10. Ford had a similar problem in Brazil when the Pinto flopped. The company found out that Pinto was Brazilian slang for tiny male genitals. Ford pried all the nameplates off and substituted Corcel, which means horse.
11. The name Coca-Cola in China was first rendered as something that when pronounced sounded like Coca-Cola: Ke-kou-ke-la. Unfortunately, the Coke Company did not discover until after thousands of signs had been printed

that the characters used meant *bite the wax tadpole or female horse stuffed with wax*, depending on the dialect. Coke then researched 40,000 Chinese characters and found a close phonetic equivalent, Ko-kou-ko-le, which can be loosely translated as *happiness in the mouth.*

12. The Kentucky Fried Chicken slogan *finger-lickin' good* came out in KFC's first Chinese campaign as eat your fingers off.
13. An American tee-shirt maker in Miami printed shirts for the Spanish market, promoting the Pope's visit. Instead of the desired *I saw the Pope!* (el Papa) thousands of shirts proudly proclaimed in Spanish *I saw the Potato! (la Papa*).
14. Hunt-Wesson introduced its Big John products in French Canada as *Gros Jos* before finding out that the phrase, in slang, means big breasts. But in this case, the name problem did not seem to have a negative effect on sales.
15. Colgate introduced a toothpaste in France called *Cue,* the name of a notorious porno magazine.
16. In Italy, a campaign for Schweppes Tonic Water translated the name into *Schweppes Toilet Water.*
17. When Gerber started selling baby food in Africa, they used the same packaging as in the US, with the beautiful baby on the label. Later they learned that in Africa, companies routinely put pictures on the label of what's inside, since many people can't read English.

Advertisers can encounter problems with the connotative meaning of signs and symbols used in their messages. For example, Pepsodent toothpaste was unsuccessful in Southeast Asia because it promised white teeth to a culture where black and yellow teeth are symbols of prestige. An American ad campaign using various shades of green was a disaster in Malaysia, where the colour green symbolises death and disease.

Tastes, traditions and customs are also an important part of cultural considerations. The customs of a society affect what products and services it will buy and how they must be marketed. In France, cosmetics are used heavily by both men and women and advertising to the male market is common. There are also cultural differences in grooming and hygiene habits of customers in various countries. For example, even though many US consumers use products like deodorant and shampoo daily, consumers in many other Western countries are not that fanatical about personal hygiene, so consumption of products such as deodorant and mouthwash is much lower than in the US.

Another aspect of culture that is very important for international marketers to understand is values. Cultural values are beliefs and goals shared by members of a society regarding ideal end states of life and modes of conduct. For example, cultural values in the US put a major emphasis on individual activity and initiative, while many Asian societies stress cooperation and conformity to the group. Values and beliefs of a society can also affect its members' attitudes and receptivity toward foreign products and services. Values such as ethnocentrism or nationalism often affect the way consumers in various countries respond to foreign brands or even advertising messages.

Religion is another aspect of culture that affects norms, values and behaviours. For example, in many Arab countries, advertisers must be aware of various taboos resulting from conservative applications of Islamic religion. Alcohol and pork cannot be advertised. Human nudity is forbidden, as are pictures of anything sacred, such as images of a cross or photographs of Mecca. The faces of women may not be shown in photos, so cosmetics use drawings of women's faces in ads. In conservative Islamic countries, many religious authorities are opposed to advertising on the grounds that it promotes Western icons and culture and the associated non-Islamic consumerism.

A number of countries ban or restrict tobacco advertising of various products. In Europe there has been longstanding ban on advertising for prescription-drug products, which is designed to keep government subsidised health care costs under control. The ban prevents prescription-drug companies from mentioning their products even on their websites or in brochures, although some relaxation of these restrictions is being considered by European Commission for drugs used to treat AIDS, diabetes and respiratory ailments.

While international markets are accustomed to restrictions on the advertising of cigarettes, liquor, and pharmaceuticals, they are often surprised by restrictions on other products or services. For example, margarine cannot be advertised in France, nor can restaurant chains.

Many countries restrict the media advertisers can use. In Greece advertisers can advertise toys on television only during the evening hours due to the ban on toy advertising in the morning hours. Some of the stringent advertising regulations in the world are found in Scandinavian countries. Commercial advertising began in Sweden in 1992, and both Denmark and Sweden limit the amount of time available for commercials. Many governments have rules and regulations that affect the advertising message. For example, comparative advertising is legal and widely used in United States and Canada but is illegal in some countries like Korea and Belgium. Many countries restrict the types of claims that advertisers can make, the words they can use, and the way products can be represented in ads. Government restrictions can influence the use of foreign languages in advertising as well as the production of the ad. These restrictions are motivated primarily by economic considerations.

Advertising Agencies around the World

An experienced and astute agency can help an advertiser deal with the creative, media and regulatory challenges just discussed. In Brazil, using a local agency is essential to get creative style and tone just right. In Australia, Australian nationals must be involved in certain parts of the production process. And in China, trying to work through the government and media bureaucracy is nearly impossible without the assistance of local agency. Advertisers in the United States have three basic alternatives in choosing an agency to help them prepare and place advertising in other countries: They can use a global agency, an international affiliate, or a local agency.

Globalised versus Localised Campaigns

One additional issue must be resolved. This key involves the extent to which campaign will be standardised versus localised across markets. The discussions of this issue, the question is often posed as, how much can the advertiser globalise the advertising? Globalised campaigns use the same message and creative execution across all (or most) international markets. By contrast, localised campaigns involve preparing different messages and creative executions for each market a firm has entered.

The issue is more complex than simply a question of globalised versus localised advertising. Both the brands and its overall marketing strategy must be examined. The marketer must first consider the extent to which the advertising can be standardised across markets, and then the extent to which the advertising can be globalised across markets. The degree to which advertising in international markets can use a common appeal, versus whether the ads prepared for each market must be customised, has been a widely debated issue.

Those who favour the globalised campaign assume that similarities as well as differences between markets should be taken into account. They argue that standardisation of messages should occur whenever possible, adapting the message only when absolutely necessary. For example, Mars's U.S. advertisements for Pedigree dog food have used golden retrievers, while poodles were deemed more effective for the brand's positioning and image in Asia. Otherwise, the advertising campaigns were identical in terms of basic message appeal. Those who argue for the localised approach see each country or region as a unique communication context, and they claim that the only way to achieve advertising success is to develop separate campaigns for each market.

The two fundamental arguments for globalised campaigns are based on potential cost savings and creative advantages. Just as organisations seek to gain economies of scale in production, they also look for opportunities to streamline the communication process. Having one standard theme of communication allows an advertiser to focus on a uniform brand or corporate image worldwide, develop plans more quickly and make maximum use of good ideas. Thus, while Gillette sells hundreds of different products in more than 200 countries around the world, its corporate philosophy of globalisation is expressed in its "Gillette—the Best a Man Can Get" theme. This theme is attached to all ads for men's toiletry products, wherever they appear.

In recent years several aspects of global marketplace have changed in such a way that the conditions for globalised campaigns are more favourable. Specifically, these conditions fostering the use of such campaigns are as follows:

Global communication: Worldwide cable and satellite networks have resulted in television becoming a truly global communications medium. MTV's 200 European advertisers almost run

English-language-only campaigns in the station's 28-nation broadcast area. These standardised messages will themselves serve to homogenise the viewers within these market areas.

The global teenager: Global communications, global travel, and the demise of communism are argued to have created common norms and values among teenagers around the world. One advertising agency videotaped the rooms of teenagers from 25 countries, and it was hard to tell whether the room belonged to an American, German or Japanese teen. The rooms had soccer balls, Levi jeans, NBA jackets, and Sega video games. In response to such similarity, Swatch has created a worldwide campaign aimed at teenagers that uses the same image in all the international markets and merely changes the print ads to adapt to language differences.

Universal demographic and lifestyle trends: Demographic and lifestyle trends that emerged in the 1980s in the United States are manifesting themselves in markets around the world. More working women, more single-person households, increasing divorce rates, and fewer children per household are now widespread demographic phenomena that are affecting lifestyles. The rising number of working women in Japan caused Ford Motor Company to prepare ads specifically targeted to this audience.

The Americanisation of consumption values: Perhaps one of the greatest advantages to U.S. advertisers is the Americanisation of consumption values around the world. American icons are gaining popularity worldwide, especially due to the exportation of pop culture fuelled by the U.S. entertainment industry. This trend has become so pervasive that some countries are seeking ways to shield themselves from U.S. entertainment exports. A recent meeting of culture ministers from 19 nations, including Canada, Britain, Mexico and Sweden, discussed proposals for exempting cultural "products" from international free-trade pacts. The ultimate target of this discussion by these czars of local culture was undeniably "Made in the USA" entertainment products.

All these are creating an environment where a common message across national boundaries becomes more possible. To the extent that consumers in various countries hold the same interests and values, "standardised" images and themes can be effective in advertising. Arguments against globalisation tend to centre on issues relating to local market requirements and cultural constraints within markets. The target audiences in different countries must understand and place the same level of importance on brand features or attributes for a globalised campaign to be effective. In many cases, different features are valued at different levels of intensity, making a common message inappropriate. Also, if a globalised campaign defies local customs, values, and regulations, or if it ignores the efforts of local competition, then it has little chance of being successful. Without the support of local managers, no globalised campaign can ever achieve its potential.

Developing global brands through standardised campaigns can only be successful when advertisers can find similar needs, feelings, or emotions as a basis for communication across cultures. Creating culture-free ads is an impossibility, but the global marketer must be able to draw upon enough commonality to be effective.

Conclusions

To imagine life today without advertising is merely impossible. Most of the products that we buy today are because we have seen them at some point or the other. The influence of the brands on our purchases is immense. Advertising and promotion are important parts of the international marketing programme of a multinational corporation. Advertising is generally the most cost-effective way to communicate with buyers and creates a market in other countries and this needs special attention.

In recent years, much attention has been focused on global marketing, where a standard marketing programme is being used in all markets. Part of global marketing is global advertising, where the same basic advertising approach is used in all markets. Opponents of the global (standardised) approach argue that differences in culture, market and economic conditions, and consumer needs and wants make a universal approach to marketing and advertising highly impractical. Many companies use in-between approach, standardising their basic marketing strategy but localising advertising messages to fit each market.

There are a number of decision areas in the development of advertising and promotional programmes for international markets. These include organisation, agency selection, advertising research, creative strategy and execution, and media strategy and selection. Only the right combination and the right proportions can get the recipe of success in international advertising.

Cited Works

Arens, William F, *Contemporary Advertising,* 6th ed. (Chicago: Irwin, 1996).

Beatty Goll Sally, "Global Needs Challenge Midsize Agencies", *The Wall Street Journal,* December 14, 1995, P. B9.

Belch E. George & Belch A Michael, *Advertising & Promotion: An Integrated Marketing Communications Perspective,* TATA McGraw Hill Edition.

Bovee, Courtland L. et.al, *Advertising Excellence,* New York: McGraw-Hill, Inc,1995.

Kazmi S H H & Batra S K, *Advertising & Sales Promotion,* 2nd ed., New Delhi: Excel Books, 2004.

Ray, Michael L, *Advertising & Communication Management,* Englewood Cliffs, NJ: Prentice Hall, 1982.

Russell, J. Thomas, W. Ronald Lane, *Kleppner's Advertising Procedure,* 14th edition, , New Jersey: Prentice-Hall

Philip, Kolter, *Marketing Management: Analysis, Planning & Control Englewood Cliffs,* NJ: Prentice Hall, 1997.

Moriarty, E. Sandra, *Creative Advertising: Theory & Practice.* Prentice Hall. 1986.

O'Guinn, Thomas C, et.al. *Advertising and Integrated Brand Promotion,* Third Edition, New Delhi: Vikas Publishing House.

_______________ Chris T. Allen, Richard T. Semenik, *Advertising,* South-Western College Publishing, 2000.

Sharma, S and Raghuvir Singh. *Advertising: Planning and Implementation, 2006.* New Delhi: Prentice Hall.

Walkie, L William & Paul W Farris, "Comparative Advertising: Problems & Potential", *Journal of Marketing* 39, 1975.

Weilbacher, M. William, *Advertising,* 2nd edition. New York: Macmillan, 1984.

Wells, William, Burneff Joun & Moriarty Sandra, *Advertising: Principles & Practice.* Fifth edition. New Delhi: Prentice Hall 2002.

8

Gaining Momentum, Bridging Gaps: A Discourse on Communication in Bhutan

—Chandra Shekhar Sharma

This paper talks about the different sets of media utilised for communication in Bhutan at various points of time. The first set consists of the traditional media that communicates the Buddhist values to the society. This set emerged from the monk body and influenced the culture deeply. The second set, unlike the first one, flourished in the lap of society and hence bear its point of view. Both these sets of media have fostered cultural values in the society. With the publishing of the national newspaper, the *Kuensel* in 1967, an era of modern means of communication began. But the development of media was slow. The paper argues that the modern means of communication could secure room only in post Coronation Silver Jubilee times i.e., after 1999.

The Kingdom of Bhutan has a population of about six lakhs[1] scattered over the mountainous region of 46,500 sq kms[2]. The country is landlocked, touching India in south, east and west and Tibet (China) in north. After the annexure of Tibet by China, Bhutan is the only Buddhist country remaining in the world. In case the drafted constitution is adopted in its proposed form it will become a 'secular' country. The other religions that are here are Hinduism and Christianity. One may be surprised that though the size of the country is smaller yet it has diverse cultural dimensions, mostly influenced by *Drukpa Kagju* school of Mahayana Buddhism that came here from Tibet. The cultural traits in North are different than that in south and east and the west. On travelling the country one may find different traits in the lifestyle of Bhutanese living at various places, questioning the oft-cited term 'Bhutanese culture' which hints at the presence of only one culture in the country. There are varied cultural traits in north but what binds them all is the belief in Buddhism, Buddhist philosophy and theocratic values. The southern belt is populated by the followers of Hinduism whose native language is Nepali. The cultural traits are similar to that of Hindus in India and hence far different from that of the people in the other parts of country.

Buddhism has played a significant role in the shaping of the society. It was Zabdrung Ngawang Namgyel, a Tibetan lama, who came to Bhutan in AD 1616 and unified the country that was divided into small fiefdoms. He shaped the culture, religion and society of Bhutan. And not only this he also laid a dual system of theocratic governance in which the power was equally vested in the hands of spiritual ruler and temporal ruler, who were then referred as Dharma Raja and Deb Raja respectively. So influential was he, his theocratic system and his governance that even after about 350 years of his passing away we find him revered highly by the people.

Communication in Bhutan has seen various developmental stages. The rough mountainous terrain has been challenging to the development of communication facilities. Given that about 66 per cent of the total area of the country is presently covered with forest ranging form tropical in south to alpine in north, the forest coverage in the past could have been far more challenging for communication during Zabdrung Ngawang Namgyel's time. That he was an outsider making his efforts for imbibing cultural and administrative reforms was one challenge and that the population was scattered and illiterate was another. And yet another challenge was geographical barrier to communicate his ideology, his laws and his system of governance. Ngawang Namgyel's success is an example of the success of his communication. After registering a graceful victory over Tibetan army in the Third Tibetan invasion in 1639 he was revered with the title Zabdrung before his name. With this victory his prestige and power in Bhutan increased manifold. The extension of his influence and unification of the country required him to convey his power. The first exemplary effort in the field of official communication by Zabdrung Ngawang Namgyel was in the form of his wooden seal that had engraved on it his self composed sixteen tenets. These tenets are known to Bhutanese as *Nga Chudugma* (The Sixteen 'I'). The seal was used in official documents providing them an identity as the present day letterheads do. Official seals are most often seen as testimony to official statements. It not only attests the document but also communicates the identity of the office. Zabdrung Nawang Namgyel used his seal to communicate the supremacy of his system of governance. It was a powerful medium of communication, which resulted in faith of not only existing monks of different schools of Buddhism in Bhutan but also the feudal lords and the public. The victory conveyed his power and the seal conveyed his confidence through the 16 tenets. It a matter of further research that whether the 'I' in the *Nga Chudugma* are subjective representing himself or they represent the Lord Buddha. The seal, though, has historical and spiritual significance yet it has played role in communication.

If the account recorded by H. Hyslop who was present at the enthronement ceremony of the first King on 17 December 1907 is taken as a testimony then it won't be an exaggeration to say that Zabdrung cared much for the decipherability of the text engraved on the seal because he kept the size of the seal large enough so that anyone who comes across it could read with an ease. He did not make his seal just for the namesake but as a mode to communicate. A great idea! The estimate of the care taken for readability can be made from Hyslop's following record.

> The chief lama, the tatsang Khenpo, who has possession of Dhrama Raja's seal, produced this from a casket. It is a huge thing some five inches square....." (Michael Aris 1994 p. 95)

The traces of communication with foreign world are also visible during Zabdrung Ngawang Namgyel's time, which denies the existence of the so called isolation policy of Bhutan. Zabdrung Nawang Namgyel never denied communication either with India, Nepal, Tibet or the Westerners. He perhaps knew the importance of communication and hence was open to it. He would go to villages in Bhutan establishing contacts with the people, performing *Rimdos* (Puja) for them. Though a Dharma Raja he would stay in tents with his monks and allow them and people to meet him. In 1627 two Portuguese Jesuits Estavo Cacella and

Jeo Cabral came here for the purpose of preaching, converting people's faith to Christianity and seeking routes to Tibet. The report Estavo Cacella wrote to his superior is not only the living account of Zabdrung's life and Bhutan's the then life but also unfolds the status of communication during seventeenth century. This historical report whose photocopy is present in "the archives of the Society of Jesus in Rome" has been translated by Luiza Maria Baille (1999). The report called as *The Relacao* hints over the state of communication in Bhutan. The barrier of not knowing either party's language was overcome with the help of interpreter whereas the messages to the Zabdrung from his subordinate were mostly oral. Horsemen were used to relay message to distant places. And the process appears to be much faster even in those difficult terrain because at one point in the report we find Zabdrung's people promptly arranging things at the next point of travelling after seeking instructions from Zabdrung Ngawang Namgyel who was stationed elsewhere (17).

Buddhism made its way deeper into the society. The entire monk body contributed in preserving religious scriptures, books by copying them day and night and distributing them to different monasteries. This was a painstaking effort on their part in preservation and communication. Apart from Khenpos, Lamas and Gaylongs who would propagate Buddhist canons in the society through recitation and *rimdos* different means have been in use in the society to communicate different context.

A most common example in the society is creating of smoke by burning of the cypress leaves in the open space nearby the venue of festivity or religious activity. It is normally taken as a simple gesture of purifying atmosphere with the sweet smell of the burning cypress. From the point of communication this is meant to inform the people living nearby about the performing of the religious activity so that they can come to attend it. This is a kind of semaphore so common in Bhutan that it has got much of religious value than the social. It is treated as a gesture of sanctity.

Trade basically requires 'need' and 'communication'. Further, trade becomes easier with the help of a currency that holds well for both the parties. Monetisation came to Bhutan of late in twentieth century; however Nicholas Rhodes (1999) finds some traces of usages of coins in the kingdom before the eighteenth century. Though there wasn't a nationally accepted currency yet the trade and commerce was doing well within and outside the country. India and Tibet were the two most sought after trading partners. Absence of currency wasn't a barrier for trade for it was mainly done through barter system. Bhutanese, Tibetans and Indians would go to either country for the trade. Communication wasn't a problem at all. Even at that time Bhutanese had competency in speaking the language of neighbouring countries. The languages spoken in other parts except South share wide similarities with the Tibetan language. This affinity in the languages had helped Bhutanese widely in over coming linguistic barriers. Father Cacella notes:

> ...we had much difficulty in understanding the one available- as he was not of this kingdom but from Tsaparang (Western Tibet), he did not know that language of this area which was the one we most needed because although in these kingdoms they all speak the same language there are differences in pronunciation and word endings, and the corruption of the language in some areas almost makes it foreign specially on this kingdom where the language is very changed—this kingdom being in a remote corner does a little business with other kingdoms; however, all the lamas and the people generally understand the other languages and so with the one we know we are able to communicate in all at these parts... (21)

Multilingual nature of the Bhutanese has helped them in making their contacts fluent with neighbouring societies. Jamie Zeppa (1999) also adores this quality in her travelogue *Beyond the Sky and the Earth: A Journey into Bhutan.*

Before the advent of modern education written communication in Bhutan mainly rested in the hands of administrators and monks. Literacy in traditional Bhutanese society was limited only to privileged ones and monks. Society thus relied on the oral messages passed on to it through heads or state. The dissemination of cultural values and Buddhist canons has been done through different means. Organised religious discourses like *katha* and *pravachan* in India are not a part of civil society. Lay people and women had almost no access to scriptures lest they ordain monkhood. Moreover sex was another discriminating factor for getting education and adorning monkhood to some extent. Kuenzang Choden (2005) has underlined sex as a discriminating factor in her novel *The Circle of Karma* where the protagonist Tshomo is refrained to learn reading and writing for the reason that she was a girl.

> You are a girl. You are different. You learn other things that will make you a good woman and a good wife. Learn to cook, weave and all those things. A woman does not need to know how to read and write,' father says quietly but sternly when she asks him to teach her. (21)

Though education was afar from lay people yet we can see old illiterates reciting daily prayers, observing the cultural values deep seated in Buddhist scriptures. This is the result of the effective media that have been used for ages in Bhutan. There has been different media for communicating different messages. *Dharshing* (prayer flags), the *mani dunkar* (prayer wheel), festivals, mask dances have been widely used for disseminating religious ideas and Buddhist philosophy. These have high religious esteem in the society.

The second set comprises folklores—folktales, folksongs and folk wisdom—hidden in traditional idioms and phrases. These have been widely used for religious and didactic purpose and comprise eternal part of culture. This set of media flourished not with lamas or in the premises of Dzongs but with common people and society. They have served dual purpose; firstly they disseminate knowledge and religious ideas and secondly entertainment. These two sets of communication media have been highly influenced by Buddhist concepts, hence can be clubbed together as a traditional medium of communication.

A traditional medium of communication reflects the culture in which it is produced for it is the culture and society that shapes it. In this very context the traditional media represents the aboriginal taste of cultural life in Bhutan. Secondly traditional media also cultivate mind with the cultural values.

The third group consists of modern means of communication like newspapers, radio, television, Internet, etc., which gained momentum in post-Coronation Silver Jubilee era, i.e., after 1999.

This set of media is accredited to connect Bhutan to the outer world and vice-versa. Modern means of communication has imbibed a sense of pacing-with-the-world in the Bhutanese society. The deep seating of Buddhism is attributed to the traditional medium which has imbibed a profound sense of social obligation towards the religion and made its way to the cultural canals.

The prayer flags communicate deeper components of Buddhist information. Made up of thin cloth these flags are either mounted on bamboo or tree trunks or are hanged across passess, bridges with a rope. They have religious scriptures and symbols printed over them. It is held in belief that their wavering would produce the chanting of mantras printed on them, which will be carried in all the directions by air to cast their sublime effect. Furthermore the flags are not traditionally taken off. They are rather left to wither for it will further purify the atmosphere and subdue demons. This means that prayer flags have been used to create fearless atmosphere. From the point of view of communication prayer flags have cultivated tenets of Buddhism in the society. They have deeply imbibed the messages of Buddhist identity in the society.

These have also served to imbibe a sense of realisation and gratitude towards the basic elements of human life. The five colours of prayer flags symbolise the elements necessary for sustainability of human life. Blue for sky/space, white for air/ wind/ cloud, red stands for fire, green represents water/vegetation and yellow stands for earth. At superficial level the presence of prayer flags has been interpreted as just religious (especially by the Westerners who came as tourists) but if observed carefully they communicate the requisites for the harmonical existence of mankind. A Buddhist cannot neglect the presence of prayer flags and chortens (Bhutanese name for stupas) for it is customary that any person passing by them is required to walk in such a way that these holy objects should be on his/her right side. This makes the passerby conscious about their presence and eventually the holy message these religious artifacts convey.

Similarly *Mani Dunkar*, the prayer wheels installed at different places is expected to be kept rotated. They can be found in the peripheries of lhakhangs, monastries and other holy and public places. Some are beautifully installed at the springs making them rotate clockwise with the natural flow of water. Prayer wheels also have Buddhist mantras painted or scribed over them which imbibe a sense of religious values. At other places the passersby rotate them with their right hand in clockwise direction. On completion of one rotation the stick projected horizontally at the top hits the bell, informing the circumbulator about the completion of one round. The bell not only tells of the completion of one round but also communicates a devotee's presence nearby. They have been so effective in communicating Buddhist values that people often keep miniature prayer wheel in their hand and keep it rotating while reciting *Om Mani Peme Hung*. The eight lucky symbols also convey the allegiance towards Buddhism. They preach the importance of different elements of Buddhism in human life and remind the ethics and etiquettes expected in pretext to them.

Bhutan has few festivals to its credit but each festival has a message. The first festival is Losar, the New Year which is observed in a very modest way. The main festival is Tshechu that is observed on the tenth day of a Bhutanese month to commemorate the birth anniversary of Guru Padmasambhava (popularly known as Guru Rimpoche), an Indian saint who brought Buddhism in Bhutan in seventh century. As he was born on the tenth day of a month, customarily Tshechu is observed on the tenth day. Each Dzongkhag (District) celebrates its Tshechu on the tenth day of a definite month of Bhutanese calendar. Months are fixed for dzongkhags to observe Tshechus but his year, in 2008, perhaps first time in the history of Bhutan that the Tshechu of Chhukha Dzongkhag was postponed for next month because it coincided with the first parliamentary election. Celebrated at Dzongs (District headquarters) with mask dances these create a mega public event. The three day-long festivities open with the sunrise and ends with the sunset of the third day. It provides an occasion for the people to gather at a place once in a year and hence gives an important shape to the venue. People from nearby villages come to attend it thereby giving the dzong a shape of temporary town where

> a whole community, which is actually dispersed throughout a valley, gathers at one place at a given time and socialises

> making a traditional media event in contemporary jargon (Françoise Pommaret 2006).

During Tshechu variety of mask dances are performed by the monks in the courtyard with the courtyard full of spectators. These dances in fact serve as a medium to communicate a variety of messages to the lay people and children who have no access to religious scriptures. Performed at the music of cymbals and drums these dances have a story at their backdrop and a message/ lesson/ moral at their core. The message could have been discharged in the form of storytelling session or verbal discourses by lamas but realising the size of the audience, limitations of human voice and strength of the appeal of the images different mask dances are chosen. They not only have a visual appeal but also make the lofty moral messages lighter for the audience to be grasped with the tint of entertainment. The Shinje Chham (the Yamraj dance), the Shamag Chham (black hat dance), the Legoen Chham (protector diety's dance), the Ngaging Chham, the Phole Mole Chham, Raksha mar Chham, the Drametse NgaChham, and the Shawo- Shachi Chham (the dance of deer and hound) are some of the most popular mask dances. The presentation of these dances has a didactic value in addition to religious. While some dances narrate legendary tales, some like Phole Mole chham delineate flaws in human nature. All mask dances are meant to preach the audience "the Buddhist concepts of retribution, forgiveness, compassion" (28).

There are also some dances, which are translated versions of the anecdotes present in scriptures, Drametse Ngachham, for instance. As lay people have no access to literature and religious scriptures so the important anecdotes are acted on the occasion of Tshechu for making them comprehensive enough through mask dances to elucidate them to the laypeople in its simplest form for,

> ...they are written in such a way and in a language that ordinary people are neither accustomed to, nor able to read and they cannot impact the masses as vividly as an enacted story. (29)

Françoise studies the dances explicitly. She observes dances as a 'traditional medium of information.' Her observation at one point can be taken as a conclusion:

> the taming of one's emotions, whatever be the circumstances, is a core of Buddhist message which is imparted during these dances and grounded in concrete examples with which people can easily identify; it is this strength which makes the dance performance play role of media. (29)

The second set of media comprises folklores, commonly referred to as oral tradition that flourished in the lap of civil society. This includes folktales, folksongs and sayings. Folktales that are seen as past-time activity have contributed a lot in shaping the civil society. While the mask dances and festivals are the media used by monks and administrators to communicate Buddhist philosophical ideals, folktales have been used as a common man's media and hence have variety of messages from the point of view of laypeople. The folktales involve much of the communication process including feedback. The listeners have to respond to the stories with a sound *'Umm..mm'* which implies 'that the story is listened by the audience.' This is a common response but there are some other responses too. To express their sympathy or signify their listening the listener says *'Aye,'* which roughly means 'yes' and when the story takes turn to some astonishments or reveals suspense the audience express their surprise or shock by *'Yaahlamah'* or *'ayi wha.'* Another usual say that follows the sequence is *'Aei'* or *'tse ni'* (in Bumthangkha) or *'delay'* that means 'then.' These instantaneous feedbacks ensure that the message encoded has been decoded properly. And these instantaneous feedbacks are not very natural but have been imbibed in the listener society as a required custom of storytelling or listening activity. The listeners have to respond with any of the suitable words or sound for it's a custom. Kunzang Choden (2002) reasons:

> This customs is to prevent the spirits from listening to the stories and stealing them. As long as human beings respond and indicate that the story is being listened to, the spirits cannot steal them. (xiv)

The storytelling sessions are social as well as domestic. In social storytelling sessions a group of listeners assemble at a place and a storyteller 'releases' or 'unravel' before the audience with utmost skills of the art of narration that could take the audience to the past to grasp the message hidden in them. To be noted in

Bhutan, stories are never 'told' or 'said.' (xi). Their objective in addition to entertainment is to communicate the virtues like compassion, workmanship, benevolence, honesty, mutual trust, etc. In the stories the honest trustful characters proclaim their victory and those dishonest suffer. *The Boys who went to Buy Cows,* Gyalpo *Migkarla, Bum Sing Sing Yang Donma, Ap Brapchul, Lame Monkey,* are a few examples of the stories that communicate the reward for virtuousness and criticise vices. There are stories like *The Lazy Boy* who communicate to the audience the criticism about laziness. The methodology of our folktales as media to preach dignity of labour is not spiritual but far more practical and full of illustrations. Labour is not criticised but is hailed high and is portrayed as an activity full of enjoyment. The philosophy of 'Work is Worship' lies at the soul of the stories. We do find here the 'division of labour' but we don't find here traces of calling any task mean. Nor we find people classified into castes and creeds according to the work they do in the society. Every character, whether rich or poor, male or female, able or disabled, young or old is found engaged in some productive activity. There are stories (like *The Borrowed Gho, Ashi Dunglidolma, Bo Serba Tung Tung*) with a focus of rich- poor conflict. Such stories communicate that vices are to be punished and virtues are to be rewarded despite being rich or poor. Prima facie the tales communicate the philosophy of justice in action. In stories the characters do kill wild animals, *sinpos,* and ghosts and harm the unsocial elements but their purpose is not to preach violence as a motive behind the life. They kill those who are harmful to them and all. This set of communication media observes things from the point of view of society. It doesn't criticise either retribution or the killings. It doesn't denounce materialism either.

Unlike spiritual models they communicate that possession of worldly things is also necessary to some extent in the society. Our characters become happy by possessing worldly things. They fight for worldly pleasures and their life is portrayed happy when they achieve them. Those who lose are portrayed as fools or *Tsagye. Meme Heyley Heyley, P'chekhay,* the Lazy Boy (*The Story of Lazy Boy*) are depicted as fools who go on bartering their priced possessions with less important objects.

Folksongs also served as a media to communicate messages that have influenced Bhutanese society to a larger extent. They are classified into different categories and the popular ones are *Zuendra, Boedra* and *Lozey*. *Zuendras* are the oldest songs. It's a group song accompanied with dance and has very soft body movements. The dance is performed in standing position. The content of such songs communicate pious values. They are neither love songs nor sad songs. They are aesthetic songs containing the admirations about dzongs, mountains, seasons, peaks, religion and philosophy. One of the popular *Zuendras* sings of the famous Punakha Dzong. Another Zuendra *"Choeki Tsa-Wa Mitsuk/ Choeki Tsa-Wa Tsuk"* sings of Buddhism and devotion. Another interesting Zuendra that commences with *"Ja sa boe la mi du"* is portrayal of a daughter's refusal for marriage as she finds her would-be in-laws' land sans religion. Two more Zuendras—one about Jhomolhari, the highest peak in Bhutan and the other that sings of sacred life of Gyalongs—is also popular. The matter content of *Boedra*, on the other hand, is picturesque. For example, *"shar lha ni ha le me shar"* sings of sun, "In the morning sun was shinning from the east", *" ni pha yel gangri karpo"* represents the love and reminiscences of the singer for his far village. It says, "When I see the White Mountain I remember my village." Another famous Boedra *"jigten samling nanka mile serga rinchen."* Boedra ends with a thumping of right foot and bending forward with open palms. Some Boedra are slow in tunes and are performed with soft movements. They communicate the societal affairs and morals in light manner laying emphasis on entertainment value.

Lozeys are concerned with historical aspect and have an epic nature. They communicate heroic achievements of a person or war or of an incident. The *Lozey of Pema Tshewang Tashi* and that of *Gaylong Sumdar Tashi* are widely popular in the kingdom. The former deals with the courage of a soldier moving for a war, while the latter talks of a Sumdar Tashi who has to leave his family and children to join the monk-body as a matter of monk tax.

The traditional media contributed much in the shaping of the society. It not only influenced the mass but also imbibed cultural traits that gradually became an identity of the Bhutanese society. The advent of modern media in Bhutan, especially TV, has been observed as a threat to it. With upcoming urbanisation and various other entertainment facilities like TV, films, Internet available around its aureole is shrinking (Tandin Dorji 2002, Sonam Kinga 2001, Karma Phuentsho 2000, Kunzang Choden

2002, Ross McDonald 2004). The issues of protecting them and concerns for their continued existence has been widely expressed.

Intra-societal communication in Bhutan too has an interesting aspect. The interesting practice of relaying messages verbally from one person to another, from one village to another can still be seen. One good example can be observed in case of hiring labour. Labour is not hired traditionally in Bhutan in terms of monetary payments. Absence of currency may be one reason. But another reason is the low population density distributed over valleys and terrain.

Labour has been exchanged for labour. Even the Royal government has entertained it at various times. Still in practice are *Chola, Changla, Jala, Zhabto Lemi* and *woola. Changla* is related to the collective help rendered to farmers in planting paddy saplings in the fields. *Jala* is attributed to harvesting. For either of the activity a word is passed to the villagers either by a person or by the village committee for working in a field. People work collectively in a field and the other day the owner (farmer) reciprocates by joining in the group for working in other's field. The information is mostly conveyed verbally and is respected by every able person. In lieu of work the owner provides food and drinks for the day to the group and later works in others field. Lham Dorji (2005) and Tashi Choden (2005) while exploring the attributes of civil society in Bhutan deal with these activities in detail.

Woola is a similar kind of activity related to the construction of infrastructure in the villages. In this activity one person from each beneficiary house in the village/ community works for the construction of bridge, school, lhakhang (temple), village office etc. The order for woola is officially released by the government or the village head. While in the former discussed activities the words are in requestive tone and the message is oral in case of Woola the communication is in written form. It seems that in the past this was also oral. Incase of absentia from any house the owner of the house is subject to fine.

Of Symbols in Written Communication

Written communication in Dzongkha involves different symbols. Every symbol has its name, value and particular context of usage.

While some are attributes to religious context, some are to administrative context. The symbols are widely used in various formal and informal written communications. A brief list of symbols, prepared after a preliminary survey and discussions is given in Table 1.

Sl.No.	*Symbol*	*Name*	*Usage*
1		yegu-Gogen	This is used as an initial symbol in the documents that are devoted to the triple-Gem. It shows respect and devotion of higher order in communication.
2.		yegu-Gogen	It has a similar usage like 1. Basically used in administrative communications.
3.		yegu-Gogen	It is used basically in religious scriptures (pecha). It is used in the beginning of the paragraphs of religious commentaries. Can't be used in letter-writing.
4.		Kasho-Gogen	It is used the orders issued by His Majesty the King. It is seen as in the beginning of Royal edicts, Royal decrees, etc.
5.		Shuyig-Gogen	This symbol is used in formal written communications addressed to superior officials, elders.
6.		Chirtang-Gogen	The symbol is commonly used in all formal written communications. The usage is a sign of respect rather than of formality.
7.		Drayam-Gogen	It is used in informal letters, lateral written communications and domestic letters.
8.		Thuyig-dang Genja yi Gogen	It is seen in the beginning of letters of agreement of higher administrative value. Also used before the titles of organisation.

9.			It is used as a bracket to code important supplementary information like section number, date, etc., can be used signal or in pair.
10.			It is used in the beginning of the text that have religious of spiritual significance.
11.	।	Chi She	This is a period used as a 'Full-stop'. It is put at the end of a long sentence.
12.	༎	Ni-she	It is used after short sentences that have a complete thought. Titles of the organisations, names of posts are mentioned in between a pair of Ni-shes.

Modern Means of Communication

The advent of modern means of communication can be traced back to the establishment of the first newspaper *Kuensel* that was started only in 1967 as a monthly bulletin of the Royal Government of Bhutan. It was published in India in English till 1974 as till that year there wasn't any printing presses in Bhutan. In 1974 Bhutan got a press and had it installed in Thimphu to print the bulletin. The Dzongkha edition could start in the same year with the preparation of Dzongkha blocks. *Kuensel* remained as a monthly news bulletin for years. It was only in the year 1986 that it could become weekly. Still it remained as the only newspaper of the kingdom for the policies didn't allow private or foreign media's existence. Till 2006 *Kuensel* was the only newspaper in the country and was published weekly.

The radio could make its way in Bhutan in 1973 under the name of "Radio NYAB" that broadcast news in English and some music for half an hour on Sundays. The studio was stationed in Thimphu. Before this, Bhutan established telecom services accessible to few areas in 1967. In 1979 the Ministry of Communications under RGoB took over Radio NYAB, renamed it as Bhutan Broadcasting Services (BBS) and introduced three hours daily services. An aid from UNESCO made Bhutan to start local FM station in 1987 that was also under BBS. About late 1980s when the television sets were making their way in the Asian societies a Royal Decree was issued in 1989 to ban television viewing thereby mandating to dismantle the Fishbone antennas. It was at this time that people in Bhutan were using television sets and were watching Indian and Bangladeshi channels. Bhutan was thus the only nation in the world to ban television. This was done to preserve the national cultural identity. This step of Bhutan initiated mindblogging across the globe. While there were some criticisms on this step, some sectors praised it in the wake of appalling influences of foreign media. The Government of India has been the chief donor agency for Bhutan. It has always extended its helping hand in the developmental stages of the country. The friendly ties of the two countries are exemplary for the world. In late 80s the Government of India understood that BBS required a facelift and keeping aside the 'ban' gifted a state-of-the-art new complex for BBS in 1991. In 9991 BBS shifted to this complex. *Kuensel* that was still alone newspaper in the kingdom was detached from government through a Royal Edict in 1992 and made to be operated under an autonomous corporation. Later in 1998 the government stopped its subsidy to *Kuensel* making it a self-financed corporation.

The year 1999 marked the start of developments in various fields especially in communication. It was the year celebrating Silver Jubilee of the Coronation the then king, His Majesty Jigme Singye Wangchuk. On the celebration day, i.e., 2 June 1999, Internet services started in the kingdom; hours later to the start of the Internet, television broadcast started for the first time in the Bhutanese history. This broadcast was from BBS. It was then for three hours every evening. It was in this year only that the Telecom Act was approved in the 77th session of the National Assembly. The year 2000 brought FM services to the BBS, still state a owned corporation. BBS started 12 hours radio broadcast a day. Later in the month of July of this year the Telecom department became a state-owned corporation and was called Bhutan Telecom.

The year 2003 marked Bhutan's equivalence to some extent to other neighbouring countries in a sense that on 11 November of this year celphones came into the hands of the people with the start of Bhutan Mobile Communication Service by the Bhutan

Telecom. Prior to this Bhutan Communication Authority was established in the same year. The BCA has been renamed as Bhutan InfoCom and Media Authority (BICMA) since January 2005. It is the regulatory body for telecommunication facilities and transmission of TV channels in the kingdom. It was in this year only that BBS extended its television services to four hours a day (6-10 pm).

The year 2005 was a setback to some TV channels as this year brought a ban on them on the ground of cultural implications. In the month of July, Bhutan banned some Indian TV channels that are still banned till date. In the February of this year the *Kuensel* became a biweekly and in December for the first time in the history, it started its Kanglung edition for western Bhutan.

The monopoly of *Kuensel* as the maiden newspaper in the kingdom came to an end on 30 April 2006 with the publishing of *Bhutan Times*. It is a weekly paper published on Sunday from the capital in English. On 2 June of the same year another weekly newspaper *Bhutan Observer* started its publication from Thimphu. It is published on Friday. Kuzoo FM, the first private FM Radio station that started its services in 2006, ended the monopoly of BBS Radio. Last year in 2007 another FM radio station, named as Radio Valley, kicked off its transmission and became the second private radio station the date 6 April 2008 stands witness to the launch of Tashi Cell, a private cell phone service that has ended the monopoly of B-mobile in telecom services especially cell phone services.

The saga that started with a news bulletin has now reached to three newspapers, three FM Radio stations, two cell phone operators and two ISPs (one private established in 2007). And there are miles to go ahead and more goals to achieve. The year 2008 marks the centenary of the establishment of monarchy in the country and inevitably more developmental announcements are expected. Trade and commerce has now gained momentum and this will surely enhance communication.

Cited Works

Aris, Michael. *The Raven Crown,* London: Serindia. 1994

Baille, Luiza Maria. Father Estevao Cacella's Report on Bhutan in 1627, *Journal of Bhutan Studies,* Volume 1.1.1999

Choden, Kunzang. *Folk Tales of Bhutan,* Bangkok: White Lotus. 1993

____________. *Tales of Yeti,* Bangkok: White Lotus. 1997.

____________. *The Circle of Karma,* New Delhi: Zubaan Penguin. 2005.

Dorji, Dasho Kinley. Media in Bhutan: Now and Then, *Journal of Bhutan Studies,* Volume 14 (Summer). 2006.

Dorji Lham and Tashi Choden. *Understanding Civil Society in Bhutan,* Thimphu: Center for Bhutan Studies. 2005.

Dorji, Tandin. Folktale Narration: A Retreating Tradition, *Journal of Bhutan Studies,* Volume 6. 2002.

McDonald Ross. Television, Materialism and Culture: An Exploration of Imported Media and Its Implication for GNH, *Journal of Bhutan Studies,* Volume 1. 2004.

Phuntsho Karma. On the Two ways of Learning in Bhutan, *Journal of Bhutan Studies,* Volume 2.2.2000

Pommaret, Françoise. Dances in Bhutan: A Traditional Media of Information, *Journal of Bhutan Studies,* Volume 14 (Summer). 2006

Sharma Chandra Shekhar. Echoes of Folksongs in Bhutanese Literature in English, *Journal of Bhutan Studies,* Volume 15. 2007.

Zeppa Zamie. *Beyond the Sky and the Earth: A Journey into Bhutan.* 2003.

9

Impact of Information and Communication Technology on Social Transition in Communication

—Ashok Kumar

Globalisation indicates interconnectivity of the assorted varieties of technology. These technologies have swiftly transformed this cosmos into a 'global village'. They have shrunk geographical frontiers. Nations, organisations, individuals, big businesses, and commercial corporations are incorporated by globalisation. This global era has titanic implications deliberated for society along with the following foremost points:

1. Emphasis on the escalation of communicational skills, with mounting mastery over information technology.
2. Inevitability to arrive at the frontiers of knowledge as swiftly as possible by closing existing gaps and subsequently to keep up velocity.
3. Stress on the general public to widen global consciousness and global concerns.
4. Challenges to evenhandedness and opportunities intended for diversities.
5. Augmentation of a global society and the obligation to allocate ethics that can protract benevolence in the global era.

The modern society is undergoing plentiful transformations due to quick dissemination of information and communication technologies in all walks of life, "in the knowledge age, information and intelligence become the raw materials." Information is burgeoning like a decisive resource for people in every action and at all the levels of edification, investigation, and evolution and via these means enlightening the excellence of day-to-day life. These days, it is leading individual verve in the impending century building an insightful impact on society and country.

The muse of information humanity emerged in 1970's to 1980's, and is hurriedly gaining all-embracing regard. A distinguished information sage, William Martin says, "The information society is a society in which the qualities of life as well as prospects for social change and economic development depend increasingly upon information and its leisure, education system and the market places are all influenced markedly by advanced information knowledge." One more IT idol, Manfred Kochen, has documented an assortment of distinctiveness of Information society in which: "Information is considered more important than the materials that provide information. At least half of its members are engaged in knowledge occupations and such occupations are not only based on knowledge generation."

In this era, information pitch is observer to an electrifying superfluity of technological advances, which have been responsible for incalculable enrichment in human techniques of communication. The convergence of information technology and communication technology has opened up pioneering challenges for communication in society. Technology if used appropriately has the prospective to primarily transform the approach in which the society is living. Our institutions cannot afford to neglect the accelerating swiftness of technological expansion and their liability in building an enlightened society of information and communication technology. The technology-based communication has trounced each barrier of the information access. Nowadays, the notion of resources of knowledge is shifting from bringing the human to the resource materials to taking the resource to the human.

Because of swift discoveries in the field of technology and unparalleled use of contemporary communication technologies at an extremely fast rate, the types of communication skills mostly considered necessary are bound to modernise. The high officials who aspire to swap over data and information among others within or without the institute have to opt for the excellent mode of communication matched for the rationale, whether to phone, call a meeting, meet them in their relevant offices or send them e-mail messages or a facsimile message. How greatly do these technological discoveries and several latest budding technologies impact upon the connotation of thriving communication? To what extent will, progressively more in the near future, building an acceptable variety of the communication medium become even more crucial than it has been heretofore?

Information technology has two magnitudes. First, is the access to it to be literate: to have the world at the tip of your fingers and the other is specialising in such areas to be certified? India is feeling the blits of technology where the juvenile and the elderly contend with one another to be computer savvy. Once the idea has set in then the reaction without human intervention comes, in the shapes of cyber shops, courses, etc. The query, one pauses to ask is, how will the society benefit? Are we anticipating circumstances where there will be merely e-communication, an idiom which is the buzz remark today? Acquaintance of information and communication technology is no doubt a prerequisite, this means being not only computer erudite in an international technique of communication. The community information centres, we are told in India, are yet to be fully equipped and outfitted. These centres should be viewed as community enabling centres, where the access to computer, ideally speaking enhances the excellence of life. The UNESCO text on edification in the twenty-first century states with clarity:

> Learning to know,
> Learning to do,
> Learning to be, and
> Learning to live together.

In the information era technically accomplished citizens can fabricate the well-built society. The public requires information for the professional, delicate and even leisure activities. In the fruition it inspires people to learn more and more and acquire a wide range of information.

The Net or Information Super Highway or Cyber Space or the Open Communication Infrastructure is a synthesis of thousands of computer networks, and computers have revolutionised resource distribution and access. The Internet covers an entire array of themes, and areas like trade, commerce, civilisation, edification, investigation, science and technology, and so on. The avenues for utilisation of the Internet resources by libraries are unconstrained and never-ending. The Internet provides access to a compilation of commercial and non-commercial information sources as well as bibliographic and full-text databases, tables of contents, e-journals, newsletters, audio and video clipart, multimedia walk through programmes, etc. The Internet is also one of the best ways to access the local and external resources of information.

Contemporary technology has become one of the strapping medium of managing knowledge through the strengthened capabilities of collecting, storing, processing, packaging and transmitting the information. The communities ought to incessantly modernise themselves with knowledge and skills in the areas of information resources, tools, access modes, technology management and research, and the capability to integrate each and every one for getting data and information services more proficiently and successfully.

Whilst analysing the impact of technology on education and erudition one must focus on the information civilisation in which the prominence is on the qualitative changes in every field of exertion. The education and erudition technology has progressed from classroom lectures and seminars to a range of learning items. Learning items, as defined by the International Electronic and Electrical Engineer's Learning Technology Standards Committee are "any entity, digital or non-digital, which can be used, re-used, or referenced during technology supported learning." These incorporate CDs, electronic books (e-books), e-journals, e-magazines, audio-visual aids, etc.

The present social order for all intents and purposes demonstrates that information engender supremacy, particularly when it is strewn in a petite space of time, or better still, in real time. The aptitude to access the information straight away, and the consequential products, services and wealth was conscientious for the exemplary swing brought about by the technological revolution. As soon as electronic communication is pooled with mobility, its command is multiplied. Mobility allows having access to information anytime and anywhere. As an effect of unexpected technological innovation, Personal Digital Assistant (PDA) and wireless devices are also being used as e-communication apparatus. Mobile communication is the juncture of mobile computing and e-communication that take account of anytime, anywhere assets with sturdy penetrating capabilities and rich interaction.

Information reaches to an entity in unfiltered formats raising questions on the subject of its soundness, genuineness, credibility, and trustworthiness. In addition information is accessible through several media with graphical, aural, and textual and these masquerade innovative challenges for persons in evaluating and appreciates information in an ethical and authorised manner. The indecisive eminence and intensifying magnitude of information create innovative challenges for society.

At present, India is the fourth prevalent market in the world that is attracting comprehensive insists for its information and communication technological services. Its market value is expected to be US$ 87 billion in 2008. Conversely, India suffers from telecommunication transportation bottlenecks resembling lack of bandwidth, low speed leased lines, high cost of software and slow servicing, which creates hurdles in the prompt developments of information and communication technology in India. Even though, electronic communication is being used in the commercial sectors in India for providing the in service training hitherto we have miles to go. And Gurukul online is the first educational portal for information technology industry in India.

Today, we envisage of using the dissimilar levels of technological realities to edify the natives. As technology is making headway at a breakneck alacrity, let us not impede thinking about the vulnerable victims of poverty and literacy. Therefore, this is a nonentity to experience elated regarding, the precise connotation of information and communication technology in the Third World market indicates towards up-and-coming pastoral areas and as citizens have straightforward and chief access to it.

India is a multilingual nation and nearly every one of the inhabitants knows vernacular languages. Nevertheless nearly all of the contents of e-resources are in English. That's why to formulate e-communication flourishing in India the digital transcript needs to be translated in these languages to boot. Rural community in India can get advantage merely by establishing e-communication centres with contents in neighbouring languages and accordingly the inhabitants would be competent enough to cross intellectual precincts by collaborating with learners from new cultures thereby plunging the space of digital segregation.

Whatsoever, on the other hand, may be the latest technologies that will enter in the communicational configuration in vista, amid the subsequent opportunities and challenges, the desires and necessities for efficient and successful communication at every phase of the society will not change. Face-to-face communication, of course, will persistently be an imperative preference. On the other hand, with the initiation of new video telephones, cell phones, teleconferencing and numerous latest sophisticated technologies accessible these days, face-to-face communication would not remain one of the best options of communication in the near future. In short, these annotations bring to the fore how communication can append significance, how may a link between business pay off or how may we bond simultaneously dissimilar tools of communication, so that it all add value as an intact rather than individual parts functioning beside each other.

In this way, due to swift developments in information and communication technology and globalisation of information, it is easier for entire society and individuals to access information from any where and at any time. The impact of Internet and other electronic and digital resources facilitate masses to use plenty of sources to gratify their information requirements. Consequently, technology is becoming a global precedence as society transits further into the digital information setting. Therefore, in due course, general public in every country will necessitate training in efficient and proficient information use in order to function confidently and industriously in any type of endeavour and social milieu.

Cited Works

American Library Association. Presidential Committee on Information Literacy. Final Report. (1989), Available online at: http://www.ala.org/acrl/nili/llit 1 st.html

Borton: Information Literacy: Learning How to Learn, Available online at http://www.ri.net./rtti_fellows/Borton/ Infolit.html

Davis, Keith (1981), *Human Behaviour at Word,* 6th Edition, New Delhi, Tata Mcgraw Hill.

Denver Business Journal. (1997), www.opnions.com/mags. Denver Business Journals/1-31K.

http://www.linezine.com/201features/cqmmwiyp.htm

http://www.webtools.city.edu.hk/news/newslett/wireless.htm

http://www.corporate.netversity.com/univ.asp

http://www.computeruser.com/news/03/01/02/newsl.html

http://www.gurukulonlinecom/ejournal/ejournalNov2001.pdf

http://www.prasena.com/public/eLearning%20%20Learning.doc

http://www.worldwidelearn.com/global-education.html

Information Literacy: An Overview of Design, Process and Outcomes, Available online at http://www.noodletools.com/Debbie/Literacies/ Information/ 1over/infolit 1.html

Kochen, Manfred. (1987), *A New Concept of Information Society.* London. ASLIB.

Ludlow, Ron and Panton Fergus (2000). *The Essence of Effective Communication.* New Delhi: Prentice Hall of India.

Lu-Xin-An. (2000), Public Secrets as a Phenomenon in Organisational Communication. *Dissertation Abstract International,* Vol. 61, No. 8.

Manzoni Jean-Francois. September 2002, Better Way to Deliver Bad News. *Harward Business Review.*

Monipally M.M. (2003), The Kinder Cut: A Macro Communication Strategy for Delivering News of Job Termination. *Vikalpa,* Volume 28, No.3.

Nine Bottom Lines Reasons Why ensuring Good Communication is small investment. http://www.ivysca.com/pages/10988/html.

Pani, SRD (Ed.), *University News,* Association of Indian Universities, New Delhi.

Visionary Communication: Much More than a Vision Statement. http://www.ivsca.com/pages/10988/html.

10

Role of Communication in Team Effectiveness: A Review

—Tarika Singh

The world is seemingly growing smaller as technology advances and organisations span greater geographic distances. Communication lies at the heart of organisational work. Organisation information systems—are dependent on effective communication. With the advent of team-based and flattened organisations, communication has become even more important than it was before. But sorting out how communication impacts organisations can be difficult.

Communication is so pervasive in organisational work that we often overlook it as a source of problems. It is almost impossible to open a business magazine today without some guru exhorting the benefits of communication in teams. In many situations teams can achieve more than individuals working on their own. This is because teams can bring to bear a wider range of skills and experience to solve a problem. This is possible only when team members have good communication among themselves.

Team members have been working on a problem; they have a sense of commitment to the common solution drawn after consensus. Teams are often used in the workplace due to task demands (i.e., an individual cannot complete the task alone) and a need to remain competitive in finite markets. This study focuses on the role of communication in increasing the team effectiveness.

Conceptual Frame

Communication: The exchange of information is vital to the success of two or more individuals working as a team (Dickinson & McIntyre, 1997). The purpose of communication is often to clarify misunderstandings and to acknowledge the receipt of information (e.g., grounding, the establishment that mutual understanding has occurred between listener and speaker; (Clark & Brennan, 1991) and may not always be verbal (e.g., head nods; Reid, Reed, & Edworthy, 1999). Communication is the process of sharing information. It is a kind of social interaction where at least two interacting agents share a common set of signs and a common set of semiotic rules. In a simplistic form, information is sent from a sender or encoder to a receiver or decoder. In a more complex form feedback links a sender to a receiver. This requires a symbolic activity, sometimes via a language. Communication development is the development of processes enabling one to understand what others say (or sign, or write) and speak (or sign, or write), translate sounds and symbols into meaning and learn the syntax of the language. Communication is based on the idea of respect, promises and the want for social improvement.

Basic Modes of Communication in Organisations

There are four basic modes of communication in organisation: Face-to-Face, Audio, Video Mediated and Shared Workplace. Operating face-to-face is often considered the most effective means, but it is not always practical. Therefore, viable alternatives to operating face-to-face are sought.

Face-to-Face: The medium conveying the most information is face-to-face encounters. Although this may be the preferred method of communication for many tasks (i.e., negotiation, initial meetings), it is not always practical. For instance, by default, face-to-face encounters must occur synchronously and at the same location. This proves quite difficult for two individuals operating in different time zones across different continents (Armstrong & Cole, 1995). Barring face-to-face interchanges, the telephone offers a reliable and ubiquitous alternative.

Audio: High quality interchanges are available via the telephone without superfluous equipment. High quality is imperative with audio transmissions, especially if the audio is not complimented with other media (e.g., video, shared workspace). Many studies of geographically dispersed collaboration have demonstrated the phone to be the preferred mode of communication (e.g., May & Carter, 2001). As such, users encountering barriers with other media will often resort to the telephone to clarify exchanges (Olson & Teasley, 1996).

Video-mediated: One potential alternative for team communication is video interchanges. However, there are a number of issues yet to be resolved with video-mediated communication before it is considered a viable option in enhancing teamwork. Poor bandwidth in sharing data across networks (Angiolillo, Blanchard, Israelski, & Mané, 1997), poor representation of reality within a two-dimensional space (Benford, Brown, Reynard, & Greenhalgh, 1996), and problems associated with deixis (Barnard et al., 1996) among others have been noted as problems for the use of video in assisting distributed collaborators.

Shared Workspace: The shared workspace is an often-overlooked medium available to collaborators. Sharing the object of work such as simultaneously working on a computer file (e.g., a budget spreadsheet, a new product design) can address the issues with respect to verbal and non-verbal communication when team members cannot be collocated. Collaborators as sketchpads to enhance communication of ideas use computer whiteboards (Whittaker, Geelhoed, &Robinson, 1993). A shared workspace application could aid in the non-verbal exchanges. For instance, the two most common visual gestures are pointing and emphasizing speech (Bekker et al., 1995). Both of these functions could be and have been built into shared object applications. A well-designed application will also provide feedback through and consequential communication. A collaborator "clicking on a button" communicates that the action has been completed. This can both facilitate communication and monitoring processes.

Communication Style: Some people strike us as better at expressing themselves than others. We find them naturally understandable and congenial. They may have a voice, which is shrill or sing-song. We'd all agree that there is a small range of "good" ways of speaking. This is what one can call style of communication.

Work Groups/Teams: A variety of definitions have been offered for team communication (Guzzo & Shea 1992). But the one we adopted here owes its origins to the work of Alderfer (1977) and Hackman (1987). A "work group" is made up of individuals who see themselves and who are seen by others as a social entity, who are interdependent because of the tasks they perform as members of a group, who are embedded in one or more larger social systems (e.g. community, organisation) and who perform tasks that affect others (such as customers or coworkers).

A team is a group of people working together for common objective. A team can also be defined as a reasonably small group of people, who bring to the table a set of complementary and appropriate skills, and who hold themselves mutually accountable for achieving a clear and identifiable set of goals. Teams are often used in the workplace due to task demands (i.e., an individual cannot complete the task alone) and a need to remain competitive in finite markets (Ilgen, Major, Hollenbeck, & Sego, 1993; Kozlowski & Bell, 2003).

"Team" has largely replaced "group" in the argot of organisational psychology. For many, "team" connotes more than "group". Katzenbach & Smith (1993), for example, assert that groups become teams when they develop a sense of shared commitment and strive for synergy among members. Increasingly, teams are geographically dispersed and must conduct their functions across time and space (Bell & Kozlowski, 2002; Maznevski & Chudoba, 2000).

Team effectiveness: There is no singular, uniform measure of performance effectiveness for teams. We prefer to define it broadly, as have Hackman (1987) and Sundstrom et al. (1990). Accordingly, effectiveness in groups is indicated by:

a) Group-produced outputs (quantity or quality, speed, customer satisfaction, and so on).
b) The consequences a group has for its members.
c) The enhancement of a team's capability to perform effectively in the future. A team can be considered to be effective if their output is judged to meet or exceed the expectations of the people who receive the output.

Producing a quality output is not enough to judge the effectiveness of the team. The other criterion is that the team should still be able to function effectively and the people should have an enhanced working relationship that benefits the organisation.

Factors Contributing Towards Team Effectiveness: There has been a great deal of research into the subject of team effectiveness over the last decade or so and there is a consensus on what factors must be controlled in order to set up and run effective teams.

There are four areas of group behaviour that must be addressed for teams to be effective. The team must work hard. The team must have the right mix of skills to bring to the table. These skills include technical, problem solving and interpersonal skills. The third and the most important area is that the team must be able to develop appropriate approaches to problem solving. This involves identification and analysis of the problems of workplace and finding solutions by giving free and fair environment and a system of open dialogue within the team members. The role of communication is important in how problem is communicated and how a unanimous decision is made towards the approach of problem solving is of crucial importance. To accomplish the task, it is the responsibility of the team leader to communicate it in a way that it urges team members to work for it.

The effective team needs challenging goals, which are clearly defined. When challenging goals are set, the team will mobilise its efforts to find innovative ways to achieve feats that may have been considered impossible. Framing the challenging goals is the most important motivator to sustain group effort.

The characteristics of the task should be communicated in a way that provide motivation and make the task worthwhile and interesting, which will result in an urge within each member to see and decide how it has to be done. The outcome of the task needs to be stated as a whole piece of work with a clear and visible result so that people can feel a sense of ownership. It should affect others in the organisation or impact on the external customer. This provides the team with an opportunity for self-regulation. The member decides how the work is to be done. Besides this the productivity of teams had enhanced by meaningful feedback (How well the team is performing).

Rewards are important and should be communicated beforehand so that they act as motivation for team members to work. Rewards reinforce the motivational aspects of having a well-designed task and challenging goals. Whatever form the reward takes, it is important that group effort be recognised. One should avoid the destructive effect of trying to single out individuals from the group, when there has been a group effort. The impact of rewards will be heightened if the team understands that the provision of the reward is contingent on meeting the agreed goals.

Communication: A Vital Factor for Teams

The importance of communication in teams in the workplace has emerged as an important research area over the past decade—Orasanu (1990), Foushee and Manos (1981), and Mosier and Chidester (1991) Communication between individuals is a major component and leads to higher productivity of work teams at every level of organisation. For organisations, "communication is the linking pin between plans and action" on a broader scale, communication between employees and their immediate supervisors is a key influence on employee happiness and productivity (Pincus, 1985). This is not as obvious as it may sound.

A recent survey of personnel administrators in 428 organisations ranked interpersonal skills of team members as the most important for successful job performance (Curtis, Winsor, & Stephens, 1989). Studies focus on dyadic and national training organisations concentrate on human interaction. Some scholars consider dyadic organisational communication the most important type, because it is responsible for getting most of the work done, has significant impact on the climate, and is often the source of difficulties (Goldhaber, Dennis, Richetto & Wilo 1979). Face-to-face communication can consume 70 per cent to 80 per cent time of team members in an organisation (Klauss & Bass, 1982, p. 3; Klemmer & Snyder, 1972). The communication within the work groups/teams is a vital part for innovation. DrugCorp found that "interpersonal communication provided researchers with their most important channels of access to information and stimulation of new ideas" (Zuboff, 1988)

To put it in perspective, effective interpersonal communication, as the basic social unit of an organisation, is considered a prerequisite site to a team's operation, which consumes a significant portion of the working day, and is responsible for a broad range of activities.

Importance of Communication in Effective Teams

Organisations require a co-orientation of behaviour, which involves the elicitation of behavioural coordination among communicators for the accomplishment of commonly recognised goals (Kreps, 1990).

In organisations, the higher the level of predictability between colleagues, the greater sense of comfort everyone is likely to feel about working together. The corollary to this statement also holds. The more the co-workers interact, the greater is the trust and comfort. Communication in work groups has a large number of attributes with day-to-day friendships. Concepts such as trust, belief in the importance of employees, responsibility, empathy, open climate, self-disclosure, supportive communication, and understandings are all used to explain the important factors in successful dyadic relationships in an organisation (Goldhaber, 1986). An effective team develops good synergy. When a group finally clicks and becomes a team, it will find creative ways to solve problems and come up with innovative solutions. Synergy comes about when gains from the team setting exceed the losses.

Synergy is affected by group interaction. For the synergy effect, teams must have a clear definition of the problem, know what resources it has available and the limits and understand the expectations. All these require clarity in communication within the team members. Put another way, organisations view communication as primarily work/task oriented and socio emotional/person oriented (Cummings, Long, & Lewis, 1983). Being able to get along with people is the human relations perspective. When this is combined with getting the job done, developing subordinates, and experiencing personal growth, we have moved into the human resources perspective

Communication Problems in Teams

Some problems that occur in team communication and why they happen have to be discovered. Awareness of these problems is the first step toward recognising and solving them. Employers are often the last to know about communication problems in their companies — because of communication gap. After all, when information isn't flowing down and out, it often isn't flowing up, either.

Information Deficit: In many workplaces employees suffer from an information deficit. They don't have the information they need to do their jobs. It's not that they lack data from external sources. They're missing vital information that their supervisors and co-workers have right at hand, but unfortunately don't have on the tips of their tongues. Many cases of information deficit occur because the people possessing the information can't distance themselves sufficiently from their own experience to recognise the knowledge state of those around them.

Communication Style: The problem is that we make judgements about the way people are based on the way that they speak. We consider people who speak loudly or with a high pitch to be pushy. We find people who take too long to "spit it out" to be distracted, or possibly not very bright. As these (often incorrect) assumptions become solidified, they create serious, long-term barriers to successful interaction.

Gender Differences: There are numerous accounts of real and alleged differences in the way that men and women speak and conduct themselves in conversation. There is a more serious form of miscommunication between men and women in the workplace, too: when female employees fail to respond decisively to male supervisors and peers working in a group who systematically underrate and patronise them. Instead of addressing the problem, they become defensive, or worse, reinforce the view the male holds of them.

Native Language Differences: According to a recent *Indianapolis Business Journal* article, Indiana will see a gradual increase in workers who are non-speakers or non-native speakers of English. These workers will range from highly educated, short-term-resident professionals to possibly unskilled immigrants. In situations like this, there is the obvious problem of communication with employees who lack English skills.

The Challenge of Communication for Effective Teamwork at a Distance

Communication: Communication, especially non-verbal communication, can be affected by proximity. Mutual performance monitoring, to compensate for individual deficiencies in team performance, constant vigilance is required of team members (Militello et al., 1999).). This becomes difficult when the members are geographically distributed. If this team were trained in team processes (Salas, Bowers, & Edens, 2001) and were collocated, then the problems that arose can significantly diminish.

Intra-Team Feedback: Provided team members are able to engage in performance monitoring, it is expected that they should likewise be able to provide information about the status of other teammates' functioning. Feedback refers to the giving, seeking, and receiving of performance related information among the members of a team (Dickinson & McIntyre, 1997). Empirical support exists for the positive effect of feedback on team performance (Brehmer & Allard, 1991; Rasker, Post, & Schraagen, 2000).

Back-up behaviours: In addition to providing feedback, team members must also be able to provide technical assistance when gaps and inefficiencies are noted (Dickinson & McIntyre, 1997; McIntyre & Salas, 1995). Likewise, team members must also be prepared to seek help when needed (McIntyre & Salas, 1995). Indeed, providing feedback and back-up assistance to others depends on adequate monitoring and proficiency in the other team members' tasks as well as a means to provide such assistance when distances are spanned

Non-verbal Communication: The problem of deixis (i.e., pointing or specifying from the perspective of a participant in an act of speech) is considerable in distributed environments. Deictic speech involves words that alone cannot give meaning to the sentence. Barnard, May, and Salber (1996) demonstrated that the problem of deixis is considerable while videoconferencing. Highly interactive exchanges between two or more participants usually involve non-visual communication. Sketching, or the use of sparse drawings, is a function that facilitates communication in several ways (e.g., idea sharing, coordinating). Therefore, communication may take place by simply observing the environment without consciously, verbally or otherwise physically expressing an idea.

The Essentials of Effective Communication in Teams

The value of skilful communication can be seen in the most extraordinary groups and individuals, who go beyond basic number chasing to excel in ways that lend a deeper mystique and meaning to their work. Indeed, surveys show that poor communication is one of the root causes for workplace stress, higher absenteeism, and people leaving the organisation.

Some of the essentials for higher-performing teams and individuals:

- *Get centred:* One's best instinct, communication, and decision-making come when one is centred, rather than when one is preoccupied, flustered, angry, or otherwise "off-centre." Thus, practices that help one stay centred are worth the time and effort.
- *Listen well:* Skilful listening makes other people feel heard, and it also ensures that one is getting authentic, good quality information and are making deeper and more positive connections with others.
- *Speak clearly:* Ums, ahhs, errs, uh-hmmms, and other poor habits make it difficult for people to understand what it is you're trying to communicate. This includes speaking too quickly (or speaking so slowly or softly that you put people to sleep before your sentence is finished), or speaking into your shirt or hand.
- *Think creatively:* Do you think? It's a weird question, to be sure, but it's amazing how often people don't think — they just DO or follow without putting any updated thought into their doing or following. Asking questions, among other things, is one great way to stimulate creative thinking. For example, one can ask, does my approach to this need to be updated? Have I fallen into a rut? What other solutions are possible for this problem? How else could I be seeing this?

— *Be receptive:* Be open to what others are saying or offering, or to potential solutions that might be just on the other side of your perception.

— *Inquire skilfully:* Asking good question is a facet of skilful listening and creative thinking. Skilful inquiry is different from interrogation, where you're basically grilling someone in order to dismantle a belief or idea that you don't agree with.

— *Stay relaxed:* Choose whatever strategies appeal to you to help you stay relaxed, no matter what is happening around you.

— *Be mindful:* This is a lovely way of saying, "Pay attention!" Cultivating mindfulness is simply learning to pay attention to what you're doing.

— *Have intention:* Knowing your intention, and understanding someone else's intention, will help you be more conscious of what you're doing or saying something, which means you'll be able to be more effective and skilful.

— *Be genuine:* Being genuine can include speaking honestly, being friendly, saying "No" when you feel like saying "no" or expressing excitement or sadness or sympathy when you feel it.

Conclusion

Communication is the *modus operandi* of social and commercial intercourse. Human beings have the urge to convey feeling, ideas and thoughts. Communication can be improved, but doing so is not always an easy process. It requires time, will, and motivation. Perhaps the most difficult obstacle is the fact that good communication requires us to think very deliberately and consciously. Communication is nothing more than bridging that gap. There are many steps that can be taken to ensure a successful outcome from a team effort. One should understand and encourage honest communication about ideas and impacts, and the barriers will disappear. This will result in better communication, a more open exchange of ideas and potentially the creation of a better product or service. In summary, communication is necessary to get the work done. One means for understanding the different uses of interpersonal communication is to examine its task, person and socio-emotional functions.

Cited Works

Armstrong, D. J., & Cole, P. (1995). Managing distances and differences in geographically distributed work groups. In S. E. Jackson & M. N. Ruderman (Eds.), *Diversity in Work Teams: Research Paradigms for a Changing Workplace* (pp. 187-215). Washington, D.C.: American Psychological Association.

Angiolillo, J. S., Blanchard, H. E., Israelski, E. W., & ManÃ©, A. (1997). Technology constraints of video-mediated communication. In K. E. Finn, A. J. Sellen, & S. B. Wilbur (Eds.), *Video-Mediated Communication* (pp. 51-73). Mahwah, NJ: Lawrence Erlbaum Associates.

Bell, B. S., & Kozlowski, S. W. J. (2002). A typology of virtual teams: Implications for effective leadership. *Group and Organisation Management, 27* (1), 12-49.

Bekker, M. M., Olson, J. S., & Olson, G. M. (1995). Analysis of gestures in face-to-face design teams provides guidance for how to use groupware in design. *Proceedings of the Conference on Designing Interactive Systems: Processes, Practices, Methods, & Techniques, Ann Arbor, MI* (pp. 157-166). New York: ACM Press.

Barnard, P., May, J., & Salber, D. (1996). Deixis and points of view in media spaces: An empirical gesture. *Behaviour & Information Technology, 15* (1), 37-50.

Benford, S., Brown, C., Reynard, G., & Greenhalgh, C. (1996). Shared spaces: Transportation, artificiality, and spatiality. *Proceedings of the Conference on Computer Supported Cooperative Work, Cambridge, MA* (pp. 77-86). New York: ACM Press.

Bowers, C. A., Jentsch, F., Salas, E., & Braun, C. C. (1998). Analysing communication sequences for team training needs assessment. *Human Factors, 40* (4), 672-679.

Brannick, M. T., Roach, R. M., & Salas, E. (1993). Understanding team performance: A multimethod study. *Human Performance, 6* (4), 287-308.

Brehmer, B., & Allard, R. (1991). Dynamic decision making: The effects of task complexity and feedback delay. In J. Rasmussen, B. Brehmer, & J. Leplat (Eds.), *Distributed Decision Making: Cognitive Models for Cooperative Work* (pp. 319-334). Chichester, England: John Wiley & Sons.

Clark, H. H., & Brennan, S. E. (1991). Grounding in communication. In L. B. Resnick, J. M. Levine, & S. D. Teasley (Eds.), *Perspectives on*

Socially Shared Cognition. Washington, D.C.: American Psychological Association.

Cohen, J. (1988). *Statistical Power Analysis for the Behavioural Sciences* (2nd ed.). Hillsdale, NJ: Lawrence Erlbaum Associates.

Daft, R. L., & Lengel, R. H. (1984). Information richness: A new approach to managerial behaviour and organisation design. In B. M. Staw & L. L. Cummings (Eds.), *Research in Organisational Behaviour* (Vol. 6, pp. 191-233). Greenwich, CT: JAI Press.

Dickinson, T. L., and McIntyre, R. M. (1997). A conceptual framework for teamwork measurement. In M. T. Brannick, E. Salas, & C. Prince (Eds.), *Team Performance Assessment and Measurement, Theory, Methods, and Applications* (pp. 19-43). Mahwah, NJ: Lawrence Erlbaum Associates.

_____________ B. J., Yanushefski, A., Hamil, L. S., & Vick, A. L. (1992). *A Conceptual Framework for Developing Team Process Measures of Decision-Making Performance*. Orlando, FL: Naval Training Systems Centre, Human Factors Division.

Fleishman, E. A., & Zaccaro, S. J. (1992). Toward a taxonomy of team performance functions. In R. W. Swezey & E. Salas (Eds.), *Teams: Their Training and Performance* (pp. 31-56). Norwood, NJ: Ablex Publishing.

Harris, T. C., & Barnes-Farrell, J. L. (1997). Components of teamwork: Impact on evaluations of contributions to work team effectiveness. *Journal of Applied Social Psychology, 27* (19), 1694-1715.

Hollenbeck, J. R., Ilgen, D. R., Sego, D. J., Hedlund, J., Major, D. A., & Phillips, J. (1995). Multilevel theory of team decision making: Decision performance in teams incorporating distributed expertise. *Journal of Applied Psychology, 80* (2), 292-316.

Hollingshead, A. B., & McGrath, J. E. (1995). Computer assisted groups: A critical review of the empirical research. In R. A. Guzzo & E. Salas (Eds.), *Team Effectiveness and Decision Making in Organisations* (pp. 46-78). San Francisco: Jossey-Bass.

James, L. R. (1982). Aggregation bias in estimates of perceptual agreement. *Journal of Applied Psychology, 67* (2), 219-229.

_____________ Demaree, R. G., & Wolf, G. (1984). Estimating within-group interrater reliability with and without response bias. *Journal of Applied Psychology, 69* (1), 85-98.

Kozlowski, S. W. J., & Bell, B. S. (2003). Work groups and teams in organisations. In W. C. Borman, D. R. Ilgen, & R. J. Klimoski (Eds.), *Handbook of Psychology: Industrial and Organisational Psychology* (vol. 12, pp. 333-375). Hoboken, NJ: John Wiley & Sons.

May, A., & Carter, C. (2001). A case study of virtual team working in the European automotive industry. *International Journal of Industrial Ergonomics, 27* (3), 171-186.

Maznevski, M. L., & Chudoba, K. M. (2000). Bridging space over time: Global virtual team dynamics and effectiveness. *Organisation Science, 11* (5), 473-492.

McGrath, J. E., & Hollingshead, A. B. (1993). Putting the group back in group support systems: Some theoretical issues about dynamic processes in groups with technological enhancements. In L. M. Jessup & J. S. Valacich (Eds.), *Group Support Systems: New Perspectives* (pp. 78-96). New York: Macmillan.

Militello, L. G., Kyne, M. M., Klein, G., Gethchell, K., & Thordsen, M. (1999). A synthesized model of team performance. *International Journal of Cognitive Ergonomics, 3* (2), 131-158.

Olson, J. S., & Teasley, S. (1996). Groupware in the wild: Lessons learned from a year of virtual collocation. *Proceedings of the 1996 ACM Conference on Computer Supported Cooperative Work, Cambridge, MA* (pp. 419-427). New York: ACM Press.

Paris, C. R., Salas, E., & Cannon-Bowers, J. A. (2000). Teamwork in multiperson systems: A review and analysis. *Ergonomics, 43* (8), 1052-1075.

Rasker, P. C., Post, W. M., & Schraagen, J. M. C. (2000). Effects of two types of intra-team feedback on developing a shared mental model in command & control teams. *Ergonomics, 43* (8), 1167-1189.

Reid, F. J. M., Reed, S., & Edworthy, J. (1999). Design visualisation and collaborative interaction in undergraduate engineering teams. *International Journal of Cognitive Ergonomics, 3* (3), 235-259.

Salas, E., Bowers, C. A., & Edens, E. (Eds.). (2001). *Improving Teamwork in Organisations: Applications of Human Resource Management Training*. Mahwah, NJ: Lawrence Erlbaum Associates.

______________, Dickinson, T. L., Converse, S. A., & Tannenbaum, S. I. (1992). Toward an understanding of team performance and training. In R. Swezey & E. Salas (Eds.), *Teams: Their Training and Performance* (pp. 3-29). Norwood, NJ: Ablex Publishing Corporation.

Stout, R. J., Salas, E., & Carson, R. (1994). Individual task proficiency and team process behaviour: What's important for team functioning? *Military Psychology, 6* (3), 177-192.

Suh, K. S. (1999). Impact of communication medium on task performance and satisfaction: An examination of media-richness theory. *Information & Management, 35* (5), 295-312.

Whittaker, S., Geelhoed, E., & Robinson, E. (1993). Shared workspaces: How do they work and when are they useful? *International Journal of Man-Machine Studies, 39* (5), 813-842.

11

Customer Evaluation of After-Sales Service Communication Mode: An Empirical Study of Gender Consequences in Mobile Services at Gwalior

—*Vijay Kumar Pandey*

Gone are the days when males were the dominating factor in purchasing and using. Now females play greater role in purchasing and using product. Several analyses of consumer behaviour suggest that males and females differ in their processing of information (Holbrook, 1986; Palmer and Bejou, 1995); particularly, males and females respond differently to alternative consuming tasks and stimuli (e.g., pictures versus words) (Meyers-Levy, 1989). Females respond to non-verbal stimuli by evoking more associative, imagery-laced interpretations and more elaborate descriptions than males (Gilligan, 1982). This phenomenon suggests that the fundamental gender differences may contribute to the moderating role for attitudes and after sales service communications; to understand this relationship, so that organisations can do the necessary change and keep pace with the changing need of the customer, this study at Gwalior (Madhya Pradesh), on mobile services provided by different companies is a step ahead.

Introduction

1.1 Conceptual Framework

Several analyses of consumer behaviour suggest that males and females differ in their processing of information (Holbrook, 1986;

Palmer and Bejou, 1995); particularly, males and females respond differently to alternative consuming tasks and stimuli (e.g. pictures versus words) (Meyers-Levy, 1989). Females respond to non-verbal stimuli by evoking more associative, imagery-laced interpretations and more elaborate descriptions than males (Gilligan, 1982). This phenomenon suggests that the fundamental gender differences may contribute to the moderating role for attitudes and after sale service intentions, because products promoted bring about different stimuli and imagery-laced interpretations versus those of products demonstrated in a physical store. Accordingly, females are more sensitive to relevant information than males when making judgements (Meyers-Levy and Sternthal, 1991), causing subsequent purchase attitudes and intentions rendered by males and females to vary.

Now the companies have realised that female needs are different from the males. It is for that Idea Company has offered special SIM card for women. We know that other companies will also follow the suit. This also has the effect when a female is communicated to the company for service and service provider is male or female and also when a male is communicating to the company for service and service provider is male or female.

After-Sales Service Satisfaction

The consumer's satisfaction is an effective reaction to an incident during the dispensing of a service. In other words, satisfaction or dissatisfaction is derived from a given experience with a service encounter and, subsequently, from the comparison of such an experience with a given standard about which consensus does not exist, i.e., what was expected (Oliver, 1980), norms based on experience (Woodruff *et al.*, 1983; Cadotte *et al.*, 1987), or what was desired (Spreng *et al.*, 1996). Regarding the evaluation of the delay in the service, we should distinguish the following relationship:

Satisfaction with service → repurchases intentions.

In general, it is considered that satisfaction explains the likelihood that consumers will purchase the service again (Szymanski and Henard, 2001). Thus, Oliver (1997) studies loyalty as a result of customer satisfaction and proposes three phases of satisfaction (cognitive, emotional and connotive) which culminate in loyalty of action. This positive relationship between satisfaction and repetitive purchase is demonstrated by Bearden and Teel (1983), among others. The logic underlies in the "exit-voice" theory (Hirschman, 1970), which assumes that the dissatisfied clients have the option of never using the services of the supplier again ("exit" behaviour) seeking the services of another company.

1.2 Review of Literature

Gender identity, sometimes referred to as an individual's psychological sex, has been defined as the "fundamental, existential sense of one's maleness or femaleness" (Spence 1984). Since gender is culturally derived, gender identity is similarly rooted in cultural understandings of what it means to be masculine or feminine (Firat 1991; Lerner 1986). For many years, sex and gender were thought to be inseparable—that is, men were masculine and women were feminine. But what consumer behaviour researchers, among others, recognised long ago was that some men were more feminine than masculine while some women were more masculine than feminine. In the postmodern culture in which we now live, this separation of gender from sex is even more apparent.

Untangling the intricate threads of masculinity and femininity began in the 1930s when the first assessment of gender identity was attempted (Terman and Miles 1936). It was not until the 1960s, however, that gender identity made its first appearance in consumer-related studies (Aiken 1963; Vitz and Johnston 1965), and with the emergence of new conceptualisations of gender identity in the mid-1970s (e.g., Bem 1974; Spence, Helmreich, and Stapp 1975), the study of gender identity in consumer research intensified, continuing into the 1980s and 1990s. Even when criticism of the most frequently used gender identity measures, the Bem Sex Role Inventory and the Personal Attributes Questionnaire, surfaced in the 1980s (see, e.g., Gill et al., 1987; Marsh and Myers 1986).

However, significant gender identity findings in consumer research have been rare, causing some as early as the mid-80s to suggest that the inclusion of gender identity in consumer research is unproductive and should be abandoned (Roberts 1984). Several reasons have emerged to explain the lack of significant findings. For example, some have suggested that the operationalisation of gender identity has stymied research (Palan, Areni, and Kiecker 1999); contributing to operationalisation problems may be the inappropriate use of terms resulting in conceptual ambiguity. Gould (1996) suggested that the inappropriate interpretation/ application of gender identity to consumer research variables produced contradictory findings.

In more recent literature, the potential contribution of gender identity research to the understanding of consumer behaviour has been questioned since the meanings of masculinity and femininity have blurred (Firat 1993). Two other concepts, gender role and gender role attitudes, have at various times been mistaken to be synonymous with gender identity in consumer behaviour studies (Fischer and Arnold 1994), when, in fact, they are not.

Gender role refers to the culturally derived behaviours and activities associated with masculinity or femininity that individuals choose to adopt. A gender role attitude refers to an individual's beliefs about the roles, rights, and responsibilities of men and women. While gender identity is certainly related to both gender roles and gender role attitudes, it does not necessarily have to be congruent with gender role or gender role attitudes (Deaux 1985; Fischer and Arnold 1994). For example, it would not be unusual for a woman to report a more favourable attitude toward egalitarian gender roles in the home than toward traditional gender roles, but at the same time be engaging in behaviours associated with a traditional feminine gender role; empirical measurement of that same woman's gender identity might show that she identified equally with masculine and feminine personality traits. The review is grounded in the theoretical models of gender identity with the specific goal of providing a framework to address the question: "To what extent are differences in gender identity useful in explaining meaningful variations among consumers?"

Multifactor Gender Identity Theory: Contradicting Bem's theory is the belief that gender-related phenomena are multifactor in nature with desirable gendered personality traits constituting but one factor (Feather 1984; Spence 1984, 1991; Taylor and Hall 1982). Accordingly, masculinity and femininity are conceptually distinct from gender role expectations, attitudes, preferences, and behaviours, and the use of the BSRI and the PAQ, which measure masculine and feminine traits should be limited to studies measuring variables relevant to instrumentality and expressiveness. This is consistent with Spence who maintains that neither the PAQ (1984, 1991, 1993) nor the BSRI (1993) is appropriate as an indicator of global gender-related constructs.

The underlying assumption of multifactor gender identity theory is that gender identity is a combination of gender-related phenomena, associated in varying degrees with each other, such as gender-related attitudes, interests, and role behaviours and gendered personality traits. Not only is gender identity multifactor, but also each gender-differentiating factor has a different developmental history that varies across individuals because the factors are impacted by multiple variables that are not necessarily gender-related (Spence 1993). Consequently, the specific array of gender-congruent qualities that people display can be quite variable within each sex (Spence 1993), although both men and women do develop gender identities and a sense of belongingness to their sex that is maintained throughout the life span (Green 1974).

Thus, the differentiating feature of multifactor gender identity theory from gender schema theory is that, in multifactor theory, the measurement of gender identity requires measuring several different factors (that is, personality traits, gender attitudes, gender role behaviours, etc.); if only one factor, such as gendered traits, is measured, then the applicability of that factor is limited to situations where only that one factor is relevant. Gender schema theory, on the other hand, maintains that it is the measurement of only one facet, a masculine and feminine personality trait that is needed to indicate multiple gender related concepts.

The finding of significant gender differences provides additional support to psychological theories, stating that males and females have different gender-based perceptions (Venkatesh and Morris, 2000) which can influence their preferences and decisions during after sales service.

1.3 Objectives of the Study

1. Development and standardisation of a measure for evaluating perception towards gender.

2. Evaluating relationship between communication mode and gender.
3. To open new areas for further research.

Research Methodology

2.1 The Study

The study was exploratory in nature with survey method being used to complete the study.

2.2 The Sampling Design

2.21 *Population:* Population included consumers in Gwalior region.

2.22 *Sampling Frame:* Since the data was collected through personal contact the sample frame included mobile users divided into two categories, i.e., male and female.

2.23 *Sampling Element:* Individual respondents were the sample elements.

2.24 *Sampling Technique:* Purposive quota sampling technique was used to solicit responses.

2.3 Tools Used for Data Collection

Self-designed questionnaires were used for evaluating customer perception towards gender. Data was collected on a likert type scale, where 1 stands for minimum agreement and 7 stands for maximum agreement.

2.4 Tools Used for Data Analysis

Item to total correlation was used to check the internal consistency of the questionnaires. Reliability and validity tests were applied to check the reliability and validity of the questionnaires. Z tests was applied to find out significant differences among the groups, factor analysis was applied to find out the under lying factors in the questionnaires.

3. Result and Discussion

Internal Consistency Test

Iterative item to total correlation was applied on the responses received from the respondents for male-to-male, male to female, female-to-male and female-to-female. The items having more correlation value than the cut off value and all the correlation coefficients became significant, and the items were retained for further analysis.

S.No	*Statements*	*Accepted / Dropped*
1	Attitude	Accepted
2	Stages needed for talking	Accepted
3	Motivation technique	Accepted
4	Regular information about discount	Accepted
5	Information about billing	Accepted
6	Speed of handling queries	Accepted
7	Clarity of voice	Accepted
8	Solution to the problem	Accepted
9	24 hrs. facility	Accepted
10	Uninterrupted discussion	Accepted
11	Call divert facility	Accepted
12	Call hold facility	Accepted
13	Call wait facility	Accepted
14	Info. junction	Accepted
15	Activation charges	Accepted
16	Time taken for personal services	Accepted
17	Knowledge	Accepted
18	Regular information	Accepted
19	Toll free facility	Accepted
20	Detailed solution	Accepted

Reliability Test

Reliability test was carried out using SPSS and the reliability test measures are given below:

Reliability Tests for Communication of gender effect on after sales services Questionnaire (Items 20)

1. Cronbach Alpha: 0.493
2. Split half: 0.794

3. Guttman: 0.745
4. Parallel: 0.493
5. Strict Parallel: 0.411

The reliability of the questionnaire was found to be high.

Validity Test

Validity tests for gender effect on after sales services questionnaire

Validity of the questionnaire was checked using face validity method and was found to be high.

Factor Analysis

Since there were many factors, therefore principle component factor analysis with Varimax rotation and Kiser normalisation was applied. The factor analysis resulted in eight factors for gender effect on after-sales services questionnaire and the factors were named according to the common nature of statements. The details about the factors included the Factor number, Factor name, their Eigen values, Items under each factor and their Item loading is given in the table below:

Factor No.	*Factor Name*	*Eigen Value*	*Items*	*Item Loading*
1	Information Centre	2.606	14, Info junction	0.795
			9,24 Hrs. facility	0.666
			19, Toll free facility	0.615
			4, Regular info.	0.557
2	Features Packed	2.417	17, Knowledge	0.830
			7, Clairty of voice	0.820
			15, Activation charges	0.455
3	Facilities Provided	2.303	2, S stages needed	0.795
			12, Call hold facility	0.815
			5, Info. about billing	0.547
4	Customer Care Services	1.749	10, Unirrupted discussion	0.870
			20, Detailed solution	0.773
5	Unique	1.584	3, Motivation techniques	0.830
			13, Call waiting facility	0.770

(Contd...)

(Contd...)

6	Grievance Solution	1.439	8, Solution to problem	0.839
			18, Regular info	0.686
7	Prompt	1.270	16, Personal services	0.866
			6, Speed of handling	0.744
8	Customise	1.135	1, Attitude	0.825
			11, Call divert facility	0.823

Z Test

Gender	*Mean*	*Standard deviation*
Male-Male	3.866	0.5378
Male-Female	3.483	0.428519
Male-Male	3.866	0.5378
Female-Female	3.784	0.454281
Male-Male	3.866	0.5378
Female-Male	3.569	0.448227
Male-Female	3.438	0.428519
Female-Female	3.784	0.454281
Male-Female	3.438	0.428519
Female-Male	3.569	0.448227
Female-Female	3.784	0.454281
Female-Male	3.569	0.448227

	Z- Value	*Significant/Insignificant*
Male-Male Male-Female	4.403	Significant
Male-Male Female-Female	0.8257	Insignificant
Male-Male Female-Male Significant	3.003	
Male-Female Female-Female	3.927	Significant

(Contd...)

(Contd...)

Male-Female Female-Male	1.495	Insignificant
Female-Female Female-Male	2.389	Significant

Hypothesis Testing

Test-1

H0: Gender effect of communication; male on male and male on female.

Ha: The hypothesis is rejected since the Z Value (4.403) is more than the cut off value, i.e., 1.96 at 5 per cent level of significance level. Therefore we can say that there is significant effect of males on male and male on females.

Test-2

H0: Gender effect of communication; male on male and female on female.

Ha: The hypothesis is accepted since the Z value (0.8257) is less than the cut off value, i.e., 1.96 at 5 per cent level of significance level. Therefore we can say that there is insignificant effect of male on male and female on female.

Test-3

H0: Gender effect of communication; male on male and female on male.

Ha: The hypothesis is rejected since the Z Value (3.003) is more than the cut off value, i.e., 1.96 at 5 per cent level of significance level. Therefore we can say that there is significant effect of male on male and female on male.

Test-4

H0: Gender effect of communication; male on female and female on female.

Ha: The hypothesis is rejected since the Z Value (3.927) is more than the cut off value, i.e., 1.96 at 5 per cent level of significance level. Therefore, we can say that there is significant effect of male on female and female on female.

Test-5

H0: Gender effect of communication; male on female and female on male.

Ha: The hypothesis is accepted since the Z value (1.459) is less than the cut off value, i.e., 1.96 at 5 per cent level of significance level. Therefore, we can say that there is insignificant effect of male on female and female on male.

Test-6

H0: Gender effect of Communication; female on female and female on male

Ha: The hypothesis is rejected since the Z Value (2.389) is more than the cut off value i.e. 1.96 at 5% level of significance level. Therefore we can say that there is significant effect of female on female and female on male.

Implications

1. This study is intended to be useful contribution to understand the gender difference among:

   Male-Male

   Male-Female

   Female-Female

   Female –Male

   and to simultaneously evaluate their communication mode.
2. It is also intended to be useful contribution for further researches because it provides a link between theory and practice.
3. This study will also be useful to those companies who wanted information specifically regarding difference in male and female communication.

Suggestions

1. The study has been done by taking only a sample size of 200; hence it may not represent the full India.

2. The study has been done in Gwalior region only so it is suggested to take larger area or other region so that more appropriate results can be obtained.
3. The study has been done by taking only one demographic variable that is gender. Some other demographic variables can also be used such as age, family size, etc.

Conclusion

The study resulted in standard and reliable questionnaire for evaluating after sales services between the genders. The study also rebuilt the fact that there is no different perception towards after-sales services, when male is communicator and male is listener and male is communicator and female is listener, male is communicator and male is listener and female is communicator and male is listener, male is communicator and female is listener and female is communicator and female is listener, female is communicator and female is listener and female is communicator and male is listener but there is significant difference in the evaluation of after-sales services between two categories when male is communicator and male is listener and female is communicator and female is listener and male is communicator and female is listener and female is communicator and male is communicator.

Cited Works

Aiken, Lewis R., Jr. (1963). The Relationships of Dress to Selected Measures of Personality in Undergraduate Women. *The Journal of Social Psychology* 59: 119-128.

Ashmore, Richard. D. (1990). Sex, Gender, and the Individual. *Handbook of Personality: Theory and Research*. Ed. Lawrence A. Pervin. New York: Guilford Press: 486-526.

Bem, Sandra L. (1981). *Bem Sex Role Inventory: Manual*. Palo Alto, CA: Consulting Psychologists Press, Inc.

Bem, Sandra L. (1974). The Measurement of Psychological Androgyny. *Journal of Consulting and Clinical Psychology* 42: 155-162.

Cross, Susan E. and Hazel R. Markus. (1993). Gender in Thought, Belief, and Action: A Cognitive Approach. *The Psychology of Gender*. Eds. Anne E. Beall and Robert J. Sternberg. New York: Guilford Press, 55-98.

Deaux, Kay. (1985). Sex and Gender. *Annual Review of Psychology* 36: 49-81.

DiMingo, E. (1988). The Fine Art of Positioning, *The Journal of Business Strategy*, 34-38.

Dobni, Dawn and George M. Zinkhan (1990). In Search of Brand Image: A Foundation Analysis, in Advances in Consume Research, 17, Marvin E. Goldberg, Gerald Gorn, and Richard W. Pollay, eds., Provo, UT: Association for Consumer Research, 110-119.

Easlea, B. (1986). The Masculine Image of Science With Special Reference to Physics: How Much Does Gender Really Matter? *Perspectives on Gender and Science*. Ed. J. Harding. Philadelphia: Falmer, 132-158.

Feather, Norman. T. (1984). Masculinity, Femininity, Psychological Androgyny, and the Structure of Values. *Journal of Personality and Social Psychology* 47: 604-620.

Firat, A. Fuat. (1993). Consumer After Modernity: Transcending the Feminine. Gender and Consumer Behaviour, Second Conference Proceedings. Ed. Janeen Arnold Costa. Salt Lake City, UT: *University of Utah Printing Service*, 198-205.

_______________ (1991). Consumption and Gender: A Common History. *Gender and Consumer Behaviour, First Conference Proceedings*. Ed. Janeen. Arnold Costa. Salt Lake City, UT: University of Utah Printing Service, 378-386.

Fischer, eleen and Stephen J. Arnold. (1994). Sex, Gender Identity, Gender Role Attitudes, and Consumer Behaviour. *Psychology & Marketing* 11 (2): 163-182.

Gardner, Burleigh B. and Sidney J. Levy (1955). The Product and the Brand, *Harvard Business Review*, 33 (March/April), 33-39.

Gill, Sandra. Jean Stockard, Miriam Johnson and Suzanne Williams (1987). Measuring Gender Differences: The Expressive Dimension and Critique of Androgyny Scales. *Sex Roles* 17 (7/8): 375-400.

Hanna. J. G (1980). A Typology of Consumer Needs. *Research in Marketing*, 3, 83-104.

Keller, E. F. (1983). Feminism and Science. *The Signs Reader: Women, Gender, and Scholarship*. Eds. E. Abel and E. Abel. Chicago: University of Chicago Press, 109-122.

Keller, Kevin L. (1993). Conceptualising, Measuring, and Managing Customer-based Brand Equity. *Journal of Marketing* 57, 1-22.

Levy, Sidney J. and I. O. Glick (1973). Imagery and Symbolism, in *Marketing Manager's Handbook*, Stewart Britt II, ed., Chicago: Dartnell, 961-969. 8.

Malinowski, (1944). *A Scientific Theory of Culture,* Chapel Hill, The Univ. of North Carolina Press.

Marsh, Herbert W. and Margaret Myers (1986). Masculinity, Femininity, and Androgyny: A Methodological and Theoretical Critique. *Sex Roles* 14 (7/8): 397-430.

Martinis, Pierre (1958). "The Personality of the Retail Store," *Harvard Business Review,* 32 (October), 47-55.

12

Corporate Communication: Dynamics of Corporate Interface in the Globalised Scenario

—*Roopa Shinde* and *Anurag Joshi*

Communication is a process by which a person can express his ideas and information to others. There are various forms of communication like verbal and non-verbal; in verbal we use oral and written communication and in non-verbal we use body language, signs and symbols to convey the message.

Communication happens at many levels (even for one single action), in many different ways, and for most beings, as well as certain machines. Several, if not all, fields of study dedicate a portion of attention to communication. So when speaking about communication it is very important to be sure about what aspects of communication one is touching upon.

Definitions of communication range widely, some recognising that animals can communicate with each other as well as human beings, and some are more restricted, only including human beings within the parameters of human symbolic conversation. Organisations have struggled to find the best way to get company communications to their employees for years. These communications can range from notices of service interruptions to announcements of corporate events. But is anyone really listening? Communication is a two-way street; it requires a sender and a receiver. If no one is listening, you're just a crazy person talking to yourself.

Anyone involved with corporate communications needs to be aware of their receivers' habits and idiosyncrasies before deciding on message and medium. It wouldn't make sense to use technology-based communications with an audience who's not tech-savvy without first providing them with adequate training; or to post an important announcement on a bulletin board when most users rely solely on their intranet for news. An understanding of the audience will help determine the best medium to use in order to get your message across. This paper introduces corporate communication, its applications and functions.

Communicating to hundreds, sometimes thousands, of recruits within an organisation is no small feat. This challenge is further complicated in organisations with a global presence, where corporate headquarters is responsible for delivering the same message to satellite offices in geographically dispersed locations. But it's not enough to just create the message. Corporate communication is an essential aspect of an organisation and one that can determine the success of a business.

Functions of Corporate Communication

For a business to run efficiently, good lines of communication must be established between management and staff, from top to bottom, as well as suppliers, investors and even customers. Corporate communication is an important consideration in change management and corporate governance. For more on corporate communication we have to understand the different steps involved in this process.

Medium and Message

Effective corporate communication involves not only the message itself, but also the medium that carries and delivers it. It's these two components of a communication that dictate whether employees will receive and understand it. But one shouldn't fool oneself in thinking that there's some long process of deliberation when one receives one of these messages. Most corporate communications will grab the attention of an employee for no more than a few seconds — if at all. It's within that very narrow window of opportunity that they will decide whether to read something or toss it aside. Corporate communication is the method by which large and medium-size companies communicate with customers, stakeholders and employees. The reputation of a company and its products are built through the messages disseminated by the company to employees, customers and the public.

Building Reputation

Corporate communication makes the company visible and gives its products an image and reputation a customer can identify with. Customers and employees also get to know and feel good about the company they are working for and doing business with. Customers need to know about the company; its management; its method of manufacture; its mode of functioning, and the company's philosophy and values. They need to know its products and services so that they can trust what the company stands for and confidently buy, consume and use their products.

Stakeholders, investors, shareholders, partners and suppliers, employees, government, NGO's, local community, industry and customers — any individual or group which can affect or be affected by an organisation's activities needs to feel a sense of involvement with what the company is doing; the more they know, and the more open the communication with them, the more they trust and feel involved and responsible for the company in which they have a stake.

It is obvious that to establish and sustain trust, corporations must actively engage the public, their customers, their employees, and their partners on the social, financial, and environmental accomplishments and actions of their organisations. They must demonstrate and communicate their clear commitment to these three fundamental efforts in every aspect of their corporation. Reputation is an asset of immense value. The fact is that reputation is the product, at any particular moment, of a fermenting mix of behaviour, communication and expectations.

The public increasingly wants to know about the companies that stand behind the brands and products presented to them. And to use their consumer power to reward 'good' companies and punish 'bad' ones. In company reputations, familiarity does not breed contempt. All other things being equal, the better known you are, the better disposed your target audience will be towards you. This applies to all audiences in all countries.

Systematic management of social issues is much less widespread in the corporate world. To avoid risks to their reputation, businesses need to understand the stakeholders' concerns about issues both under their direct control, such as employment policies, and under their influence, such as of the impact of their supply chains on the environment and society. The issue of corporate social responsibility is rapidly climbing domestic as well as global political agendas.

Environmental issues are clearly one aspect of corporate responsibility. Environmental policy has, however, progressed much further than in the context of human rights and social responsibility. There is a much more directly applicable set of standards and accepted procedures, and there is a body of experience to show the degree to which business incorporates environmental concerns.

Media Relations

Effective media relations are vital to the success of any corporation's overall communications strategy. A sound media relations programme can deliver huge benefits to a corporation. Madan Bahal emphasizes upon the importance of media relations as a usual practice at Adfactors:

> At Adfactors PR, we place huge emphasis on deploying superior media relations skills for our clients. We specialise in developing strategic media relations programmes that effectively deliver the client's key messages through relevant media to their target audiences. In each significant market of India, our consultants maintain close relationships with regional, national and the relevant international media to maximise communication opportunities for our clients.

He further adds:

> Our teams understand the media and what makes news. They know how individual media will treat a particular piece of information and have the expertise in matching the client's messages to the right media vehicles. While our

> superior skills in communicating with the traditional media are well known, we are now expanding our repertoire to address the opportunities represented by emerging interactive media. We also provide media training for client executives to help them develop and deliver messages effectively in interactions with the media.

Efficient Employers

Employees are most important to the organisation; without them the company cannot run. Both the management and employees must appreciate this interdependence. So, both management and employees at all levels must develop a sense of inclusion, a sense of willing cooperation and a united pursuit of the company's values and goals. This is done through two-way internal communications up and down the hierarchy.

Corporate Citizenship and Ethics

Corporate Social Responsibility (CSR) is a concept whereby organisations consider the interests of a society by taking responsibility for the impact of their activities on customers, employees, shareholders, communities and the environment in all aspects of their operations. This obligation is seen to extend beyond the statutory obligation to comply with legislation and sees organisations voluntarily taking further steps to improve the quality of life for employees and their families as well as for the local community and society at large.

As recently as a decade ago, many companies viewed business ethics only in terms of administrative compliance with legal standards and adherence to internal rules and regulations. Today the situation is different. Attention to business ethics is on the rise across the world and many companies realise that in order to succeed, they must earn the respect and confidence of their customers. Like never before, corporations are being asked, encouraged and prodded to improve their business practices to emphasize legal and ethical behaviour. Companies, professional firms and individuals alike are being held increasingly accountable for their actions, as demand grows for higher standards of corporate social responsibility.

The Driving Forces Behind Corporate Social Responsibility

Globalisation

To understand where corporate social responsibility will take us in the twenty-first century, we need to understand why it is climbing the global policy agenda so effectively. A brief look at the driving forces illustrates both the dynamism and complexity of corporate social responsibility. If we have to sum up in just one word, globalisation springs immediately to mind. Globalisation provides undeniable benefits, while tens of thousands of protestors in Seattle's last fall effectively conveyed to the world the flip side of the coin. Sceptics hold that current globalisation trends are forcing us to live in an economy rather than a society. Whatever view one takes, however, globalisation appears to be an irreversible process that challenges existing societal patterns both at home and abroad Revolutions in technology and communications to companies and non-governmental organisations. State actors are still potent players, but gradually reduced, at least in relative terms.

Specific Driving Forces

The pressures that globalisation is putting on existing political and economic structures create a fertile ground for a range of more specific driving forces underpinning the corporate social responsibility agenda. Suffice it here to summarise a number of important trends, which together form a momentum moving corporate social responsibility deeper and deeper into corporate boardrooms.

Opportunities and Challenges for Companies

Companies worldwide, which depend on well-regulated and relatively free world markets in order to attain their commercial goals, cannot take such beneficial rules of the game for granted. Public grievances against globalisation's dark side threaten to erode the legitimacy of World Trade Organisation. The corporate world has yet to take full account of the erosion of the notion of security and predictability that globalisation implies for important population groups all round world. The corporate world will have to build nothing less than a social contract with the broad range of stakeholders represented in the streets as well as corridors during the trade talks.

Developing an Effective Response

A risk effective approach

While much of the value derived from the development and implementation of a corporate social responsibility strategy revolves around image related factors such as brand, reputation and stakeholder trust, a company that focuses its effort primarily on image related activity in order to enhance stakeholder perceptions runs a significant risk that the reality does not match the perception.

A risk-effective approach to corporate social responsibility requires the right balance to be struck between communication and profiling around corporate social responsibility issues to enhance the way the company is perceived, with actual on the ground delivery of corporate social responsibility-related performance improvement. Corporate social responsibility includes most importantly the place of ethics in management of employing organisations. Ethics is not something foreign to management but exists at its core, and relates to the wide range of values and purposes involved in the formulation of business policy just referred to.

Leadership and Communication

Leadership, a critical management skill, is the ability to motivate a group of people toward a common goal. These items will help you develop your skills as a leader. *The Fundamentals of Corporate Communication* by Richard Dolphin gives professionals and students in marketing a comprehensive and incisive overview of what modern corporate communications is, and what it can achieve. The author has drawn on extensive business experience in the area and wide ranging research in major corporations to produce an authoritative account of best practice - backed by numerous cases and examples. The book demonstrates how corporate communications affects today's marketing mix and explains how it can support wider marketing objectives. The key elements are covered in depth: Who are the key audiences in the present business climate, the role of corporate image and identity in the communications process, how communication informs and affects corporate strategy development, what are the tools of modern communications—from lobbying to brand building using communications in a crisis, and who should be communicator and why? The book is both highly practical (it is grounded in real business issues), and rigorous in covering the concepts accessibly. It will be an essential text and reference for practitioners and students of marketing.

Every industry is witnessing unprecedented levels of competition. As competition intensifies, companies must work hard to differentiate themselves from their peers. The companies must carve out a unique position in the minds of their key stakeholders based on their visions, values, unique strengths and the value that they bring to the lives of customers, shareholders and communities they serve. Maximising shareholder value alone is not enough.

Each company must identify and consistently project the unique value that it brings to the marketplace. As the pace of change intensifies, and as managements respond to these changes with newer products and services, the companies have to redefine themselves for their present and future stakeholders. In today's times perception is reality, and the company's reputation capital is perhaps its most important asset. If the reputation of a well-known company is damaged the company can wither and die in a matter of months, destroying shareholder value and hurting the interests of virtually every category of stakeholders. Conversely, even a lesser-known company which builds a solid reputation can thrive and grow by competing effectively in the marketplace for customers, employees, vendors, desirable business partners and capital. In the process, the company is able to deliver sustained shareholder value. Every action of a company has a bearing on its reputation. In such an environment, active and deliberate corporate reputation management is a necessary extension of traditional brand management. After all, the primary brand is the overall corporate brand.

Tata Consultancy Services Ltd, a leading IT services provider, has implemented a digital platform in its offices throughout India, the United Kingdom and the Netherlands. TCS is part of Asia's largest conglomerate, the TATA Group. With a presence in 34 countries across six continents and a comprehensive range of services across diverse industries, TCS is one of the world's leading information technology companies. DigiFour Technologies, a Scala Certified Partner in India, has implemented Scala's Info Channel Platform in 70 TCS locations. The Digital Communication Channel informs and educates TCS employees on major corporate activities including corporate announcements, staff programmes, company performance and achievements.

The strategy is to develop an effective centrally controlled internal communication system that had the flexibility to support relevant dynamic content and instantaneous changes. The channel would act as the most preferred form of information for employees.

Successful corporate management in the new millennium is essentially about managing accelerated pace of change. When companies develop strategies for responding to changes, managements, particularly in the developing world, often overlook the importance of communicating the change initiatives to employees.

In most Indian companies employee communication often means a monthly or a quarterly newsletter. In most cases, the standard contents are the CEO inaugurating some irrelevant internal function, or coverage of employee picnics or family events and other material which has little impact on equipping the employees to understand and adapt to the company's strategic initiatives. If strategy must succeed it is imperative that the entire organisation understand it and work in tandem for achieving corporate goals. Effective employee communications is the difference between unlocking and blocking the full potential of the organisation.

Crisis/Risk

Like every other plan, a crisis plan has to have a trigger. When a crisis hits, there has to be a responding process that moves it to the team leader in a matter of minutes. The team leader then needs to activate the team, if necessary, as soon as possible. In a crisis, time is a luxury you never have. The official company crisis plan may include a lot of the right ingredients such as the spokesperson, crisis team members, a list of telephone numbers, and perhaps even a list of potential crises. It might even hit as to who is to do what in a crisis. A crisis plan should include all these points and a lot more. But crisis plans, for the most part, are just too broad. At the very best, they are merely the starting point for handling a crisis. A crisis arises because of a conscious business decision. Decisions are made knowing it will create public relations problems. Plant closings, layoffs—these fall into that category. Other crises are beyond control—fires, recalls or sabotage, for example.

Here is the list of crises that could happen and that could be viable part of a crisis plan:

- Government investigation
- Controversial law suit
- Accusation of discrimination based on race, sexual preference or gender
- Product recall
- Serious injury to someone within or outside of the organisation
- Protest
- Strike
- Physical violence between co-workers
- Insider trading scandal
- Theft by an outsider (ideas or physical assets)
- Embezzlement
- Hostile takeover
- Outbreak of food poisoning caused by a company (maybe even at a company picnic)
- Death of top executive
- CEO gets arrested for drunk driving
- Natural disaster
- Plane crash
- Congressional hearings make something that was legal illegal, and a company is used as an example
- Plummeting stock price
- Major interruptions in service

- Computer system crash, causing loss of all data
- One of the employees is accused of a high profile crime
- Sexual harassment case
- Fire
- Explosion
- Chemical spill
- Radiation leak
- Caught in a lie
- Union grievance

Corporate Identity

Corporate identity can be broken down into four components; corporate strategy, corporate culture, organisational design, and operations. Strategy is the overall plan that determines the company's product/market scope and the policies and programmes it chooses to compete in its chosen markets. Corporate culture is the shared values and beliefs that the organisation's members hold in common as they relate to each other, their jobs, and the organisation. It defines what the firm personnel believes is important and unimportant, and explains to a large degree why the organisation behaves the way it does.

Organisational design refers to the fundamental choices top managers make in developing the pattern of organisational relationships. It encompasses issues such as whether basic tasks should be organised by function or product division, the company's overall configuration, the degree of decentralisation, the number of staff personnel, the design of jobs, and the internal systems and procedures. Operations, the fourth and final component of corporate identity, are the aggregate of activities the firm engages in to affect its strategy. These activities become part of the reality of the corporation and can influence its identity in a wide variety of ways.

Conclusion

Corporate communication is an attitude towards communication or a set of mental habits that employees internalise. The result is good communication practices that permeate an organisation and our present communication with all its constituencies. Reputation equals rational expectations (based on product and performance) plus emotional expectations (based on behaviour and perception). Corporate social responsibility is achieving commercial success in ways that honour ethical values and have respect for communities and the natural environment. In its simplest terms, many equate corporate social responsibility with being a good corporate citizen by supporting worthwhile community causes.

Cited Works

Bahal, Madan 2005, *Knowledge Driven Communications,* Ad factors PR Pvt.Ltd.p.2 http://prnewswatch.com/2005/09/ 27 October 2005.

Bromley, D.B., (2001). Relationships between personal and corporate reputation, *European Journal of Marketing,* 35 (3/4), pp. 316-334.

Harrison, J. and E. Freeman, 'Stakeholders Social Responsibility and Performance—Evidence and Theoretical Perspectives', *Academy of Management Journal, 1999,*

M.J. Hatch, & M.H. Larsen, (Eds.). *The expressive organisation: linking identity, reputation and the corporate brand* (pp. 66-74). Oxford: Oxford University Press.

13

Emphasising the Role of Technology in the Modern Scenario

—Priyanka Tripathi

It is a commonplace saying in modern scenario that the world has become a global village. Indeed discussions lead to probe into the factors contributing to the evolution of nations coming up together forming a globalised world. If one has to find a key contributor, the unanimous choice would be 'communication'; also no one may deny the role of technology in pacing the communication process. Communication is important when it comes to individuals, organisations or countries. Language varies –from English to Dutch or from French to Hindi but the underlying idea remains the same 'transmission of ideas'. What one communicates through language is significant but at the same time non-verbal communication does not lag behind. They go hand in hand with language. The cultural interactions that have taken place is not a result of some agenda on globalisation but a natural proceeding of the progression of society. It is this reason that would have perhaps made Edward Hall write: "Culture is communication and communication is culture."[1]

All technology influences language in ways that are not always obvious. Adhering to this phenomenon English also is influenced including other languages as well though it gains its importance upon other languages because of its wide ranging speakers .In technical excellence, it's only the language that is understood by most people. To explain it in an elaborated way, one can cite the following example: "We use aeroplanes to fly people and goods around the world. And we try to make this safer and more efficient by developing an air-traffic control system. That's language and technology working together for the common good. (And English is the language used in that system globally.")[2]

If English is not the first language of a country, it will certainly be the second language. If one takes the example of country like –India there is a boom in technology. Every year many professionals go abroad as their part of job sometimes and at times for their job itself. The language they have to be proficient in is English. In fact, this is the state of several other developing countries and India can be cited as just an instance representing all. Unless they have the fluency in English language, it would not be possible to work in the contemporary scenario.

In the same context it is also significant to discuss what technological progress means. Does it only mean the advancement in the IT and manufacturing sector? Or is it just fast means of transportation and communication? Absolutely not. It does not denote a single, unchanging and specific thing. It represents, rather, a very general group of things - which includes a very extensive array of other things, some of which alter over time. A country truly becomes technologically progressed when technology necessarily becomes the part of the academic curriculum. The teachers and students use it in significant ways to augment knowledge. The previous certainties of an education system defined by four classroom walls and solid boundaries are disappearing, giving way to global interdependencies and complex systems that require agility, sensitivity and creativity. Thus, teachers are expected not only to have an in depth knowledge of the subject they teach but also the understanding of high-tech skills of how to access, evaluate, analyse, and synthesise vast quantities of information. Various benefits out of electronic curriculum had been invariably discussed. Tim Shortis suggests these points in *The Language of ICT* as the distinctive features of electronic text:

> Enables storage and transmission of diverse information.
> Includes electronic typed text and/or digitised information.
> Allows instant communication across geographical space.
> Can be linked to other electronic texts and processes.

> Keeps a record of its "history" automatically.
> Echoes previous genres and technologies.
> *Challenges notions of fixity and authority.*[3]

However, as the world is changing not at a generation-to-generation pace but in year-to-year pace, life in general and education in particular becomes more and more complex. Educators prepare for a technology-rich future and keep up with change by adopting effective strategies that infuse lessons with appropriate technologies. Michele Jacobson writes:

> We no longer live in a world in which information is scarce, and the teacher's role is to deliver content to children. Overwhelmed by information from a wealth of sources, students desperately need the skills to create new knowledge, not just consume the old.... The old certainties of a world defined by four classroom walls and impermeable boundaries have disappeared forever, replaced by global interdependencies and complex systems that require flexibility, responsiveness, and imagination.[4]

But technology is not all in all when it comes to teacher-student equation. It varies from teacher to teacher and to the capability of students as to how they utilise the source. Else instead of adding value, it can be a complete distraction to students. Many a time the expectation that a teacher and students and even the educator goes through is very high. It often does not generate the desired result. So it's important that every teacher has a vision of his own when it comes to the usage of technology in teaching. One doesn't have the same mind set, so when any technology penetrates into our daily life our reactions may be different. Some are quite keen about technology, seeing it as the tool most essential to smooth the progress of more comprehensive educational reform. Others see it as a passing trend, more an interruption from school reform than anything else.

As this article discusses the role of English language in the modern scenario, one can take the example of upcoming Digital Language Lab to justify the conditions partially. It's a set-up with more or less a self-learning process with teacher's participation almost negligible. The students are required to go through exercises and answer it. The answers are digitally evaluated and the explanation to wrong answers also comes the same way. To a general perspective the process in a short span of time becomes monotonous as the process is too mechanical. To avoid monotony, teachers combine their own designed exercise totally generated from their own ideas containing pictures, famous personalities and things associated with the technically equipped communication lab. This is definitely diverging from what they had been doing but it's a usage of the same technology to make the process more interesting as well as informative to the students. In the context of incorporating technology in English, several studies have taken place. Melanie Shoffner in her article *Preservice English Teachers and Technology: A Consideration of Weblogs for the English Classroom* writes:

> When English teachers effectively integrate technology into their classrooms, however, they have the opportunity to engage students positively in the learning process. As the literature attests, technology can encourage students to work within and across multiple literacies, providing opportunities for new understandings and broader applications in the English classroom (Kim & Kamil, 2004; Myers & Beach, 2004; Patterson, 2000). The use of interactive technologies can support collaborative learning, within and beyond the English classroom (Carroll & Bowman, 2000; Hogue, Nellen, Patterson, & Schulze, 2004; Sipe, 2000). Certain technologies can also offer constructivist learning experiences (Coppola, 2004; Wenglinksy, 2005), where students are allowed, if not required, to construct their own understanding of the subject at hand in order to complete the technological task. [5]

In any case it's a medium and not a device to make the students grasp their chapters. As Marshall McLuhan says, "The medium is the message."[6]

Also, there has been ample analysis on the negative effects that the immense usage of technology may cause in. A teacher's individuality as an intellectual is often ignored when it comes to the usage of technology. There is generally a perception that if there is classroom learning through technological devices the teacher's role is minimised. So that area too should not be neglected while taking massive efforts to convert traditional teaching to something that can be delivered via the computer. In considering research on technology, Kathleen Fulton noted in her article *A Framework for Considering Technology Effectiveness* that the following caveats must be taken into account while preparing for a technologically rich curriculum:

- The technology keeps changing; as hardware and software evolve, new educational opportunities appear.
- Educational technologies are used in classroom settings, which rarely provide optimal conditions for their use.
- Research findings and results are often inappropriately generalised across grade levels, students, subject matter, types of technologies, and applications.
- The teacher is a key variable in technology implementation and effectiveness.
- Technology's impact on teachers and their practice should be considered as important as student effects because students move on but teachers remain to influence many generations of students.[7]

If one throws light on the academic curriculum in general, technology has dramatically changed the ways we educate, inform and entertain. Computers and information technologies have apparently revolutionised nearly every aspect of daily life. How we obtain news, how we order goods and services and how we communicate? It is both rational and expected that technology should also help us in leading the way to improve teaching and learning in schools. Educational technology, especially computers and computer-related peripherals, have grown tremendously and have permeated all areas of our lives. From banks to hospitals, from industries to universities everywhere technology dominates. Use of the Internet plays a major role in every sphere of life.

But still technology doesn't necessarily advocate itself in all contexts. It's developed with a purpose of advancement and not to hamper the traditional practices in any case. In fact, that is the key theme of the educators who have introduced in the curriculum. E-learning thus, is the order of the day. To quote John Bowen from his essay *Seven Steps for a Successful Change*:

> Successful change is a real challenge because no one reacts well to change except the person that is driving it. When change comes, we all tend to immediately put our hands up and try to figure out how to avoid it. Behaviourists tell us that 80 per cent of us are reactive thinkers who will do anything to avoid change. Twenty per cent of us are creative thinkers, meaning we initially try to avoid the change, but then examine and judge whether it's a good change or a bad change. If we think it is a good change we will incorporate it into our lives. If creative thinkers believe it is a change for the worse, they will just figure out ways to go around it. It's important to recognise that most of us, in reacting to change, want to slow it down; but if we accelerate it, we can move ahead.[8]

Though spoken in the context of Alberta, a province in Canada, the statement of Bowen can be generalised to all, signifying the importance and adaptability of technology in not only academics but in our daily life in general: Our human survival depends on our ability to learn new things and use ideas to solve problems in deeply ambiguous and confusing situations; and it depends on our ability to teach our children how to do this.[9]

References

1. Matthukutty & Monipally *Business Communication Strategies* (New Delhi Tata McGraw-Hill Publishing House, 2006), p-45
2. http://www.universalteacher.org.uk/lang/languageand technology.htm#overtime,2 February 20, 2008.
3. http://www.universalteacher.org.uk/lang/ languageandtechnology.htm#overtime,2 February 20, 2008.
4. http://www.citejournal.org/vol2/iss3/currentpractice/article2.cfm, February 20, 2008.
5. http://www.citejournal.org/vol7/iss4/languagearts/article1.cfm, February 20, 2008.
6. http://www.universalteacher.org.uk/lang/ languageandtechnology.htm#overtime, February 20, 2008.
7. http://ideanet.doe.state.in.us/olr/pdf/appresearchkful.pdf, August 26,2007
8. http://www.cegworldwide.com/articles/ArtSevenSteps.php, August 26,2007
9. http://www.citejournal.org/vol2/iss3/currentpractice/article2.cfm, February 20, 2008.

14

Cyberspace and Identity: A Study of Hari Kunzru's *Transmission*

—Anupama Kaushal

The most celebrated thing of the present times is the "information superhighway"[1], the cybernet. The access to cyber world affected by computer electronics has made possible the scope of uniting the world in an expansive family as cyberkin. Today man is not living in separate soapboxes, cut off from the other countries, culture and language of the world. The interaction made available by cybernet is not only on the national level but the Internet has made possible the interaction between the individuals of the world. This man-to-man interaction has been a boon especially for the diasporas. The connectivity that it has provided has made them feel less lonely and more at home in an environment outside their home, country, culture and language. So, it has become not just a means of connection but a necessity which provides and maintains the emotional support required by the expatriates. But it urgently gave occasion to the issues of identity of coalitionalism and in separation within electronics and transnational frame. Along with providing a space for progressive and responsible globality, it could be exploited for personal self interest, which Gayatri Spivak, calls *the new pax electronica*[2]. In the following discussion, I would focus on the impact of electronic technologies on the issues of identity concerning expatriates with special reference to Hari Kunzru's novel *Transmission*.

The explosion in electronic technologies not only assisted in the growth of IT professional diaspora in developed countries but it also made easy availability of personal computers and internet. This forces us to rethink the complex subject of identity of diaspora in digital terms. These new technologies removed the relative isolation of the diaspora by providing them an opportunity to establish a link not only with the natives but also with the other diasporas. As Deepịka Bahri opines:

> The geographic disconnection with the homeland, the historical rupture with the homeland's national time and cultural confusion produced by migration, when subjected to the logic of net, begin to produce alter and altering cyber localities that recreate a geographic and historic connection with the lost nation and culture.[3]

This facilitates the expatriate to establish a connection with his own country, culture and the other arrived diaspora and thus makes him feel less lonely and forlorn. The cyber fraternity also empowers him to subscribe, unsubscribe and re-subscribe at his own sweet will, absolutely optional. Along with it a relative anonymity is sanctioned while expressing the views which are difficult to express in front of the real society. In this way Internet communication facilitates to operate in different settings and in different positions. It simultaneously provides "a space for a dialogue on different aspects of the identity of natives as well of the diaspora for it provides 'a space for psychic sharing, and even healing, the Internet can afford the comfortable hothouse ambience of a sympathetic confessional, the unchecked uncensored liberty of the locker room, a forum for debate and discussion, for all three at one time or another. For those struggling with identity in exile, the digital dialogic of electronics net provides countless opportunities for exchange and exploration of options". [4]

The second novel of Hari Kunzru, *Transmission* deals with varied aspects of identity affected and facilitated by this world wide communication system—cybernet. Arjun Mehta, a software engineer confident of his talent and merit, is all set to rock America with his specialisation in databodies. In India Arjun is desperate to secure a good job in America, and as he is above the ordinary student, he faces troubles:

> Listen Mehta. You don't know how many positions Databodies has open. Perhaps there are several. The Americans have a skill shortage. They want as many programmers as they can get. (p.07)

But Arjun is not the only applicant, there are several like Arjun who are misguided by such agencies with a fake promise, "I am going to send you to America and start making you rich....You start to become who you always dreamed of becoming....good programmers like you are gold just over there" (p.10). All the actions of Noida fizz through Arjun's sensorium without leaving a trace. *Love's Dream* (p. 13). Neglecting his mother's emotions and father's apprehensions, Arjun sets off for America, "Amrika ! Becoming his dreams" (p. 11). But unfortunately his expectation and confidence get a heavy jolt when he becomes aware of the fact that there is no red carpet welcome for him but on the contrary he will have to search for a job for himself in America, a place which doesn't value him or his qualifications.

Hari Kunzru has made reality dawn on the masses about the popular notion that America is a land of endless scope for IT professionals. Arjun runs high and low but secures only a petty job on a lease of two months. Facing great mental trauma owing to differences on the cultural level and on his headlong fall to the ground of bare reality, his personality is drastically changed. Arjun Mehta, the confident software engineer in his own land has become a lowly begging man in some other land. Still he decides to stand on his own legs to make a place for himself as V.S. Naipaul writes, "But we remade the world for ourselves."[5]

Eventually he secures a job in a prestigious company, Virugenix, but the post and salary are still not up to his qualifications and expectations. A personality which is not ready for any compromise in his country bows down to agree for a job which he would never have accepted in his own country. But he agrees as he has no options left "Living his dreams was proving hard." (p.38). But still as something is better than nothing, he grabs the service with a hope of promotion. And that hope seems to become a reality when a certain virus in the AV section (the coveted post) comes as an opportunity to prove his self and worth. He gives his earnest help in the AV section. But the team leader, Darryl Gant, sums up his efforts, in eradicating the virus, with polite thanks. Arjun is struggling continuously not only to raise his rank in the company but also to adjust in that different cultural set-up:

> Apart from Clay most of the AV team were not particularly gregarious creatures. People did their thing and other people left them to get on with it .... Away from the top floor Arjun's social life was limited .... In cafeteria, like many of his colleagues, he tended to eat alone. A lot of people in the AV team shunned the communal areas of the campus altogether.... Though Arjun followed the workaholic Virugenix ethos... in his rare moments away from his cubicle he sometimes craved conversation. He tentatively struck up nodding acquaintanceships with a Bengali who worked on firewalls and a Dilliwalah who did something or the other for the diagnostic product team. He even took up an invitation to dinner with the Dilliwalah's family, but though he took the precaution of preparing a list of conversation topics, the evening was not a success. (p.56)

Though his identity has got suppressed in the alien non-social environment, yet still an in-house socialising does exist through the circulation of entertaining data sets. By and large the thing is picking up speed and a hope of some success is getting strong. Meanwhile, unfortunately, there is a crisis in the company:

> By Tuesday morning he was probably the only Virugenix employee still unaware that the company had issued a profits warning, the stock price had tanked, and the board

> had pledged to cut operating costs across all divisions. Everyone else, the whispers and the starers, knew what they meant. (89)

Before Arjun can understand, he is out of the job with a grace period of two weeks. Bewildered he beggs but to no avail, " Please, if I lose this job I 'll have to go back and I can't go back ... you don't mean it. What if things change? You'll need me then" (p.92). Going back to India is an impossibility because his prestige would get affected. It is a general notion in India that America is a land of endless scope for IT professionals. When Arjun left India for America, he was regarded by everyone as a worthier person than the other Indian relatives. And proving himself a failure in front of his own people meant real shame. Being in a foreign land means being in exile where there is no sense of belonging, so an expatriate feels no sense of prestige or esteem in front of the strangers. It becomes possibly easier for a diaspora to bow down in front of those ethnicised aliens in order to hide his failure from his own people. So, Arjun is transformed from a confident middle class Indian engineer to a meek, begging immigrant. Helplessness makes him incapable to understand the indifferent, calculative firmness of American decisions, where there is no place for humane considerations. So in his fight for survival, he creates, in anonymity, nine viruses of Leela Zahir (an upcoming Indian actress and Arjun's heartthrob) to make him feel desired in the company. Cyber identities are fleeting and evanescent, so are insubstantial. The identity of virtual fantasy is not susceptible to any distinctions. It is possible to disappear and remain hidden from the real society. It provides a freedom of shedding the limiting markers of identity and makes possible the use of the Internet for various personal and social goals.

Arjun Mehta creates a fake cyber identity in order to accomplish this mission. In the beginning he creates just one virus of Leela to make his worth realised in the company. But this time the company calls its own people to meet out the situation. In his frustration he issues nine viruses one after the other, anonymously. This is not the first time that Arjun has done such an act. Prior to his visit of America he had erased the traces of such acts in India:

> All his best toys were now etched on the little silvered disks ready to travel in solid state to America. Next he cleaned up: he deleted his data from Aamir's machine and before exiting the NOIT system ran a script that erased all traces of his session from the school's logs. Behind the walls of his secret garden which existed not so much apart from as between the legitimate areas of the college network, his various experiments were still running their course, stealing spare processor cycles from idle machines, storing themselves in tiny splinters on dozens of different hard disks. Together these fragments formed an interstitial world, a discreet virtuality that could efficiently mask its existence from the students and teachers doing their online business round about it. It was a world which could look after itself for a while, until its creator had time to check on it properly. Until he was successfully installed in California. (p.28)

The blocking of this worldwide communication system by Arjun indicates not only the helplessness of a misappropriated immigrant in his failure to fulfil his desire of playing a role in the world but also an outlet to suppressed anguish and anger of a meritorious periphery against the ethnicity and inhumane attitude of the centre. A positive, aspiring young software engineer who came to America to prove his worth to the world, thus, becomes a criminal and fades into anonymity, dodging the American communication system and authority: "One persistent report, mostly from Pacific Rim countries, has a young man fitting Mehta's description accompanied by a South Asian woman of a similar age ..... According to conspiracy theorists there is only one possible explanation, only one pattern that makes sense." (p.281)

Hari Kunzru has used various film references in the narrative. They serve as a medium of connection of the expatriates with their home-country and roots. Arjun's sticking of posters of Indian filmstars on the wall and downloading their pictures on his website are examples of it. Especially in Arjun's case, when it is impossible for him to remain in close connection with his own family – this Indian film fraternity is the only means of connection for him with his Indian roots. When in India he used to download Hollywood actresses on his website but in America he is all for his own country's actresses especially, Leela Zahir. The issuance of Leela virus shows the anguish of an Indian boy against Western world. Leela Zahir, a temperamental young lady, chooses cybernet as a means to escape from the strangulating environment around her, to meet her lover, Arjun. Thus both get united probably, in their Elysian world of romance. So, the cybernet, the worldwide communication system, serves to expand the narrower margins of Arjun's and Leela's identity to make them the migrants of perfection, as Edward Saīd says: "The man who finds his homeland sweet is still a tender beginner; he to whom every soil is as native one is already strong; but he is perfect to whom the entire world is a foreignland."[6]

Where the Internet can serve as a medium for rapid mobilisation, connection, expression of self, mutation, relative isolation or an instant worldwide communication, it has made the present world appear like a place where anything can happen and anything will at the click of a mouse.

References

(All the textual references have been taken from Hari Kunzru's *Transmission*. London: Penguin Books. 2004. The page numbers have been mentioned in brackets.)

1. Pal Vinay: *Politics of History on Internet: Cyber – Diasporia Hinduism and the North American Hindu Diaspora.* Indialog Publication Pvt. Ltd. : New Delhi : 2001: p. 179.
2. Spivak Chakarvatri Gayatri: Love, Cruetly and Cultural Talks in the Hot Peace. Parallax 1: 1995 : 1-31.
3. Bahri Deepika: *The Digital Diaspora: South Asians in the New 'Pax Electronica'*. Indialog Publication Pvt. Ltd.: New Delhi : 2001: p. 223.
4. Ibid. p. 225.

5. Naipaul V.S., *The Engima of Arrival,* London, Viking, 1987, p. 310.
6. Said Edward, *Culture and Imperialism,* London: Chatto and Windus, 1993, p. 406-07.

15

Corporate Communication: Emergence and Challenges

– R.C. Parida & D.P. Panda

Communication has always been of critical importance to the success of corporate reputation and is one of a company's most valuable and enduring assets. It plays a central role in the achievement of key business objectives such as creating shareholder value, attracting and retaining and motivating high-quality people, enhancing reputation with all audiences, marshalling stakeholder support on public policy issues, creating consumer preference for products and services, etc. The theory and practice arising from corporate communication lie at the heart of effective strategic management, planning and control.

Introduction

Communication is a process in which we all take part since our birth. People express their thoughts, feelings, and imagination through spoken and written languages. As human beings we all use communication to establish linkages with others. Information and communication management have gained unique importance due to communication revolution triggered off by developments in electronics and spurred by the launching of space satellites. Similarly business executives communicate through writing, speaking, conferences, reports, manuals etc. Corporate communication is the process of facilitating information and knowledge exchanges with internal and key external groups and individuals that have a direct relationship with an enterprise. It is concerned with internal communications management from the standpoint of sharing knowledge and decisions from the enterprise with employees, suppliers, investors and partners, agencies. Corporate communication and social accountability have become significantly more important since last two decades. Communication itself is one of the primary responsibilities in many careers, like customer relations, selling, labour relations, selection, training, public relations, etc. The present paper emphasizes on the corporate communication, its emergence, internal corporate communication, techniques of corporate communication and challenges.

Corporate communications may include: analyst relations, internal communications, investor relations, corporate governance (communications aspects of corporate governance), issue management, change management (communications aspects of growth management, mergers and acquisitions, etc., litigation (communications on/around litigation), crisis communications, etc. Corporate communication (vital areas are) include: (i) Enterprises use annual reports as corporate communication tools; convey information related to results, processes and relationships of the enterprise. Typically, these communications occur on a yearly basis. (ii) Corporations use electronic and print newsletters to share corporate diversity hiring practices and information on new hires. (iii) Enterprises use corporate Intranets to create a corporate communication platform to formalise processes around.

Emerging Trends in Corporate Communication

Corporate communications have become a strategic asset both in manufacturing and service industries. Corporates understand this vital need and have also designed the services to provide the results and long-term benefits for the corporate clients. Enterprises located on multiple sites, spanning and ever growing territory, wish to offer all users the same services (speech and data communications) and support mutual interactivity in their work. Enterprises use annual reports, accounts, and statements as corporate communication tools to convey information related to results, processes and relationships of the enterprise. The fundamentals of corporate communication assist professionals and students in marketing a comprehensive and incisive overview of what modern corporate communications is, and what it can achieve. Due to the demands of stakeholders, customers, media, government agencies business organisations are vigourously concerned about their public image. In multinational companies (MNCs) and large business houses, executives devote three to four hours daily in corporate communication, conferences, reports, manuals, advertising, bulletins, etc.

Communications extend beyond political boundaries and new communication services are emerging; professional telematics, security, mobile communication services, electronic document interchange with business partners: suppliers, distributors, goods carriers, etc. A strategy for clear communication in today's corporate environment, in the days of liberalisation, privatisation, and globalisation (LPG) is the call of the time.

In the globalised economy, English is an international language of the business and 750 millions of people do speak English in professional setting, and over about one billion more are in the process of learning it as a second language. The clear and confident English communication skills now are more than ever critical for the success of global organisations. The emphasis on corporate communication is building a company's reputation among its stakeholders.

Corporate communication involves much more than just motivating employees and dispensing good public relations. The aim of corporate communication is building a company's reputation among its stakeholders. Communication has always been of critical importance to the success of companies and corporate reputation and is one of the company's most valuable and enduring assets. It plays a central role in the achievement of key business objectives such as creating shareholder value, attracting, retaining and motivating high-quality people, enhancing reputation with all audiences, marshalling stakeholder support on public policy issues, creating consumer preference for products and services, and minimising the impact of crisis on company's financial position and business prospects. Many companies are reassessing their communication budgets, moving away from traditional, functional approaches to public relations and public affairs, and pursuing internal and external corporate communication strategies. The theory and practice arising from corporate communications lie at the heart of effective strategic management, planning and control. How an organisation communicates with its employees, its extended audiences, the press, and its customers brings its values to life. Recognising the impact of the new digital media technologies on corporate management and the monitoring and evaluation of corporate identity, corporate advertising, organisational reputation and overall performance, communication is now a wealth to the enterprise. Corporate communication encodes and promotes strong corporate culture, coherent corporate identity, reasonable corporate philosophy, genuine sense of corporate citizenship, an appropriate and professional relationship with the press, quick, responsible ways of communicating in a crisis, understanding of communication tools and technologies, sophisticated approaches to global communications.

Internal Corporate Communications

Internal communication is said to be the lifeline of a business. All business activities are internally and integrally communicated to different levels of management. It has strategic importance to the running of the firm. The benefits of internal communication are outlined below:

- It helps in sharing information with numerous offices across multiple sites, locally, nationally and internationally.
- It provides an information access point for mobile and non-desk-based employees.
- Internal communication facilitates event and activity information.
- It promotes internal marketing of new processes and procedures.
- It processes knowledge and information sharing.
- It prompts sharing business and corporate information.
- It helps in sharing local office information.

Techniques of Corporate Communication

Corporate communication is the process of facilitating external groups and individuals, and information and knowledge exchanged with internal groups have a direct relationship on an enterprise. It is concerned with internal communications management from the standpoint of sharing knowledge and decisions from the enterprise with employees, debtors, customers, suppliers, financial institutions, investors and partners. There are several techniques of communicating an organisation's image with its end users. Remember that corporate identity is not just something that private sector organisations strive for; it is also very important for many public sector organisations. There are many ways used for corporate communication; however, the following are popular techniques of corporate communication:

- *Mission statements:* Mission statements aim to encapsulate what the business is about and what it wants to be associated and identified with. The mission statement is used not only to communicate an external identity but to bind together staff in a common culture and identity.
- *Packaging:* Packaging is becoming increasingly important not just to maintain quality and to protect products but as a form of communicating messages about the company as well. Colgate, for example, now supplies toothpaste in a small container that sits easily on bathroom shelves as opposed to the traditional tubes (which are still available).
- *Logo:* Most organisations now have logos. The design of this is very important. It often communicates messages that are subtle and may rely heavily on an understanding of our psychology. For example, having three parts of a company's name all in the same size and font may communicate a different message to one which has the first word larger and in a different colour to the other two. Logos are intended to ensure that the company becomes instantly recognisable even if there is no writing or words to convey the message. Logos may contain a name but a good logo may not need any words to communicate the company, organisation or message.

Communicating in Corporate Communication

Effective communication is now the corporate buzzword. Every firm tries to communicate effectively without any ambiguity. Since corporate communication is already narrated now we shall focus on how to make communication more effective. Effective and professional communication is the lifeblood of any good business. Not only can it drive sales and motivate the staff, it can also improve the morale, engage employees and increase efficiency. Effective corporate communication involves not only the message itself, but also the medium that carries and delivers it. It is these two components of a communication that dictate whether employees will receive and understand it. Most corporate communications draw the attention of an employee for no more than a few seconds - if at all. It is within that very narrow window of opportunity that they will decide whether to read something or toss it aside. Employees are processing more information than ever before — information dealing with their projects, their clients, and their industry as a whole. With all this information competing for employees' attention, does a single corporate communication stand a chance of making it through? Organisations have struggled to find the best way to communicate with their employees for years. These communications can range from notices of service interruptions to announcements of corporate events. But is anyone really listening? Communication is a two-way street: it requires a sender and a receiver.

For effective communication editing is must. Written business communication often requires the input of more than one person. When editing another's works, various factors are taken into account; do not change the meaning; be careful when substituting, deleting or adding a word, phrase or even punctuation. Changes in the text might significantly alter the writer's meaning. If not certain about revisions, check with the writer first. The writer should keep a copy of the original for verification in case discrepancies occur, and each draft should be clearly marked with a number or revision date. When editing, do not change the style unless it is inappropriate. Although some uniformity is often desirable within a department or company, we all have the right to our own "voice". Be careful not to over-edit. Be sure all changes are justified. Saying the same thing in another way is not justification for changing another person's writing. The revision should be better, not just different. The editing should be an editing with empathy. Consider using a very light, thin mechanical pencil when editing. If the revisions are easy to be seen, use bright green, orange or purple ink. Red ink can evoke a negative emotional response.

The ego is to be controlled. Remember that an editor's role is that of a co-pilot, not a pilot. Editing must be with an open mind, a big heart and a light hand. Moreover the following are some tips to make corporate communication more effective:

— There should be face-to-face communication, as necessity.
— Balance between upward and downward communication.
— It is shaped for intended people.
— Difficult words to be avoided.
— Clarification and simplification should be guiding factors.
— Feedback should be promoted for communication.

Skills of Corporate Communication

Whether anybody is a manager, a sales professional, a human resource specialist, a health care professional, an administrative assistant, an educator or entrepreneur, he can learn to lead by example and win respect with every word spoken. In today's fast-paced business environment everyone is being asked to do more with less. People are torn between managing the frustration and stress of the added responsibilities and maintaining the proverbial positive mental attitude. With proactive word power we do not have to feel positive to produce great results. Instead of being in denial, people learn to identify and channel the energy of authentic emotions and reactions into productive actions and problem solving that propel them forward. They learn to tap into a well of creative energy that supports accomplishment.

Table 1: Communication Skills for Different Jobs

Job Type	*Communication Skills*
Secretary	Must be proficient in reading and writing skills.
Finance associate/ professionals	Must be able to communicate clearly to clients and others.
Product manager	Develop & communicate product strategies.
Personnel manager	General knowledge of proposal preparation: good oral /written communication skills.
Production manager	Ability to write, ability to read, listening to grievances, ability to conduct interviews.
Sales representatives	Excellent oral communication and follow-up skills, ability to draft proposals.
Other executives	Ability to communicate precisely to colleagues/ friends/employees.

(*Source: Communication Skills,* Rao & Das, p.3)

Proactive word power trains people to think and speak and empowers them to bridge their differences with respect and without judgement. It trains people to listen with an understanding that builds trust and cooperation. It is easy to understand and to apply. As we look to the future for ever better ways to improve performance, leadership and teamwork and to handle the accelerating changes we face communication problem both at work and at home. We must understand the significant ways that interpersonal communication impacts our lives. The following table outlines communication skills for different positions.

Clarity: Clear writing is writing that cannot be misunderstood. Clarity means there can be no ambiguity in your writing. When the writing is clear, your words can have only one meaning. That gives the very first impression about the firm. May it be financial statements, analysis reports, statutory reports and documenters, clarity must be maintained.

Brevity: Mark Twain, the famous American writer, wrote to a friend, "Sorry for the long letter. I did not have time to write a short one." Brevity does not mean writing the perfect first draft; it means editing to cut repetitious and unnecessary information; rather it means using as few words as possible to convey the meaning. If a word is to be deleted and it does not change the meaning, do so. All business communication, may it be from inside or outside, must be to the point and easily understood. In corporate reporting this aspect is taken into account for presentation.

Simplicity: Use easy words and short sentences to convey the meaning. When possible, use words of one and two syllables. Many times when sellers use words with three syllables or more, they often burden the mind of readers. The fact is that simple writing is a sign of clear thinking and hard work. Writing that is wordy and rambling is a sign of a writer who does not care or does not know any better. Using simple words does not mean one should limit the vocabulary.

Empathy: The way for effective communication for more selling is to be sensitive towards receiver's needs, feelings and perceptions. This is what psychologists call empathy in communication, implying putting legs in the other's shoes or projecting oneself into the viewpoint of the other person. When the sender of the message looks at the problems from receiver's point of view, much of the misunderstanding is avoided.

Challenges

Communicating to hundreds, sometimes thousands of employees, within an organisation is a challenging task. It is also a great task to communicate with millions of outside people. This challenge is further complicated in organisations with a global presence, where corporate headquarters is responsible for delivering the same message to satellite offices in geographically dispersed locations. But it is not enough to just create the message. In today's often frenetic working environments communicating clearly is a challenge. 'Information overload' is a common phenomenon. With numerous channels and cluttered air space, messages can get diluted or lost altogether. It is also vital to communicate quickly and effectively whether they are mobile, non-desk-based or in other offices across the country or the world. Anyone involved with corporate communications needs to be aware of the receivers' habits before deciding on the message and medium. It would not make sense to use technology-based communications with an audience who are not tech-savvy without first providing them with adequate training; or to post an important announcement on a bulletin board when most users rely solely on their intranet for news. An understanding of the audience will help to determine the best medium to use in order to get the message across. The internet is considered revolutionary since it has pushed communication at an unprecedented and incredible speed at multiple levels. Also the ability to communicate well is a valuable asset for most of the activities in business management.

The advent of e-mail changed the way organisations communicated with their employees in a big way. Rather than post to send out large quantities of paper-based announcements, a single e-mail message could be sent to all employees at the same time, regardless of their geographic location. E-mail is the biggest advancement in corporate communication. But there are many barriers to its effectiveness. There is perhaps no bigger contributor to this decline than spam. E-mail has the ability to alert every employee once a communication is sent, but there are uncontrollable factors that hinder its effectiveness as a corporate communication medium. E-mail has been contaminated by so much junk that it is difficult to get an important message across. Users might give a company announcement a cursory glance and pass it by thinking it is just more unsolicited mail; or they might setup e-mail filters so restrictive that the message never even makes it through. With the sheer volume of e-mail that comes pouring in daily, employees may simply treat these types of internal communications as white noise and ignore them. And with the time-sensitive nature of corporate communications, it might be too late when users finally discover the message.

The significance of corporate communication factor induced many enterprises to organise and structure their networks with an "information systems management" in order to optimise and integrate their dedicated networks through a common digital approach. Designing and managing these structures on a daily basis and the supported services is an increasingly complex task. To manage business well is to manage its future. The future management implies management of information and communication. Mega challenges faced by the corporate world in the field of communication are:

- The pace of fast changing technology
- The challenging of consumerism
- The growing concerns of quality control
- Information technology revolution
- Communication to consumers, middlemen and resellers

Boosting Communications in Business

1. *Boost the employees confidence.* Nobody can afford to have their staff suffer from the lack of confidence. By providing a non-native English speaker an ability to speak up clearly, articulate the thoughts, and precisely express the ideas, organisations do increase a self-confidence of each of the clients. A client-sponsoring the organisation, in turn, benefits from the increased productivity and the greater passion for the success because of good corporate communication.
2. *Increase the customers' satisfaction.* We spend a lot of the time and resources for acquiring and retaining the customers.

Exemplary customer service is the foremost goal of a modern global corporation. If the company does have the multinational employees or the non-native English-speaking executives in the client-facing roles, clarity in the communication becomes vital. It enhances the customers' satisfaction.

3. *Avoid the worst nightmare.* We ever imagine that a single miscommunication can damage the company beyond repair? Single incorrectly spoken or a mispronounced word could cost the company valuable time and money. By training effectively the employees and the executives to communicate clearly, the firm would benefit immensely.
4. In a global world an effective communication strategy should account for geographical and cultural diversities. Effective network should be developed.
5. Today corporate communication is taking on multiple forms and expression - online, printed, spoken and visual. Each of these forms has its unique characteristic. The understanding application of these helps in working with an aim for creating high impact collateral development and management programs that will reach and resonate with the audience groups.
6. In trade, industry, commerce, the service sector corporate and its executives have to exert to upgrade communication skills constantly. In the present-day context and competing business, corporate communication has immense contribution for long-run survival and managerial excellence.
7. Language tells, sells. The three watchwords of good writing are Clarity, Brevity, and Simplicity (CBS). The clear writing is "writing that cannot be misunderstood." Most of the time our goal is to write clearly. But sometimes we intentionally want to be vague. Clarity, brevity and simplicity are the three goals of effective communication for more selling and must be followed in the organisation.

Conclusion

Executives are constantly looking for breakthrough strategies that will give their companies a competitive edge. Once those strategies are formulated they become operating plans and departments are charged with carrying out specific activities. It is up to individual employees to execute within their daily jobs in support of those plans. But what happens if the strategies are not well communicated throughout the organisation? What if employees lack essential skills to accomplish their work? What if cultural barriers stand in the way of progress? Global firms like Honda, Ericsson, Tata, General Motors, etc., have made significant progress and success in business due to effective corporate communications. With advent of information technology (IT) communication convergence linking voice, video and data, the time for bringing a product to market has been compressed into weeks and months, rather than years. Corporate communication is a strategic management function that enables sharing of information and knowledge exchange with both internal and external groups. Effective and efficient communication with partners, prospects, customers, channels, employees, investors, shareholders and other stakeholders lays the foundation of a successful marketing plan and survival of the business.

Works Cited

Bahl, S., 1996, *Business Communication Today*, Sage Publications, New Delhi.

Chander, S, 1992, *Corporate Reporting Practices*, Deep & Deep Publications, New Delhi.

Fernandez, Joseph, 2004, *Corporate Communication: A 21st Century Primer*, Sage Publications, New Delhi

Prasad, L.M., 2002, *Principles of Management*, Sultan Chand & Sons, New Delhi.

Michael J. Rouge, 2001, *Business Communication: A Cultural & Strategic Approach*, Atlantic Publishers & Distributors (P) Ltd, New Delhi.

Rao, Dr. Nageshwar & Das, Dr Rajendra P., 2005, *Communication Skills*, Himalaya Publishing House, Mumbai.

Sherlekar, S. A., 1998, *Marketing Management*, Himalaya Publishing House, Mumbai.

Villanilam, J. V., 2004, *More Effective Communication*, Sage Publications, New Delhi

Websites:"http://en.wikipedia.org/wiki/Corporate_communications"; alexcommunications.com

16

The Role of Development Communication in Reaching the Grassroots in India: An Appraisal

—Koyel Ckakrabarty

The over-discussed Shakespearean expression from his play *Julius Caesar*, "I came, I saw, I conquered", seems to represent the generalised spirit of one of the most sensational and worldwide phenomena called 'Globalisation'. In this postmodern world where 'things fall apart' and 'centre cannot hold', globalisation seems to be a single force behind all nations impinging upon almost every aspect of human living—social, cultural, political, environmental—thereby reducing the barring gap between them. Indeed, globalisation doubtlessly stands as one of the most important agents in upbringing a synthetic evolution in the world and human history which the two-millennium world has ever witnessed.

The word 'globalisation', though mainly related to economic market penetration and dispersion, nevertheless has penetrated into the grassroots of cultural entity of almost every country where even the illiterate and poor know the taste of coca-colaisation of today's indigenous living. But winning entails an implication of losing something. And thus, globalisation which has won over almost every part of the world has its evident effects of losing and losing all that it has won over. And here lies the invisible ogre, inside the translucent survey of the social change, which despite being heavily polished and sophisticated, unhesitatingly trespasses the 'Other' giant's periphery and slouches slowly over the 'Other' culture, economy, political, social spheres, directly or indirectly, leaving very little scope for the 'Other' to realise and make up what is unknowingly getting lost or extinct.

Globalisation can be grossly coined into a word 'collation' where the basic demographical existence of any human being is synthetically tantalised either to get hybridised into an 'Other's' cultural and social existence or entirely be beaten by one's identity so as to become synchronised into a unipolar world. In such a pronounced evolutionary trend-wave where multi-cultural, multi-lingual and multi-economic system work and are in a way hegemonised to dissolve into one another, the Darwinian cliché 'the survival of the fittest' with its positive and negative consequences are obvious and prominent. And as for its resultants, a New World Order is bound to reveal with all its comprehensive meritorious and de-meritorious factors that directly fall into the critical perspectives of the critics, raising a host of brain-hammering questions like, 'to be or not to be' in the new world order: 'that is the question'.

Perhaps one of the most alarming inventions that the history of human evolution had ever witnessed is communication. With the realisation of the ongoing undercurrents of immense possibilities of development under the phenomenon of globalisation, Communication has gained in importance the more not only for dissemination of thoughts and information but also for making the world a global village and globalising every aspect of human existence. It is quite interesting to note that neither communication nor globalisation is a new phenomenon, and human beings have been exploiting their advantages since times immemorial. Communication, as a process of 'dissociation of message' in the modern electronic and technological modes, has overtly been exploited in the trend wave of globalisation where the occurrence of globalisation as a commercial phenomenon, at the first instance, has been promoted by communication vice-versa through mass media. Mass media, its effects, though may be fiercely debated as well as globalisation itself, has been tremendously exploited in this renewed age of globalisation to meet vicarious ends and to influence the human demographic existence heavily in all sections of society. This includes culture, education, entertainment, sports, art and crafts, media, production and industry, science, technology external and internal affairs and so on. Thus, just like communication which bears its prehistoric past in its post-modern applications, globalisation too now has animated its old apparel making communication its wand, changing and propagandising all kinds of new orders under the glamorous social tag called 'development'. And when in the 1950's the realisation of the need to develop the world with the emerging media services came into focus, development communication as a distinct discipline emerged.

The word communication comes from the Latin word *communis* meaning commonness. Successful and effective communication is only possible when all the needed parameters for communication, like interest, motive, language, physical and psychological conditions of listener and speaker, are common. It is also a successful communication when the speaker and listener through a dialectical process and argumentative technique reach a point where one is either motivated by the other or both the views are synthesized. According to I.A.Richards, in one of his essays, "Communication takes place when one mind so acts upon its environment that another mind is influenced and in that another mind an experience occurs which is like the experience in the first mind and is caused in part by that experience."

Trickling down the ages, it is an ever convinced fact that effective communication can bring about development. Browsing over the Western models and theories of communication, from the time of Aristotle to Everett Rogers, from a simple Shannon-Weaver sender-receiver model to Nora Quebral, it proves that communication serves as the bottom-line for development and progress. Development is perhaps one of the most fiercely debated concepts in the contemporary social sciences, which has evolved since World War II. From a narrow economist term, it has outgrown into a comprehensive dynamic one, taking within its ambit natural environment, community, social relations, education, production , culture and welfare, though the approach of development depends upon local culture and national circumstances and not on outside models. That communication is an important input in development, is unanimously accepted by the sociologists, psychologists and economists, who say that proper use of communication can foster the pace and development of a country. The United Nations Conference on

Freedom of Information, in 1948, called freedom of information, one of the basic freedoms, and free and adequate information, the touchstone of all freedoms. It was generally believed that for free and adequate information in any country there must be adequate development of mass.[1] Nora Quebral, also known as the 'Mother of Development Communication', defines Development Communication as "the art and science of human communication linked to a society's planned transformation from a state of poverty to one of dynamic socio-economic growth that makes for greater equity and the larger unfolding of individual potential" in *Bulletin of Science Technology and Society*, USA (2001), highlighting the prominent yet varied aspects and scopes of development through communication in an under developed country. Developmental communication is thus a process of developing the society through not only affecting or influencing behaviours of individuals or groups towards certain desired goals and objectives, necessary for the betterment and benefits of the entire society, but also reaching the entire mass population of the country through proper channelised means. It refers to the communication processes, strategies and principles within the field of international development, aimed at improving the conditions and quality of life of people struggling with underdevelopment and marginalisation.

The development paradigm that united international development community in the 1950s and 1960s, sought to explain and facilitate the transition from traditional to modern societies. This dominant paradigm was based on the observation that the differences in per capita income between developed and underdeveloped nations could not be explained in terms of differences in natural resources or other factors outside human control. The developed nations were taken as the ideal. Development consisted of an attempt to increase productivity, economic growth and industrialisation by capital-intensive investments, sometimes tied to administrative reforms. The favourable effects of these innovations would 'trickle down' from the elites to throughout the society. In the process, the culture would be transformed from 'traditional' to 'modern'. This strategy led to programmes of capital-intensive investment in industry and to assessment of development in terms of GNP, per capita income, and proportion of GNP in industrial products rather than in agriculture or rawmaterials. But the real individual development of the people in this procedure could not claim positive results to a huge extent in the underdeveloped countries because the attitudes and folkways of traditional people were ill suited to the demands of modern society and this created a gap in the proposed strategy. Here the historical background, indigenous culture, underdeveloped mindset and other local parameters were not taken into consideration. Communication, through broadcasting, was taken as the most indispensable tool to make the underdeveloped modern. That is, the dominant paradigm evinced a model that allows a flow of communication in only one direction, from top to bottom ignoring the flow of information in the opposite direction, thereby portraying one of the biggest lacunas in the model.[2]

With the failure of the working of the dominant paradigm system in the underdeveloped countries, a new paradigm or alternative paradigm model of development came up in the 1970s. The model now stressed on six major terms of improvement in the quality of life for the individuals in the underdeveloped countries. The shift of emphasis from the Western countries upholding them as role models, to a unique blend of local and traditional values with modernism, was the main motive of the alternative paradigm. Popular participation had now been asserted in the local levels, a stress on self-reliance, self-development and self-management were taken as primary objectives; equal distribution of economic gains was another objective to reduce the economic gap. Traditional media and 'Society specific' models as suited to individual country, for transmitting message and receiving feedback, were emphasized; attention was now given to social and international structural factors that impede development, rather than concentrating exclusively on deficiencies of individuals or nations. Participation was the key characteristic of this new paradigm system of development, which initiated novel forms of interaction among various groups within society. It took communication as a process of social interaction through a balanced exchange of information. Participatory communication has the advantages of including those groups of individuals who plan for development as well as those, for whom the development is meant, thereby leaving ample scope not only to 'adopt' but also to interfere, repair, care for the machinery and amenities they receive as part of development efforts. New paradigm development theorists take participation in development projects as an educational process that starts with an analysis of reality follows with a rejection of the ideology of the elite classes and finally leads to motivation of the unprivileged population toward concerned action for social change.[3]

In India, Bhattanayaka stressed that the essence of communication lay in achieving commonness and oneness. The Indian concept of communication is deep-rooted in the primitive age of Indian civilisation itself, when Bharat Muni, in around second century BC, expressed his views on aestheticism discussing communication and literature, in his book *Natya Shastra*, also taken as the fifth *Veda*. Bharat insists that a 'Sahridaya', i.e. one who has one heart can understand the 'bhabas' and 'rasas' in a 'dhavani', i.e. in a text or form of speech. He asserts a need for 'Sadharanikaran', meaning simplification or identification of meaning, which will appeal to all kinds of people, irrespective of the literary barrier, and senses. This kind of communication is a support system to the government or the developing authority, as the message can reach to every corner of the nation only because of its effective work-methods, that is, channelising and motivating of the public in a simplest form.

India has witnessed remarkable instances of effective social-communicators who had boosted the common people for improvement by classic communicative means in various fields. Musing back through the ages, we can focus on how great men like the Buddha, Ramakrishna Paramahamsa, Vivekananda, Lord Chaitanya, and many others had tried to enforce changes both in human and social aspects of life only by persuasion and communication. Social development in the pre-independence era got its tempo with the great minds like Raja Rammohan Roy, Bal Gangadhar Tilak, Dayanand Saraswati, Jyotirao Phule, and Mahatma Gandhi, who played a great role in the upgradation of the marginalised. The Arya Samaj, Satya Sodhak Samaj and the workers of the Indian Congress stood up for the social consciousness in people and with the coming of the Mahatma the entire Indian mass was motivated into social and political awareness. In fact, it was Mahatma Gandhi who had planned a meta-model of development for the country in proper and after independence the government convinced the first five-year planning based on the very Gandhian meta-model of development through the panchayati raj system.

Gandhi's concept of "Sarvodaya" describes a democratic socialistic pattern of economics and institutions suited to the conditions, realities, and needs of Indian society. His development strategy had sought to preserve Indian values and ways of life rather than replace them with Western models. He stressed on rural reconstruction rather than heavy, urban industrialisation that would incorporate the labour-oriented methodologies of production and utilisation of indigenous resources, devoid of exploitation. His original model, records Uma Narula, was an attempt to produce powerful village communities by initiating participatory communication, developing self-reliant village republics in the form of panchayats, enforcing reforms of land ownership, and encouraging the development of rural industries (p.68). The village was seen as the unit of social planning with self reliance providing basic necessities of food, shelter clothing, education and justice. Good of the community was prioritised rather than private profit. Village and cottage industries would provide employment to the non-farmers and the natural and necessary co-operation among villagers in everyday matters of social, economic and political life would produce popular participation. The Gandhian model suggested vigorous attempts to mend, and if need be replace, outlived social, economic and political institutions. In their place, the society would strive for justice, freedom and equality for all citizens (Narula: 1986, 68).

The folk or traditional arts of India have from the ancient times been used for moral, religious socio-political purposes. It is a classic communicative medium which appeals to the personal and emotional level of the people, avoiding any cross-cultural hurdles, expensive entertainment programmes and above all, the message is dispersed in a familiar format and content in local and colloquial dialects to a homogeneous group, surpassing all literacy and socio-economic barriers. It is quite interesting that India, though have witnessed many ages of folk representations since times immemorial, yet development activities with the help of folk communication have not much been into practice except for the religious cause.

Gandhi was first to use inter-personal communication as a medium to influence the folk media which as its outcome spoke about Gandhian philosophy and ideals so as to influence India into social and political development of the country. He was an intuitive social worker, far ahead of the Western development theorists, and was well aware of the power of communication. He weighed and measured the Indian colonial situation and the existing psychological and physical state of Indians and concluded that the accurate means to reach them was by the folk media and group communication. He achieved easy identification with the masses through "Sadharanikaran" or simplification of his message, through common religious symbols, *Vedas*, myths and of course making his life very simple so as to establish an easy identification. In a word, Gandhi's development module was mainly based on 'villageism'.

Gandhi, though not in-person, but in ideologies, teaching, views, had reached the stage and in hearts of people through various forms of Tamasha, Jatra, Keertan, Nautanki, Pala, Yakshagana, Ramlila, Raslila, Puppetry, and Street Theatre, to name a few folk forms, at all corners of the country. Gandhi's social activities were development oriented and his idealism, democratic, rural and homogeneous in nature. His interpersonal and non-violent persuasion and conversation techniques describe a top-down 'advisory' role for the government but also include bottom-up channels from the people to the government and bottom-bottom channels among the people themselves. The model aimed at raising the consciousness of the people against exploitation, injustice and poverty, encourage consciousness for socio-economic equality and social change, and enable the people to articulate their needs for development.

Gandhi realised that three aspects of the traditional social structure were identified as contributing to the problems of people. First, system of bonded labour and tremendous exploitation of the poor by the existing zamindari or feudal structure, second, the rigid caste system that made the low caste doubly marginalised, and finally, the traditional attitude toward family, children, living style and population problem. Development activities related to redemption of untouchability, casteism, practising of spiritualism, Hindu-Muslim unity, and healthy living conditions, spinning of the charkha, mass education, and women emancipation were some of the basic social changes that Gandhi strived to attain in rural India. He set up several organisations for the promotion of specific causes—Cow Protection Society, One Language, One Script society, All India Spinner's Association Harijan Sevak Sangh, All India Village Industries Association etc., carried on voluminous correspondence, wrote practically everything under the sun, conducted prolonged experiments on sex, food, etc., and was in general was involved with several other activities which he thought would lead to the moral regeneration of society.[4]

Active participation that Gandhi sought to establish among the rural folk was implemented by mainly two ways. First, by the local party workers and the Gandhi followers who brought up certain social evils to the surface and gathered public opinion and remedies based on Gandhian ideals thereby bringing about social changes and second, by the religious interpretation of Gandhi among masses. Through rumours Gandhi's ideas were spread far and wide by the local people, 'opinion' leaders', holy men, media, literary writers and Gandhian representations in which he was portrayed with miraculous powers, power to heal and revive, power to thrash out the British away from the country, the power of immeasurable good and holiness. In many cases, Gandhi had never known about the development activities going on in remote villages but definite changes in hygiene, education, spinning and restriction to consumption of liquor, tobacco, swearing, etc., were noticed.

The idea of self-purification and Sanskritisation has been similarly noticed where prophesies from the Devi or God has been witnessed, in different districts of India, moving on par with the Gandhian instructions of self-purification by physical and dietary restraints. New rules to observing of vegetarianism, cleanliness, daily-bath, washing hands after defecation, etc., were noticed to have been followed by the God-fearing people in the name of 'Ganhi baba' (Saint Gandhi; local dialect of Dhangars in Bihar) thereby making oracles and resolutions more rigid. Even the name of Gandhi and his prescribed guidelines were means enough to resolve the village disputes. On this Shahid Amin reports, "The 1910's movements and organisations of Hindi, Hindu Culture and social reform—'nagri sabhas', pathshalas (vernacular schools), 'gaushalas' (asylums for cattle), 'sewa samithis' (social service leagues) and 'sudrak sabhas' (reform associations) of various sorts provided the support and cover for nationalist activity" all backed by popular Gandhi belief even in the rural villàges and undeveloped regions. "Each type of these socio-political movements served nationalism in its own way, but there was a considerable amount of overlapping in their functions and interests...Yagya (sacrifice) was performed; a Sanskrit Pathshala and a gaushala endowed with financial support from traders, arrangements made for the orderly running of Ramlilas and melas, and panchayats set up for the arbitration of disputes"[5] (p.10).

Since independence, the Indian government has made concerted efforts to meet physical needs to improve the quality of life of people together with a stress on the development of the national economy. The UN General Assembly in 1948 emphasized that information media have an important part to play in education and in economic and social progress generally and that new techniques of communication offer special opportunities for acceleration of the education process. Consequently, governments, especially of newly emerged developing countries, were urged to include in their economic development plans adequate provision for development of national information media. UNESCO was specially called upon to play active role and support programmes and activities leading to development of communication systems in the developing countries. In India three experimental projects> The Etawah Project (1958), The Nilokheri Experiment (1950), "Grow More Food" Campaign (1951) in India, based on Gandhian meta-model, were conducted to pilot future development. The Etawah project in Uttar Pradesh, with its object to enable economic sufficiency through agricultural up gradation and improved quality of life with active participation of the people, stressed on realistic planning, based on the characteristics of the local situation. Communication was to play a role in mobilising, education and persuasion of the people. It was taken as a tool to provide opportunities for coordinated activities within and among the villages and mass and government. Flow of message included both top-down model vice-versa. Communication channels were mostly interpersonal consisting of village-level workers, extension agents. Through mass meetings, Kisan Melas (farmer fairs), use of folk songs and

Emphasis was on education, employment and communications through satellites and with the introduction and wide availability of cable television networking in India, mass communication served as a greatest route to development communication. Private channels were also taken into consideration who could impart the social message. Education or eradication of illiteracy was one of the greatest campaigns that this five-year plan clung on to. Moreover, employment and family planning were main agenda beside education. A "Book Bazar on Wheel" was launched by the Publication Division. The Directorate of Field Publicity which targets its publicity effort mainly to the rural areas and has a large network, organised nearly 3.13 lakh film shows, arranged song and drama programmes, held 2.15 lakh photo exhibitions and 3.03 lakh oral communication programmes, thus reaching an estimated audience of over 30 crore during the Seventh Plan period.

In the Ninth Five-Year Plan (1997-2002) Social Welfare dealt with the welfare and development of those vulnerable groups who failed to cope up with the rapid socio-economic changes and were lagging behind the rest of the society. The Ninth Plan proposed to adopt a three-fold strategy specific to each group, namely, empowering the disabled, reforming the social deviants and caring for the other disadvantaged. One of the major objectives during the Ninth Plan was women empowerment which was taken as agents of social change and development. With increasing literacy, awareness about opportunities, reduction in family size and time required for childbearing and child rearing, it was likely that there would be increasing number of women who would seek employment on full time or part time basis. Their entry into this sphere of economic activity and income generation will be of considerable significance especially to small scale sector, home-based agro, and agriculture and handicrafts production. While encouraging this development, it became essential to take steps to prevent economic exploitation of women; and so efforts were suggested to prevent or reduce the potential adverse health impact of dual stress of household work and economically productive activities on women also. The social sector planning ensured to lessen poverty rate. Appropriate policies and programmes were formulated together with adequate investments plannings so that poor and vulnerable segments of the population could access essential commodities and facilities based on their needs and not on the ability to pay.

With the technological advances and instant global reach, communications and the media had become an integral part of Indian life. With the convergence of the communication, broadcasting and electronic technologies, the challenges faced by this sector were equally wide ranging in view of the rapidly changing media scenario and a fiercely competitive environment. The main objectives of communication as tools for development were mainly based on consolidation, technological modernisation and better and more relevant programming. For Information and Films Media, the main thrust was on better services to the public. Further, units such as the Song and Drama Division and the Directorate of Field Publicity helped to bridge the information gap in areas which have limited access to electronic and print media. The experiences of the Eighth Five Year Plan have guided the strategies and policies to be adopted for achieving the objectives for the Ninth Five Year Plan. An increasing involvement of the government in the film industry was envisaged. Another important area that was in highlight was the augmentation and modernisation of training facilities in the country especially in the fields of film and television production. Information technology which was fast emerging as the technological infrastructure for global integration and rapid development of all sectors of economy had special projects in this plan. Recognising the impressive growth, the country had achieved in IT since mid-eighties, its immense potential for future growth and its importance as an agent of transformation of every facet of human life, a high priority had been accorded to the development of this sector. The Ninth Plan would aim to make India a global IT super power and a front-runner in the information revolution.

The Tenth Five-Year Plan(2002-2007) can in one word be called as development of urban sector through modernisation with a keen eye on the rural sector for improvement. The Internet and media are taken as the latest weapons to kill backwardness and enlighten the educated. With the fast growth of literacy and socio-economic awareness, the rate of educated unemployed rose high. With the positive effects of globalisation, the outsourcing of resources by the multinational companies from India through the information technology resulted into a high rise in India's GDP and per capita income. But this could motivate a certain sector of the society who were IT-literate and they faced a sudden rise in economic growth. The other vast section of the population being computer-illiterate could not access the boons of communication through the Internet and thus the government led high stress on computer literacy both in the urban and rural population. Media and press who now had become the chief source of entertainment, tried to motivate the public into social development for the social good. Films and theatres though privatised also bear a social responsibility to educate and aware. Radio now was popularised by the frequenting of the FM channels. Communication is now used by the media as the source of feedback, especially SMS system through mobile phones is used to weigh a public opinion through open voting system. Telecommunication is highly attended and attempts are being made to equip every nook and corner of rural sectors with facilities of electronic media and computer exposure. In this planning where people could easily connect the media or join live with the media channels any time through telecommunications, for giving the feedback on certain issue, government policy and whatsoever matters, media channels became the chief mirror of politico-socio-economic scenario in India besides providing entertainment. With the introduction of Right to Information by the Supreme Court in the year 2000, communication as a tool to disseminate messages and reciprocate feedback from the public became the biggest resource. Private investment in the field of communication was boosted. Digitalisation of the communication system and its optimal use was a major thrust area. This plan other than stressing on the development of the socio-economic conditions of the educated unemployed, stressed on the conservation of environment and prevention of its destruction.

The Eleventh Five Year Plan (2007-2012) is the current addition last year whose basic emphasis is on upgradation of the existing socio-economic facilities band and its optimal utilisation. This plan is a fertile development of the past achievements and the government hopes to cover the loopholes of the previous endeavours by better communication system and essential social possibilities.

Developmental communication, as the complementary procedure to development, has been adopted and adapted by

India from the very first year planning. Though soon after Gandhi's death and First Five-Year Plan, the entire development notion changed from alternative paradigm of development to one of dominant capitalism, yet the alternative social angle to develop people by dint of education, self-reliance and training has not been dismissed. Folk communication was used before and is now used in the same way only through the electronic medium to reach out to the grassroots for development. Birth control campaigns, marriages of women after a matured age and education campaigns through an animation series "Meena" has become quite popular. In Mumbai AIDS control campaign through television has been very successful. In West Bengal through 'Buladi', the AIDS control mascot, as a social health worker proved a super agent to spread awareness. Television channels Doordarshan, Prasar Bharati or Gyan Bharati as agents of government tried to motivate the farmers and villages about the social needs to development to a reasonable extent. The popular most television serial *Humlog* (1984-85), featured in the Doordarshan, portrayed the themes of family planning, family harmony, gender equality and national integration. Similarly, *Thinka Thinka Sukh*, a radio presentation highlighted woman emancipation gender equality, family harmony and HIV prevention. Moreover, the private channels through vicarious means are spreading social messages to the people and children to define their social responsibility. Sony and Star TVs too project messages to women emancipation, birth control, prevention of environment, etc.

One classic positive developmental function can be explained by a simple example in the modern scenario where media like a Magic Bullet influences the illiterate ignorant people of Bihar on the issue of vaccinating pulse polio to children. The result that the Government Health Division, campaigns, kiosks, posters and political leaders could not achieve, because of certain tribal or rustic superstitions, religious prejudices, fear and taboos previously, could be achieved to a much unexpected greater degree only by the mass media campaign of Pulse Polio, marketed on television, by the most popular actor on screen, Amitabh Bachchan. Surveys conducted by the UNICEF and the media showed an unexpected rise in polio intake in the state of Bihar in the year 2004-05. On interviewing the reason for such an

17

Ethical Challenges in Information Technology Age

—A.A.Khan & QamarTalat

INTRODUCTION

We are living in the so-called information age which can be described as an era where economic activities are mainly information based. This is due to the development and use of technology. The main characteristic of this era can be summarised as a rise in the number of knowledge workers, and a world that has become more open in the sense of communication and trans-border flow of information at lightning speed. This paradigm shift brings in its wake new ethical and judicial problems which are related to issues such as the right of access to information, right to privacy, and protection of the economic interests of the owners of intellectual property.

ETHICS

In this age of IT, it has become mandatory to safeguard our ethical responsibilities. The ethical actions of a person can be described in general terms as those actions that are performed within the criterion of what is regarded as socially, morally and legally acceptable within the framework of a particular society or nation. It relates thus to the question of what is good or bad in terms of human actions. According to Spinello (1995, p.14) the purpose of ethics is to help us behave honourably and attain the basic good that makes us more fully human.

The Concept of Privacy

In addition to ethics, the concept of privacy too has become a force to reckon with. Privacy can be defined as an individual condition of life characterised by exclusion from publicity (Neetling et al., 1996, p. 36). The concept follows from the right to be left alone (Stair, 1992, p.635; Shank, 1986, p.12). As such, privacy can be regarded as a natural right which provides the foundation for other legal rights. The legal right to privacy is constitutionally protected in most democratic societies. This constitutional right is expressed in a variety of legislative forms. Examples include the Privacy Act (1974) in the USA, and the Data Protection Act in England. Privacy is an important right because it is a necessary condition for other rights such as freedom and personal autonomy. There is thus a relationship between privacy, freedom and human dignity. Respecting a person's privacy is to acknowledge such a person's right to freedom and to recognise that individual as an autonomous human being. The duty to respect a person's privacy is furthermore a prima facie duty. In other words, it is not an absolute duty that does not allow for exceptions. Two examples may be cited in this regard. Firstly, the police may violate a criminal's privacy by spying or by seizing personal documents. Secondly, a government also has the right to gather private and personal information from its citizens with the aim of ensuring order and harmony in society (Ware, 1993, p.205). The right to privacy as an expression of individual freedom is thus confined by social responsibility.

Different Concepts of Private Information

Based on the definition of privacy, aspects which are of specific relevance for information based society must be emphasized. The first is the fact that privacy as a concept is closely related to information. According to Neethling (1996, p.35) privacy refers to the entirety of facts and information applicable to a person in a state of isolation. The fact that privacy is expressed by means of information implies that it is possible to distinguish between different categories of privacy, namely— private communication, information which relates to the privacy of a person's body, other personal information, and information with regard to a person's possessions. Each of these categories is briefly dealt with.

Private Communication

This category of privacy concerns all forms of personal communication which a person wishes to keep private. The information exchanged during an interview between a user and a service provider can be seen as an example.

Privacy of the Body (Westin, 1967, p.351)

This normally refers to medical information (Neethling, 1991, p.35-36). This means that a person has the right to be informed about the nature of an illness as well as the implications thereof. Such a person further has the right to privacy about the nature of the illness and can not be forced to make it known to others. The only exception is when the health, and possibly the lives of others may be endangered by the specific illness— such as the case may be where a person is HIV positive and the chance exists that other people may contract the virus. This category of information is of specific importance for an information professional working in a medical library.

Privacy of Personal Information

Personal information refers to those categories of information which refer to only that specific person, for example name, address, and financial information. This type of information is of relevance to all categories of information professionals.

Information about One's Possessions

This information is closely related to property right. According to this a person does have control over the information which relates to personal possessions in certain instances. For example, a person may keep private the information about the place where a wallet is kept.

THE EXPRESSED WILL TO PRIVACY

This is an important aspect of the issue of privacy. It implies an explicit desire for privacy. This desire is important for the delimitation of privacy. In short, the desire for privacy implies that privacy will only be an issue in cases where there is a clear expression of a desire for privacy. For example, a personal conversation between two persons will be regarded as private as long as there is an expressed will to keep it private. The moment that this will is relinquished, the information is no longer regarded as private. The same applies to the other categories of personal and private information. If a person makes a private telephone number (as a form of personal information) known to a company, it is no longer regarded as private information. It can then even be seen as business information which may legally be traded in. This expressed will to privacy acts, therefore, as a very important guideline for the information professional regarding the delimitation of privacy. Here, it is also important to distinguish between privacy and confidentiality or secrecy. The confidential treatment of information is not only applicable to the above-mentioned four categories of private and personal information; it may refer to any category of information, such as trade secrets.

Influence of Technology on Processing of Personal and Private Information

Definition of Information Technology

Before the influence of the use of technology in the processing of personal and private information can be dealt with, it is important to define information technology. According to Van Brakel (1989, p.240), information technology is the gathering, organising, storage and distribution of information in various formats by means of computer and telecommunication techniques based on microelectronics.

Ethical Implications in the Processing of Information

Although technology has a major impact on the gathering, storage, retrieval and dissemination of information, its main ethical impact relates to accessibility and or inaccessibility and the manipulation of information. It creates the possibility of wider as well as simultaneous access to information. By implication, it becomes easier to access a person's private information by more people. On the other hand, a person can be excluded from necessary information in electronic format by means of a variety of security measures such as passwords. Technological manipulation of information refers, among others, to the integration of information (merging of documents), the repackaging thereof (translations and the integration of textual and graphical formats), and the possible altering of information (changing of photographic images) by electronic means. The use of technology in the processing of information can therefore not be seen as ethically neutral. Christians (199, p.7) refers to the use of technology as a value laden process. Kluge (1994, p.337) comments that technology has changed the ontological status of a document with accompanying ethical implications. By this he specifically refers to the manipulation of information by means of technology. Brown (1990, p.3), however, on the other hand, indicates that the ethical problems that are caused by the use of technology do not imply "that we should rethink our moral values." The impact of the use of technology on the privacy of people manifests itself in a variety of areas. These include the following:

- *Electronic Monitoring of People in Workplace*: This relates to personal and private information as discussed earlier. The justification by companies for the use of such technology is to increase productivity. Stair (1992, p.655), however, in the discussion of this practice, clearly points out the ethical problem pertaining to the use of these technologies. According to him peoples' privacy in the workplace are threatened by these devices. It can also lead to a feeling of fear and of always being watched.
- *The Interception and Reading of E-mail Messages*: This poses an ethical problem which relates to private communication of an individual. It is technically possible to intercept E-mail messages, and the reading thereof is normally justified by companies because they see technology infrastructure as a resource belonging to the company and not the individual, and secondly, messages are intercepted to check on people to see whether they use the facility for private reasons or to do their job.
- *Merging of Databases Which Contains Personal Information*: This is also known as data-banking (Frocht & Thomas, 1994, p.24). By this is meant the integration of personal information from a variety of databases into one central database. The problem here does not in the first place arise

personal information. Related questions are as follows— does a user have the right to verify any personal and private information that is being held by an information professional, and if so, what are such person's rights regarding the correcting (in cases of the incorrectness thereof) of this information, and does the person have the right to know who is using that personal and private information and for what purposes?

Applicable Ethical Norms

Applicable ethical norms which can act as guidelines as well as instruments of measurement must be formulated to address these ethical issues. The following norms can be distinguished— truth, freedom, and human rights. They are discussed briefly:

- *Truth:* Truth as an ethical norm has dual ethical application. First, it serves as a norm for the factual correctness of information. As a norm it thus guides the information professional regarding the accurate and factually correct handling of private information. Secondly, truth is an expression of ethical virtues such as openness, honesty and trustworthiness.
- *Freedom:* According to this norm a person has the freedom to make choices in terms of freedom of privacy and freedom from intrusion. As a norm, however, it may not become absolute. Therefore, the choice to privacy from intrusion may not restrict the freedom of others.
- *Human rights:* This norm is closely related to freedom, but can be regarded as a more concretely applicable norm. Applied to privacy it means the juridical acknowledgment and protection of a persons' right to privacy. As an individual human right it also protects the individual from unlawful interference from society.

Ethical Guidelines for the Information Professional

Based on these norms, practical guidelines for the information professional can be formulated. Before the formulation of these guidelines, two fundamental aspects must be taken into consideration, namely the recognition of a persons' autonomy and freedom, as well as the fact that legal guidelines on privacy do not offer a complete framework for ethical actions of the information professional with regard to the handling of personal and private information.

The concept of autonomy and freedom has already been dealt with. With regard to the juridical guidelines the following comments can be made. Firstly, once a person's private and personal information has been made known publicly, such information is no longer, according to the law, viewed as private. This implies that the information can legally be dealt with as trade information. There is, therefore, from a juridical perspective, no ethical sensitivity on the issues of autonomy and freedom of the individual with regard to his right to privacy. The second remark relates to the content of legislation itself; immense growth in and development of information technology give rise to the fact that legislators fall behind in the tabling of appropriate legislation on the protection of personal privacy. Bearing in mind these two aspects, the following practical guidelines can be laid:

- As an acknowledgment of the autonomy and freedom of the individual the information professional must act on the assumption that the client regards as confidential all personal and private information that is handled by the information professional. This implies that the information professional acknowledges the right of the client to control to a certain extent, any personal and private information. This is based on the norm of freedom.
- The client must, on a regular basis, have access to all private and personal information that is held and used by the information professional. The reason for this is to provide the client the opportunity to verify the accuracy of the information. It is then the responsibility of the information professional to see to it that necessary corrections are made and again verified by the client (Fouty, 1993, p.290) based on the norms of freedom and human rights.

The merging of personal and other private information of an individual into a different database than the one for which it was originally collected must be done with necessary caution (Schattuck, 1995, p.310). This is specifically applicable in situations where the client is not aware of such merging or the implications thereof. The appropriate action would not only be to inform the client about such a merging and the implications thereof, but also to give the client the right of access to the information on the central database, and the opportunity to change the information where it is incorrect, and the right to know who is using the information as well as the purpose of such use based on the norms of human rights, freedom, and truth.

The information professional must notify the client explicitly of the intended purposes of the use of all personal and private information. This implies the client's permission. Different avenues exist for seeking such permission. Spinello (1995, p.122) prefers the method of implicit informed consent. According to this principle, companies or information professionals that have collected information about a person must diligently inform that person about the various uses of the information. Clients must then be given an opportunity either to consent to these uses or to withhold their consent. The burden is on the client to respond, and a lack of response implies consent. However, the client must be granted the opportunity to withdraw consent (Amidon, 1992, p.67) based on the norms of freedom and human rights.

No unnecessary private information must be gathered. This is not only for logistic reasons but also to prevent the unnecessary violation or exposure of a person's privacy based on the norm of freedom.

Personal and other private information that is no longer necessary for the function for which it was collected must be destroyed (Branscomb, 1995, p.71) based on the norms of freedom and human rights.

When the rendering of a specific service or product to a person is refused on the grounds of personal information (e.g. creditworthiness), the reason for this denial must be made known to the person based on the norms of truth and human rights.

A person's information must be handled with the necessary confidentiality. This implies security and control of access to the information, of the right to use it, as well as the right to change or add any information (Fouty, 1993, p.290) based on the norms of freedom, truth and human rights.

A private policy must be formulated consisting of the following elements— the categories of information that must be regarded as private and personal, the levels of confidentiality (e.g. who has access and use of which information), a clear explanation of the purposes of the use of the information, and the description of the procedures to ensure the accuracy of this information based on the norms of freedom, truth and human rights.

Conclusion

It can thus be concluded that the use of technology in the processing of information poses important questions with regard to a person's right to privacy. This right is directly linked to the right to freedom and human autonomy. These problems relate mainly to the accessibility of information and the manipulation thereof. This is of specific relevance to the information professional who deals with private and personal information. Practical guidelines in the handling of these problems can be formulated according to the norms of freedom, truth and human rights.

References

Amidon, P. (1992). "Widening Privacy Concerns." *Online,* 16 (4), pp. 64-67.

Baker, L. (1992). "Needed: An Ethical Code for Library Administrators." *Journal of Library Administration.* 16 (4), pp.1-17.

Benjamin, L.M. (1991). "Privacy, Computers and Personal Information: Towards Equality and Equity In an Information Age." *Communications and the Law.* 13 (2), pp.3-16.

Branscomb, A.W. (1994). "*Who Owns Information?: From Privacy to Private Access.*" New York, Basic Books (A division of Harper Collins Publishers).

Christians, C.G. (1991). "Information Ethics In a Complicated Age." *Ethics and The Librarian.* Proceedings of the Allerton Park Institute, 29-31 October 1989, University of Illinois, Graduate School of Library, Edited by: F.W. Lancaster. Vol.31.

Collier, G. (1994). "Information Privacy: Just How Private Are the Details of Individuals In a Company's Database?" *Information Management and Computer Security.* 3 (1), pp. 41-45.

Focht, K.T. & Thomas, D.S. (1994). "Information Compilation and Disbursement: Moral, Legal and Ethical Considerations." *Information Management and Computer Security.* 2 (2), pp. 23-28.

Fouty, K.G. (1993). "Online Patron Records and Privacy: Service vs Security." *The Journal of Academic Librarianship*. 19 (5), pp.289-293.

Froehlich, T.J. (1994). "Re-thinking Ethical Issues In an Online Environment." *Proceedings of Online Information*, 6-8 December 1994, Edited by: D.I. Raitt & B. Jeapes. Oxford, Learned Information. pp. 415-422.

Goode, J & Johnson, M. (1991). "Putting Out the Flames: The etiquette and law of E-mail." *Online*. 15 (6), pp. 61-66.

Kluge, E.H.W. (1994). "Health Information: The Fair Information Principles and Ethics." *Methods of Information in Medicine*. 33, pp. 336-345.

McGarry, K. (1993). *The Changing Context of Information: An Introductory Analysis*. 2nd edition. London, Library Association Publishing.

Neethling, J. (1991). *Persoonlikheidsreg*. Derde uitgawe. Durban, Butterworths.

Neethling, J., Potgieter, J.M. & Visser, P.J. 1996. *Neethling's Law of Personality*. Durban, Butterworths.

Rosenberg, R.S. (1993). "Free Speech, Pornography, Sexual Harassment, and Electronic Networks." *The Information Society*. 9, pp.285-331.

Shank, R. (1986, Summer). "Privacy: History, Legal, Social, and Ethical Aspects." Library Trends. pp.7-15.

Shattucks, J. (1995). "Computer Matching Is a Serious Threat to Individual Rights." *Computers, Ethics and Social Values*. Edited by: D.G. Johnson & H. Nissenbaum. New Jersey, Prentice-Hall. pp. 305-311.

Smith, M.M. (1994). "Online Information ethics: Online Searching and the Searching Self." *Proceedings of the 15th National Online Meeting*, May 1994. Edited by: M.E. Williams. Medford, NY, Learned Information. pp. 399-405.

Spinello, R.A. (1995). *Ethical Aspects of Information Technology*. New Jersey, Prentice-Hall Inc.

Stair, R.M. (1992). *Principles of Information Systems: A Managerial Approach*. Boston, Boyd & Fraser.

Van Brakel, P.A. (1989). *Inligtingstegnologie: Verkenning van navorsingstemas*. Suid-Afrikaanse Tydskrif vir Biblioteek- en Inligtingkunde, 57 (3).

Ware, W.H. (1993). "The New Faces of Privacy." *The Information Society*. 9 (3) pp.195-211.

Westin, A. (1967). *Privacy and Freedom*. New York, Atheneum.

Zorkoczy, P. (1990). *Information Technology: An Introduction* (2nd Edition). London, Pitman Publishing.

18

Advertising and Globalisation in India

—B. Utpal

Advertising has been defined as any paid form for non-personal presentation and promotion of ideas, goods or services by an identified sponsor (American Marketing Association, quoted in Bennet, 2000, p.117.) and more narrowly as any human communication intended to persuade or influence buyers in their purchase decisions (Cheng, 1996, p.74). Advertising lies at the juncture where culture and the economy interact. Its primary purpose is to sell products and services by stimulating purchasing behaviour, and it does this by using strategies that rework culture, creating aspirations and desires for products.

Major environmental factors that have an impact on advertising are economy, demography, culture, political and legal system. Advertising is itself a cultural product which increasingly affects social attitudes, defines social roles, and influences cultural values. Influenced by these factors, advertising evolved and developed a particular profile in Western industrialised society in the 20th century as a means of stimulating the consumption of products generated by new and expanding industries. In recent decades, advertisers from the industrialised nations have increasingly targeted international markets, expanding the consumption of foreign products and bringing about widespread cultural change. In this context, it will be interesting to make a short study of the contemporary profile of advertising in India.

There has been a long tradition of advertising in India, with newspaper advertising dating back to the 19th century. The first advertising agency established in India was B. Dataram and

Company in 1905, followed by The India-Advertising Company in 1907, Calcutta Advertising agency in 1909, S.H. Bensen in 1928, J. Walter Thompson Associates through its Indian associate, Hindustan Thompson Associates in 1929, LINTAS (Lever International Advertising Services) in 1939, and McCann Erikson in 1956 (Pashupati and Sengupta, 1996). Under the more socialist political environment of the 1960s and 1970s there was little incentive for companies to advertise because advertising was not tax deductible. The first advertising appeared on state television in 1976. With the opening of the economy in the 1980s there was a growth in the number of alliances with multinational agencies and a correlative expansion in advertising, though foreign participation in agency ownership was limited. In 1987, LINTAS, the 2nd ranking agency, held only 4 per cent of its subsidiary, as did Ogilvie and Mather. (Pashupati and Sengupta, 1996). At the time, foreign controlled corporations had the dominant share of total advertising expenditure, and 80 per cent of these were in the consumer goods sector. Advertising was very concentrated with the top 50 advertisers accounting for 80 per cent of the advertising spending and the top 10 advertisers made up 40 per cent of that figure and 32 per cent of the total. Pharmaceutical companies were also significant advertisers at this time (Sachdeva, 1984). There was a massive expansion in advertising in India in the mid 1990s and increased competition among multinationals made big budgets a necessity. New entrants in the market, for example Samsung, had to spend heavily to raise brand awareness (*India Business Intelligence,* 1997).

The profile of advertising agencies in India changed dramatically in the 1990s. Prior to that advertising was dominated by Indian agencies, but since 1990s, foreign agencies have increasingly come to dominate Indian advertising. In 1992-1993, 11 of the top 20 Indian agencies were affiliated with multinational agencies and those agencies were allowed to own stock in the local companies since the early 1990s (Pashupati and Sengupta, 1996, p.167). In 1990 the key companies that were the top advertisers in India were also the leading advertisers internationally—Unilever, Procter and Gamble, and Nestle (Belch and Belch, p.739). In 1992-1993 the monopoly of a small range of product categories was associated with a few companies which dominated the advertising scene. Hindustan Lever had a major impact on the content of programming and the initiation of new programmes, associated with their power as the major advertiser on television (*Advertising Club of Bombay Diary*, 1994, quoted in Pashupati and Sengupta, 1996, p.172).

The advertising industry has expanded rapidly in recent years. Growth was 23 per cent in 2000-2001 and the top 5 agencies in 2000-2001 earned 47.2 per cent of total revenue (Emerging Markets Economy, 2002, August 1). Foreign companies were seen to be initiating more aggressive advertising campaigns and recent growth in advertising has been driven by television advertising, especially satellite channels many of which are free-to-air, which means they depend solely on advertising for their revenue (Sehgal, 2000). Foreign brands are definitely impacting on local brands through competition and takeovers. Some of the greatest competition is in the biggest advertising categories— soaps and detergents, and soft-drinks. Procter and Gamble, Unilever and Colgate Palmolive are competing for the soaps and detergents market. Procter and Gamble has made a strategic alliance with Godrej Soaps, the leading Indian maker of soaps and detergents. Coca Cola and Pepsi are fiercely competing for the soft-drink market. Both companies are increasingly targeting the youth market. Coke made losses in India for many years but was starting to make a profit since the late 1990s (Kripalani, 2003). The 1990s also witnessed increased government spending on advertising and government departments are featured in the client lists of major agencies. The government is advertising in areas such as tourist promotion, army recruitment, AIDS awareness, and is using international agencies in joint ventures (Indiantelevision. com/2001). The service sector of the country is rapidly expanding. Since the privatisation of banking and insurance, there has been a spurt of growth in advertising in these areas. After a new code of conduct was issued in the early 1990s, Indian political parties have emerged as major clients for the advertising sector (Srinivas, 1999).

The usage of the different advertising media has changed in recent decades, largely due to changes in technology. In the early decades of the 20th century, print was the key medium, as it is today, though its influence is declining in relation to television. The impact of media— television, radio, print, outdoor, and

Internet is influenced by different factors. Literacy and income levels are important for print advertising. According to the World Bank, literacy levels in the country are improving. While in 1995, 53.3 per cent of the population was literate, it rose to 58.8 per cent in 2002. Language is another factor influencing television access. The figures for print advertising expenditure are on the increase. Press advertising accounted for 58 per cent of the total advertising expenditure in 1999 as compared to television which accounted for 34 per cent (Srinivas, 1999). By 2004, the share of television increased to 41.8 per cent (www.agencyfaqs.com/www1news/stories/2004). It is also worth the note that between 1991-2002 magazine advertising spending rose from US $245 million to US $968 million (www.magazineworld.org/members/2002).

The increase in spending on television advertising can be directly linked with the growth of the media since its introduction in 1959 in Delhi (CIA, 2002). A regular service was introduced in 1965, but until 1982 it was confined to major cities. The first Indian satellite was launched by NASA in 1982, and by 1984 transmitters covered 30 per cent of the population, and by 1991 that figure reached the 76 per cent mark. There was only one channel until 1984 when a second channel was set up in Delhi, Bombay, Calcutta and Madras (Pashupati and Sengupta, 1996). In 1989 Vilanilam estimated that even if there were 30,000 village community sets, as there were over 500,000 villages, television coverage was by no means extensive in rural areas. The cost of a television set in 1989 at approximately US $800 was four times the average annual per capita income. He saw that the television was still targeting the top 10 per cent of viewers. There was major expansion in television in the early 1990s and the importance of television advertising has increased dramatically. Satellite and cable television were introduced in the 1990s. Cable penetration grew from 20 million to 32 million homes from 1998 to 2000. It may however be noted that actual access to television is much wider than can be estimated from ownership data. Some advertisers find it more effective to use television rather than print to reach consumers, partly because of the low literacy rate. Hindustan Lever found that it cost Rs 5 to reach 1000 people through television, compared to Rs 100 through print. Hindustan Lever spent 60 per cent of its budget on television, and 25-30 per cent on print and 10-15 per cent on other media, which is the major pattern of most of the major consumer goods producers. There is some regional variation though, for example in Kerala, where literacy levels are higher there is a higher use of print advertising (*India Business Intelligence*, August 1997). Advertising spending on television increased to 118 per cent from Rs 23.9 billion in 1996, to Rs 49 billion in 2000, 25 per cent of which was spent on the satellite channels. (Sehgal, 2000).

Outdoor advertising has been important in major cities and is also common in rural areas. Outdoor advertising during 1993-1997 averaged about 5.5 per cent of total advertising budget, which is similar to international trends. In big cities demand for outdoor media exceeds supply, and costs are relatively high. Both billboards and films are seen as 'reminder' advertising (Srinivas, 1999). Billboards have tended to be hand painted, and still are in rural areas, but new methods are now being used in cities. The latest advertising frontier is the Internet and minor players have also entered the arena because of relatively low cost and a global reach. Some of the largest advertisers in India are exploring different strategies and media in an attempt to enter the vast rural consumer market, where even a small percentage of market share amounts to millions of consumers. Media alternatives such as video vans and point of purchase video display are an attempt by major advertisers to communicate to rural purchasers in their local language, rather than Hindi and English, the main languages on television and print (*Unnikrishnan* and Bajpai, 1996 and Kilburn, 2000).

The range of products that are most advertised reflect socio-economic profile of the population and disposable income levels. Low cost repeat purchase consumables dominated advertising in India as they do in most emerging economies. The first companies to move into new markets in developing countries tend to be in the areas of low cost repeat purchase consumables— cigarettes, fast food, personal products, cleaning products, soft drinks and pharmaceuticals. The changes in the advertising product profile in India in the 1990s reflect changes in the levels of disposable income that occurred in the 1990s for some groups as well as legal changes. According to Srinivas, areas of fierce competition in Indian include soft drinks, toothpaste, soaps and detergents (Srinivas, 1999). In 1992, 90 per cent of the most advertised products were repeat purchase consumables with bath soaps and laundry detergents accounting for 45 per cent of the market. Other products included soft drinks, suiting and textiles, tires, chocolates, cigarettes, tea. The category suiting and textiles reflected the local custom of the people to have their clothes made rather than buying them ready-made (Pashupati and Sengupta, 1996, p.171), but later in the decade this category was no longer a leading advertising product. There was a slight variation in the profile of products advertised on television. In 1993 75 per cent of television advertisements were for five major groups of products— toiletries and detergents, cold drinks, foodstuffs, cosmetics, and health products. Audience research unit at Doordarshan confirmed that 30.1 per cent of advertising was for toiletries and 21.1 per cent was for food and beverages. Consumer durable advertising was seen to be educating the future consumers (Bajpai and Unnikrishnan, 1996).

By the mid 1990s, the key products in terms of overall advertising spending in descending order were, personal care, electronics, cigarette and tobacco, automobiles, pharmaceuticals, food and dairy products, breweries and distilleries, with the strongest growth being in the figures for electronics and cigarettes and tobacco (A&M media report, quoted in the Economist Intelligence Unit Limited, 1997). Products most advertised on Doordarshan included cosmetics, and soap and detergents, while the satellite channels in 1997 tended to attract alcohol, consumer durables, and expensive clothes (*India Business Intelligence,* 1997). In order of importance in 1999 the key products advertised were, soaps and detergents, household appliances, consumer electronics, food and beverages, cosmetics, pharmaceuticals, services and entertainment (Indian Society of Advertisers, Srinivas, 1999). It is interesting that cigarettes and automobiles slipped off the list of most advertised products. Alcohol was banned from print but allowed in pay television until January 2001 (*Multichannel News,* May 2001). Cigarette and tobacco advertising was permitted in print in the 1990s and was banned in December 2000 (Sehgal, 2001).

Advertisers have attempted to improve the sales of products by changing purchasing behaviour, which involves changing traditional values and creating desire for new products. The dominance of foreign advertising means that expenditure is increasing on foreign products and consumers are purchasing more branded products than before. In 1991, Srikandath studied the values depicted in Indian television advertising and concluded that the main values being promoted were technology, modernisation and consumerism. Bajpai and Unnikrishnan found that television was playing a significant role in the expansion of consumer values in Indian society, that children are effectively being groomed to become future consumers, and that values that were being promoted supported those aims— individualism and nuclear family (Bajpai and Unnikrishnan 1996, pp.229-233). Shoma Munshi studied the portrayal of women in the Indian media through a combination of interviews and content analysis, and found that traditional women's roles in the family were being subverted, often with humour and ironic subversion. Women were being given more power through consumerism and traditional roles of women as wives, mothers and daughters-in-law were being modified to reflect social changes (Shoma Munshi 1998).

Body image is another area targeted by advertisers. Hindustan Lever Limited (HLL) used a campaign to sell lipstick aimed at changing the traditional concept of beauty which focuses on hair, skin and eyes, and to make lips the focus of attention. Their television advertisement featured a woman at a tennis match blowing a kiss, her lips being on the large screen, and the crowd going wild. The slogan was: "who's watching your lips today." HLL promoted Fair and Lovely skin whitening cream by linking dark skin colour and career prospects, though thinly disguised as dark skin under the eyes being the problem that was holding the woman back from a career as an air stewardess. This advertising blends the old and the new, promotion of career for women, and also the association of success with pale skin. It won't be acceptable in many Western countries where appearance is no longer legally acceptable as hiring criteria, and reference to skin colour would be a taboo. Procter and Gamble is also using the idea of changing values and perceptions, and in its promotion of Whisper sanitary napkins, it uses information booklets on hygiene and beauty care (Mila, 2002). Another change is reflected in the clothing sector with an increased emphasis on ready-made clothing for women, rather than the traditional sari. In cities traditional male dress is uncommon and most Indian men have adopted western clothing.

Traditional Indian values are seen to still play an important role in advertising in India where they are used to attach value to products (Srinivas, 1999). The portrayal of children in magazine advertisements is higher than in other countries, such as the United States and France. The Indian consumer profile differs from the West, in that it is need driven and this is reinforced by the fact that social welfare system is very fragile, and frugality and savings are valued much, hence extravagant and excessive claims are not seen to be appreciated (*India Tradepoint*, 1995). Language is another area of cultural impact. Indian advertising on television tends to be in Hindi, English or a blend of the two. This bias means that many groups are excluded and reflects the middle classes who are the primary target audiences of advertisers (Bajpai and Unnikrishnan, 1996). Coke has been using a blend of English and Hindi in its advertising, called 'Hinglish' which is seen by *Business Week* as reflecting the fact that the Indian consumer likes a blend and it is part of its latest attempt to focus on the youth market and to make profit after many years of making losses (Kripalani, 2003).

Advertising in India has been concentrated on two key media— print and television, with print on the decline and television on the ascendancy. Advertising is targeted at the group that can be reached through these media. Products tend to be advertised to groups that can afford them, or who are potential purchasers. Advertising strategies vary with the intention of the marketers, especially the international advertisers, their agencies and analyses of the target market. In the early phases of international entry into the Indian market, they targeted the affluent Indians with significant purchasing power and those with disposable income for repeat purchase of consumables and increasingly expanding market of consumer durables. Television advertising was seen to play on the foreign obsessions of many Indians in the early 1990s as well as significantly increasing their desire for advertised products (Bajpai and Unnikrishnan, 1996, p.305). Most academic research into advertising strategies seem to have been studies of print advertising, mainly in magazines, which are admittedly easier to document than more ephemeral television advertising, but which are targeted more at affluent groups. The National Council for Applied Economic Research has identified the "very rich and consuming classes" in India as part of an international class with similar lifestyles and consumption habits. This group is educated, travels, owns houses, cars, consumer appliances, and in India, have servants. Advertising in certain media, especially magazines, is likely to target this group. A cross cultural comparison of magazine advertising in the US, and India and other countries in the late 1980s saw more visual similarities than differences in advertising practices of print advertisements. The magazine profile included *Business India, Reader's Digest, India Today, Femina,* and *Woman's Era* (Cutler et al, 1992).

In a comparative content analysis of magazine advertising in India and the U.S. in 2002, Khairullah and Khairullah found the dominant cultural values to be similar and thus made a case for standardisation of advertising, i.e., using advertising in India primarily developed for the American market. The product range of the advertisements was limited to airlines, cars, cigarettes, computers and hotels (2002). These products have been identified as the most likely to be characterised by standardised advertising (Belch and Belch, 1990, p.754). Another study by Chandra *et. al.*, which investigated whether American standardised advertising was suitable for the Indian market in 2002, found that market segments were similar to the US, and that India had a strong middle class with Western product experience. They recommended the use of American advertising in India, especially in a diverse market. They see that one reason companies use standardised advertising is that they view emerging markets as less significant, and use standardised advertising to cut costs (Chandra, Griffith and Ryans, 2002). Sehgal states that advertising campaigns are seen to be getting much more aggressive and focused in recent years (2000a) which is probably because advertisers are beginning to appreciate the size of the markets and the potential profits to be made in India. There has been considerable increase in market research by key advertisers, with companies like Ogilvie Mather setting up OgilvieOne a marketing agency to help with consumer research, and the establishment of international marketing firms such as MindShare a WPP agency which was launched in India in 2001. MindShare is estimated to have cornered 30 per cent of the Indian advertising market within a year (Media Asia, 2002). There seems to have been less academic research into the advertising of cheap repeat purchase consumables of less affluent markets, though there has been considerable market research by key advertisers (Munshi, 1998). HLL has been the largest advertiser in India almost every year for decades, and personal products are the biggest category in advertising. As the average income in India is still low, a key strategy by large companies like HLL has been to reduce the size of their packages, and sell tiny sachets of detergent and shampoo. This makes the product accessible and gets consumers accustomed to using the product (Kripalani, 2002).

According to *India Business Intelligence* (The Economist Intelligence Unit Limited, 1997), the advertising industry in India has moved from focusing on demand creation to brand creation and the promotion of specific products. The most successful strategy prior to 1997 was seen to be simple and straightforward messages stressing product benefits. An example may be given of Rexona Deodorant sold at Rs. 60, compared to other brands selling at Rs.150-200, and advertised with a campaign saying that body odour is a problem and Rexona is the answer. Another important factor is that the market also needs to be ready for the product, for example an American disposable contact lens company spent Rs 30 million in 1996-1997 on advertising but could not sell its product because of its high price (The Economist Intelligence Unit Limited, 1997). Other reasons could be that if people value frugality they may be reluctant to purchase disposable items as an alternative to reusable lenses, or that they have different values about appearance and wearing glasses. There have been significant changes in recent years and no longer does successful advertising focus only on product benefits, but works through values and value change (Smita 2002). By the late 1990s, multinational companies were seen to be customising their advertising to the Indian market. Product endorsement by celebrities, and associations with national passions like cricket were other strategies used. The Korean company L.G. sponsored the Indian cricket team in the Cricket World Cup in 2003 for example and Adidas, which had previously made their Indian advertisements in London, started making them in India in 1999, with the advertising agency RK Swamy / BBDO and using Indian cricket star Sachin Tendulkar (Chawla, 1999). L'Oreal increased its sales dramatically by using Miss India, later Miss World, Diana Hayden, along with its regular models (Fannin, 1999).

Pashupati and Sengupta state that in the 1990s the profile of rural consumers was starting to change and greater literacy levels meant brand identification was easier and more product information could be supplied. Previously visual characteristics like colour were seen to be a very important factor in identifying the product for the non-literate, for example, the use of red colour in the packaging of Lifebouy soap from HLL. In the 1990s, strategies used to tap the vast rural market included using mobile vans with television sets screening Hindi film songs interspersed with product promotions. Marketing initiatives since 2000 have been precisely targeting rural consumers, who number about 700 million. Activities include setting up e-choupals and HLL's 'Project Shakti.' Through 'Project Shakti' the company supports rural self-help groups to alleviate poverty and reduce disparities in purchasing power. The groups are provided with a range of its products like Lifebuoy Soap, Wheel Detergent, A1 Tea, Nihar Coconut Oil, and Clinic Plus Shampoo. India's rural market makes up nearly 50 per cent of HLL's total sales in India. Project Nova is Hindustan Lever's direct selling network set up to market personal care products and household cleaning products. Other HLL endeavours include expanding its massive distribution network through Project Bharat, and its network reach in rural markets through Operation Streamline (Euromonitor, 2001B). These endeavours sound a little like military operations! Consumer durable companies such as Philips India, LG Electronics, Kodak India, and Samsung India are also launching new initiatives such as Philips's battery free radio (Gupta, 2002). Ogilvie Mather has launched Programme Outreach specifically to target rural consumers and has also set up initiatives to undertake consumer research (Kilburn, 2000).

One of the key challenges for foreign markets in India has been called "de-commodification," changing the pattern of consumer buying from traditional unbranded products to branded products. This was seen as significant both by Reckitt and Coleman and Hindustan Lever. In 1999, HLL acknowledged that the potential for certain branded products was enormous. Another major area for growth was seen to be the establishment of retail outlets, as opposed to the traditional markets, which will further facilitate the sales of branded products (Subramanian, 1999). Coca Cola has tried multiple approaches in the Indian market since it returned in 1993, including buying out key local brands Parle and Thums Up. Though it has not always been able to get its advertising right, for example in 1997 a television commercial showing a child bungy jumping to get a chocolate bar had to be withdrawn after a few children died trying to imitate the advertisement (*Marketing News*, 1997).

More recently, Coca Cola has expanded efforts to market its products to internet users. It has set up a site with competitions and games with the aim of building an online community. The site is www.enjoyzone.com (Smita, 2002). Coca Cola also launched other products— another soft drink 'Sprite,' and bottled water 'Kinley'. Sprite was launched in 1999 with advertising that spoofed advertising hype and current trends in advertising, targeting the youth "in the process of establishing their identity" (Chawla, 1999). In 2001, Kinley bottled water was advertised depicting village life and military families— aimed at building emotional connections with consumers (Kripalani, 2003). The advent of foreign advertisers in India has not always been successful and according to Sehgal, campaigns that failed in its initial stages in India include those by Nike, Reebok, Johnny Walker, Sony, Panasonic, McDonalds and Coca Cola. One of the most dramatically insensitive recent campaigns was that of Cadbury-Schweppes which compared its chocolate to Kashmir: "Too tempting. Too good to share" which caused a major outrage and the advertisement had to be withdrawn (*Economist*, August 8, 2002).

Conclusion

The whole purpose of advertising is to sell products or ideas, so the massive expansion of foreign companies and advertising, whether coming from overseas or created in India, has meant the massive expansion of sale of foreign products. Liberalisation of the Indian economy in the early 1990s has led to an accelerated entry of foreign businesses and foreign advertising agencies to sell the products of foreign origin to the potentially vast Indian market of over a billion people. Though approximately 25 per cent of the population is living at or below the poverty line, the expanding potential market represented by those above the poverty line number hundreds of millions for low priced repeat purchase consumer goods, and many millions for those able to purchase consumer durables and luxury goods. Advertisers are using considerable ingenuity to develop strategies to enter these markets. By the end of the 1990s, most Indian advertising agencies had made strategic alliances with foreign agencies. Major competition is in the low end of the market between the cola giants, personal care products, and soap market, but there is also a rapidly expanding market for electronics, consumer durables, and services. Television and satellite television has been eroding the market dominance of print advertising since the 1990s, but print is still the largest media of advertising, and its reach has also expanded considerably since then. Advertising in the 1990s focused on Hindi and English speaking population, which was predominantly, educated, urban, and middle class. In the 2000s however, major companies have been using strategies to enter the rural market which constitutes the major area for expansion, and the Internet user teenage market.

The increase in advertising expenditure and the promotion of foreign products have impact on our traditional values by undermining traditional habits and behaviours, and creation of new wants and desires, often for products like soft drinks that have no nutritional benefit, and also by strategies that re-work cultural values and beliefs. Traditional roles of men, women, and children are changing as are the concepts of beauty, identity, and personal hygiene. The overall impact of massive increase of foreign advertising is the acceleration of India into the culture and ideology of consumerism, the expansion of foreign businesses into India, and export of profits to foreign corporations.

Cited Works

Ahluwalia, I.J., Mohan, R. and Goswami, O. (1996). *Policy Reforms in India*. Paris, UNESCO.

Bajpai, S. and Unnikrishnan, N. (1996). *The Impact of Television Advertising on Children*. New Delhi, Sage.

Belch, G.E. and Belch, M.A. (1990). *Introduction to Advertising and Marketing*. Burr Ridge, Illinois, Irwin.

Bennet, D. (2000). "American Culture and Advertising." Monye, S.O. (Ed). *The Handbook of International Marketing Communications.* Oxford, Blackwell.

Cateora, P.R. (2002). *International marketing.* (11th Edition). Boston. Irwin-McGraw Hill.

Chandra, A., Griffith D.A. and Ryans, J.K. (2002). "Advertising Standardisation in India." *International Journal of Advertising,* 21, (1). pp.47-66.

Chawla, I. (1999, April 12). "Marketers Shift in India." *Advertising Age International.* p.13.

Cheng, H. "Advertising in China: A Socialist Experiment." In Frith, K. (Ed). *Advertising Asia.* pp.73-102. Ames, Iowa State University Press.

CIA. World Fact Book retrieved from: http://ciagov/publications/factbook/goes/in.html#Econ

Crowther, G., Raj, P. and Wheeler, T. (1984). *India: A Travel Survival Guide.* (2nd Ed.) South Yarra, Vic. Lonely Planet.

Cutler, B., Erranilli, M.K. and Javalgi, R. (1992). "The Visual Components of Print Advertising: A Five-Country Cross-Cultural Analysis." *European Journal of Marketing.* 26, (4), pp.7-20.

Dyer,G. (1995). *Advertising as communication.* London, Routledge.

Fannin, R. (1999, 8 February). "Q&A, ask the expert." *Advertising Age International.* p.6.

Hargrave-Silk, A. (2002, June 28th). "Privatisation Expected To Fuel Adspend." *Media Asia.* p.11.

Hargrave-Silk, A. (2003, 1 October). "Benetton Moves Brief to Burnett After India Pitch." *Media Asia.* p.5.

India Business Intelligence. (1997, August). "Growing Up." The Economist Intelligence Unit Limited.

India Business Intelligence. (1998, January). "Tooth and Nail." The Economist Intelligence Unit Limited.

"India Permits Foreign Ads." (1993, October 4th). *Advertising Age.* 64 (42), p.61.

Jones, P. (Ed.). (2000). *International Advertising: Realities and Myths.* London, Sage.

Khan, M.M.A. (1995, May 15). "Enormity Tempts Marketers to Make a Passage to India." *Advertising Age,* p.12.

Kilburn, D. (2000, 13th November). "Marketing to Reach Rural India." *Marketing Magazine.* 105 (45), p.6.

Kripalani, M. (2002, 10 June). "Battling for Pennies In India's Villages:

Coke and Pepsi Struggle to Control Market." *Business Week.* (3786), p.18.

Kripalani, M. (2003, February 10). "Finally Coke Gets It Right." *Business Week.* (3819), p.18.

Khairullah, H. Z. and Khairullah, Z.Y. (2002). "Dominant Cultural Values: Content Analysis of The U.S. and The Indian Print Advertisements." *Journal of Global Marketing.* 16, (1/2), pp. 47-70.

Levitt, T. (1983). "The Globalisation of Markets." *Harvard Business Review.* 61(3). pp.92-102.

Marketing News. (1997, August 18th). "Coca Cola Pulls Ad." 31(17), p.7.

Mattelart, A. (1991). *Advertising International.* London and New York, Routledge.

"MindShare Keeps India Rivals at Bay." (2002, 13 December). *Media Asia.* p.14.

Munshi, S. (1998). "Wife / Mother / Daughter-in-Law: Multiple Avatars of Homemaker In 1990s Indian Advertising." *Media, Culture and Society.* London. (20), pp.573-591.

"O&M Buys Indian Shop to Aid WPP growth." (1997, July 14th). *Advertising Age.* 68, (28), p.31.

Pashupati, K. and Sengupta, S. (1996). "Advertising in India: The Winds of Change." In Frith, K.T. (Ed). *Advertising in Asia: Communication, Culture and Consumption.* Ames, Iowa State University Press. pp.155-186.

Sachdeva, S. (1984). Institute for Studies in Industrial Development. New Delhi.

Sehgal, R. (2000a, April) "Sunny Skies Ahead for Indian Channels." Multinational News International. 6 (4), p.10.

Sehgal, R. (2000b, July-August) "India's Renaissance." *Multinational News International.* 6 (7), p.10.

Sehgal, R. (2000c, 25 September). "India Clamps Down on Vice, Piracy." *Multinational News International.* 21 (39), p.49.

Sehgal, R. (2001, May) "Kiss and sell? Don't try it in India." *Multinational News International.* 7(4), p.8.

Slind-Flor, V. (2001b, December). "The Cola Wars, Indian Style." *IP Worldwide.* p.18.

Smita, G. (2002, 14 June). "Coke and Pepsi Take Battle to Cyberspace." *Media Asia.* p.9.

Smita, G. (2002, 12 September). "Modern Messages Told the Traditional Indian Way." *Media Asia.* p.12.

Srikandath, S. (1991). "Cultural Values Depicted in Indian Television Advertising." *International Journal of Mass Communication Studies.*

Srinivas, P. (1999). Advertising services: India. New Delhi, U.S. Foreign Commercial Service, and U.S. Department of State. Retrieved from: http://www.tradeport.org.ts/countries/isa/isar0012.html

The Economist Intelligence Unit Limited. (1998, 9 February). "Darwinian Struggles." *Business Asia.*

Vilanilam, J. (1989). "Television Advertising and the Indian Poor." *Media, Culture and Society*. London. (11) 4, pp.485-497.

World Bank. (2002). "Information and Communication Technologies: India Table." Retrieved from: worldbank.org/data

World Bank. (2004). "Information and Communication Technologies: India Table." Retrieved from: worldbank.org/data

Worsley, P. (1984). *The Three Worlds, Culture and World Development.* Chicago, University of Chicago Press.

19

Communication and Leadership: Essential Traits

—Sunil K. Rai

Communication is a process that allows organisms to exchange information by several methods. Exchange requires feedback. The word communication is also used in the context where little or no feedback is expected such as broadcasting, or where the feedback may be delayed as the sender or receiver uses different methods, technologies, timing and means. For many of the problems that occur in an organisation is the direct result of people failing to communicate. Faulty communication often causes most of the problems. It leads to confusion and can cause a good plan to fail. Communication is the exchange and flow of information and ideas from one person to another. It involves a sender transmitting an idea to a receiver. Effective communication occurs only if the receiver understands the exact information or idea that the sender intended to transmit.

Studying the communication process is important because you coach, coordinate, counsel, evaluate and supervise through this process. It is the chain of understanding that integrates the members of an organisation from top to bottom, bottom to top, and side to side. In the case of visual arts, the work, as Derrida reminds us, is conceived of as a receptacle or dwelling place for meaning, one whose borders are both clearly defined and consistently repressed to provide the spectator with easy access to its centre and seat. In this respect Derrida's philosophical inquiry is exemplary, and the structural resemblance between linguistic and visual or architectural models is reinforced, for the hierarchical relation between speeches and writing that deconstruction analyses and seeks to displace is traditionally described in terms of that between an inside and an outside. Speech is held to remain within the closed circuit defined by the speaker and listener, disappearing into the fold of immediate comprehension, forgetting the spacing that constitutes it. Writing, on the other hand, cannot but fall outside, into an unavoidable materiality, and its materiality ensures that it will function outside of the control of its producer, from where it will always threaten the integrity of the supposed intact system of speech. The means by which speech then both rejects and co-opts writing in order to perpetuate its position of priority—indeed, the means by which this operation repeats itself throughout any areas of Western thinking—has been referred to by Derrida as an 'economy', from the Hellenic (*oikos*) for 'house'. Derrida's work aims to break down or re-arrange the walls of that house, exposing its inside to previously unseen aspects of its outside, reconstructing different accommodations of space, forcing different means of access, reworking its principles of what it contains. Philosophy since Plato has concerned itself into understanding the metaphysical framework of reality, which questions and apprehends reason as its domain. Language is then subservient to philosophising; it is, all the more, a medium to communicate ideas through ages. However, there is twist of fate, a reversal from this linearity of tradition, or more precisely the retaliation of language against the 'metaphysics of conformity'.

It was Wittgenstein who then positioned language as a philosophical interest—the object of scrutiny and the subject for scrutinising philosophy in particular and reality in general. The Structuralists from Saussure and Barthes to Levi-Strauss delineated language as the reductionistic or absolutist explanation of all. That in simple term means that everything can be reduced to language—from simple utterance, myths, laws, culture, and society up to the supra-structure of relational or corelational of all these items as governed by linguistic patterns, rules and principles.

Because of this regimentation of reality in all its intelligible and unintelligible aspects, Jacques Derrida deconstructs this linguistic utopia of the Structuralists. He conceptualised difference (with an 'a') to distance itself from difference that the

Structuralists appropriated to language. For the Structuralists, there is no fixed meaning but only relational and 'differential' patterns of language. But it is contended that language is the limit of the logos (philosophy) and the text (literature). The language of debate therefore speaks of critique against the debate and the language used in the debate. The debate refers to deconstruction while the language explores the framework of which this debate runs through in reason (logos) and in meaning (text).

Communication is what we try to do speak to those near us. It involves:

- *Thought*: First, information exists in the mind of the sender. This can be a concept, idea, information, or feelings.
- *Encoding*: Next, a message is sent to a receiver in words or other symbols.
- *Decoding*: Lastly, the receiver translates words or symbols into a concept or information that he or she can understand.

During the transmitting of the message, two processes will be received by the receiver: content and context. Content is the actual words or symbols of the message which is known as language—the spoken and written words combined into phrases that make grammatical and semantic sense. We all use and interpret the meanings of words differently, so even simple messages can be misunderstood. And many words have different meanings to confuse the issue even more.

Context is the way the message is delivered and is known as Paralanguage. It includes the tone of voice, the look in the sender's eye's, body language, hand gestures, and state of emotions (anger, fear, uncertainty, confidence, etc.) that can be detected. Although paralanguage or context often causes messages to be misunderstood as we believe what we see more than what we hear; they are powerful communicators that help us to understand each other. Indeed, we often trust the accuracy of non-verbal behaviours more than verbal behaviours.

Some leaders think they have communicated once they told someone to do something, "I don't know why it did not get done...I told Jim to it." More than likely, Jim misunderstood the message. A message has not been communicated unless it is understood by the receiver (decoded). How do you know it has been properly received? By two-way communication or feedback? This feedback tells the sender that the receiver understood the message, its level of importance, and what must be done with it. Communication is an exchange, not just a giving, as all parties must participate to complete the information exchange.

Barriers to Communication

Anything that prevents understanding of the message is a barrier to communication. Many physical and psychological barriers exist:

— *Culture, background, and bias*: We allow our past experiences to change the meaning of the message. Our culture, background, and bias can be good as they allow us to use our past experiences to understand something new, it is when they change the meaning of the message then they interfere with the communication process.

— *Noise*: Equipment or environmental noise impedes clear communication. The sender and the receiver must both be able to concentrate on the messages being sent to each other.

We focusing on ourselves, rather than the other person can lead to confusion and conflict. The "Me Generation" is out when it comes to effective communication. Some of the factors that cause this are defensiveness (we feel someone is attacking us), superiority (we feel we know more that the other), and ego (we feel we are the centre of the activity).

— *Perception*: If we feel the person is talking too fast, not fluently, does not articulate clearly, etc., we may dismiss the person. Also our preconceived attitudes affect our ability to listen. We listen uncritically to persons of high status and dismiss those of low status.

— *Message*: Distractions happen when we focus on the facts rather than the idea. Our educational institutions reinforce this with tests and questions. Semantic distractions occur when a word is used differently than you prefer. For example, the word chairman instead of chairperson may cause you to focus on the word and not the message.

- *Environment*: Bright lights, an attractive person, unusual sights, or any other stimulus provides a potential distraction.
- *Smothering*: We take it for granted that the impulse to send useful information is automatic. Not true! Too often we believe that certain information has no value to others or they are already aware of the facts.
- *Stress*: People do not see things the same way when under stress. What we see and believe at a given moment is influenced by our psychological frames of references—our beliefs, values, knowledge, experiences, and goals.

Active Listening

Hearing and listening are not the same thing. Hearing is the act of perceiving sound. It is involuntary and simply refers to the reception of aural stimuli. Listening is a selective activity which involves the reception and the interpretation of aural stimuli. It involves decoding the sound into meaning. Listening is divided into two main categories: passive and active. Passive listening is little more that hearing. It occurs when the receiver or the message has little motivation to listen carefully, such as music, story telling, television, or being polite.

People speak at 100 to 175 words per minute, but they can listen intelligently at 600 to 800 words per minute (WPM). Since only a part of our mind is paying attention, it is easy to go into mind drift - thinking about other things while listening to someone. The cure for this is active listening - which involves listening with a purpose. It may be to gain information, obtain directions, understand others, solve problems, share interest, see how another person feels, show support, etc. It requires that the listener attends to the words and the feelings of the sender for understanding. It takes the same amount or more energy than speaking. It requires the receiver to hear the various messages, understand the meaning, and then verify the meaning by offering feedback. The following are a few traits of active listeners:

- One should spend more time listening than talking.
- Do not finish the sentence of others.
- Do not answer questions with questions.

- We all are aware of biases. We all have them...we need to control them.
- Never daydream or become preoccupied with our own thoughts when others talk.
- Lets the other speaker talk and avoid dominating the conversation.
- Plans responses after the other person has finished speaking ...NOT while they are speaking.
- Provide feedback, but not interrupt incessantly.
- Keep the conversation on what the speaker says...NOT on what interests them.
- Take brief notes. This forces them to concentrate on what is being said.
- Nonverbal behaviours of communication
- Without knowing the force of words it is impossible to know men." —Confucius

To deliver the full impact of a message, use nonverbal behaviours to raise the channel of interpersonal communication:

- *Eye contact*: This helps to regulate the flow of communication. It signals interest in others and increases the speaker's credibility. People who make eye contact open the flow of communication and convey interest, concern, warmth, and credibility.
- *Facial Expressions*: Smiling is a powerful cue that transmits happiness, friendliness, warmth, and liking. So, if you smile frequently you will be perceived as more likable, friendly, warm and approachable. Smiling is often contagious and people will react favourably. They will be more comfortable around you and will want to listen more.
- *Gestures*: If you fail to gesture while speaking, you may be perceived as boring and stiff. A lively speaking style captures the listener's attention, makes the conversation more interesting, and facilitates understanding.
- *Posture and body orientation*: You communicate numerous messages by the way you talk and move. Standing erect and leaning forward communicates to listeners that you are approachable, receptive and friendly. Interpersonal

closeness results when you and the listener face each other. Speaking with your back turned or looking at the floor or ceiling should be avoided as it communicates disinterest.

- *Proximity*: Cultural norms dictate a comfortable distance for interaction with others. You should look for signals of discomfort caused by invading the other person's space. Some of these are: rocking, leg swinging, tapping, and gaze aversion.
- *Vocal*: Speaking can signal nonverbal communication when you include such vocal elements as: tone, pitch, rhythm, timbre, loudness, and inflection. For maximum teaching effectiveness, learn to vary these six elements of your voice. One of the major criticisms of many speakers is that they speak in a monotone voice. Listeners perceive this type of speaker as boring and dull.

Communication Theory

Communication as a named and unified discipline has a history of contestation that goes back to the Socratic dialogues, in many ways making it the first and most contestatory of all early sciences and philosophies. Aristotle first addressed the problem of communication and attempted to work out a theory of it in *The Rhetoric*. He had primarily focused on the art of persuasion. Some of the prominent communication theories are referred here. Theories can also be studied and organised according to the ontological, epistemological, and axiological framework imposed by the theorist.

Ontology is a study of conceptions of reality and the nature of being. In philosophy, ontology is the study of being or existence and forms the basic subject matter of metaphysics. It seeks to describe or posit the basic categories and relationships of being or existence to define entities and types of entities within its framework. It is the science of what is, of the kinds and structures of the objects, properties and relations in every area of reality. Ontology essentially poses the question of what, exactly, is the theorist examining. One must consider the very nature of reality. The answer usually falls in one of three realms depending on whether the theorist sees the phenomena through the lens of a realist, nominalist, or social constructionist. Realist perspective views the world objectively, believing that there is a world outside our own experience and cognitions.

The subject of ontology is the study of the categories of things that exist or may exist in some domain. The product of such a study, called ontology, is a catalogue of the types of things that are assumed to exist in a domain of interest D from the perspective of a person who uses a language L for the purpose of talking about D. The types in the ontology represent the predicates, word senses, or concept and relation types of the language L when used to discuss topics in the domain D.

An uninterrupted logic, such as predicate calculus, conceptual graphs, or KIF, is ontologically neutral. It imposes no constraints on the subject matter or the way the subject may be characterised. By itself, logic says nothing about anything, but the combination of logic with an ontology provides a language that can express relationships about the entities in the domain of interest.

The basic categories and distinctions have been derived from a variety of sources in logic, linguistics, philosophy, and artificial intelligence. The two most important influences have been the philosophers Charles Sanders Peirce and Alfred North Whitehead, who were pioneers in symbolic logic. Peirce was also an associate editor of the Century Dictionary, for which he wrote, revised, or edited over 16,000 definitions. In calling that task "stupendous," he was looking beyond his personal experience of writing definitions in English to the task of stating complete definitions in logic, which he said was "a labor for generations of analysts, not for one." That labor, for which there was little practical application in the 19th century, is a major challenge for the 21st. Without it, there is no hope of merging and integrating the ever expanding and multiplying databases and knowledge bases around the world.

Yet as Shakespeare observed, any philosophy is destined to be incomplete. The continuing advance of science and human experience inevitably leads to new words and ideas that require extensions to any proposed system of categories. Whitehead's motto is the best guideline for any philosopher or scientist: "We must be systematic, but we should keep our systems open." Figure below shows beverage types classified according to the attributes

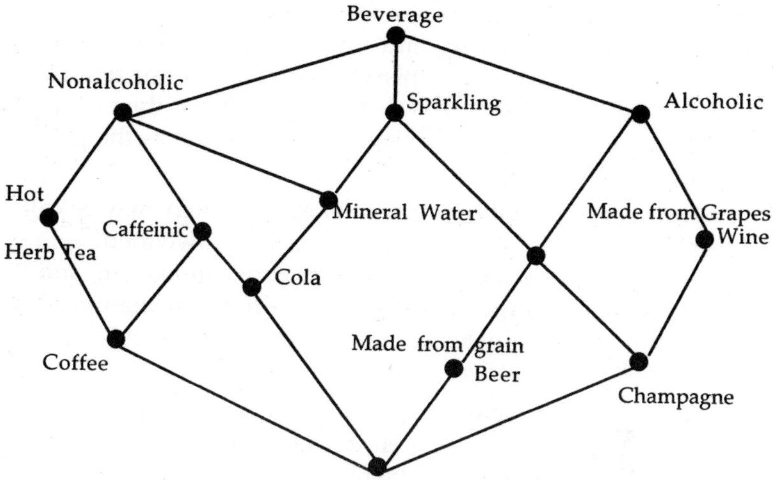

Figure 1: A Lattice Constructed by the Method of Formal Concept Analysis

below shows beverage types classified according to the attributes alcoholic, nonalcoholic, hot, sparkling, caffeineic made From Grapes, and made From Grain. This lattice was derived from the attributes by the method of formal concept analysis.

Epistemology is an examination of how the theorist studies the chosen phenomena. In studying epistemology, objective knowledge is said to be the result of a systematic look at the causal relationships of phenomena. This knowledge is usually attained through use of the scientific method. Scholars often think that empirical evidence collected in an objective manner is most likely to reflect truth in the findings. Theories of this ilk are usually created to predict a phenomenon. Subjective theory holds that understanding is based on situated knowledge, typically found using interpretative methodology such as ethnography and interviews. Subjective theories are typically developed to explain or understand phenomena in the social world.

In Plato's view knowledge is merely an awareness of absolute, universal Ideas or Forms, existing independent of any subject trying to apprehend to them. Though Aristotle puts more emphasis on logical and empirical methods for gathering knowledge, he still accepts the view that such knowledge is an apprehension of necessary and universal principles. Following the Renaissance, two main epistemological positions dominated philosophy: empiricism, which sees knowledge as the product of sensory perception, and rationalism which sees it as the product of rational reflection.

The next stage of development of epistemology may be called pragmatic. Parts of it can be found in early twentieth century approaches, such as logical positivism, conventionalism, and the "Copenhagen interpretation" of quantum mechanics. This philosophy still dominates most present work in cognitive science and artificial intelligence.

According to pragmatic epistemology, knowledge consists of models that attempt to represent the environment in such a way as to maximally simplify problem solving. It is assumed that no model can ever hope to capture all relevant information, and even if such a complete model would exist, it would be too complicated to use in any practical way. Therefore, we must accept the parallel existence of different models, even though they may seem contradictory. The model which is to be chosen depends on the problems that are to be solved. The basic criterion is that the model should produce correct (or approximate) predictions (which may be tested) or problem-solutions, and be as simple as possible. Further questions about the "Ding an Sich" or ultimate reality behind the model are meaningless.

Ferdinand de Saussure in his *Course in General Linguistics* (1916), laid down the principles of this linguistic project. The first principle elaborates the arbitrariness of the 'sign'. The concept of the sign is the kernel of language according to Saussure. 'The study of the nature of the linguistic sign helps us understand the structure of all (even non-linguistic) signs' (Selden, 76). The sign is composed of two underlying concepts—the signifier and the signified. The signifier is any spoken or written element and the idea or notion produced from this element is the signified. Thus the word tree (signifier) could signify stillness or courage (signified) depending on how the writer or the speaker produces the connection and meaning. For Saussure then, language is a system of signs with the signifier and the signified completing such system. The interplay of these two makes the language no natural connection between a 'tree' (word) and an 'acacia' (the reference). In other words, a word is formed correlatively depending on who is speaking.

Every nation has its own language, its own way of arbitrarily assigning word to mean what it is. For instance, here in the Philippines the 'tree' becomes puno but in such no way that it refers only to acacia, pine tree, etc. Each word in this signification must be thought of as it is without any reference if this 'it is' exists or refers to reality (that is, puno-acacia). 'This is common sense; otherwise we would have difficulty in explaining the existence of different languages (Selden 1989). Furthermore, a word establishes meaning through its smallest unit of sound, the phoneme. It means that what differentiates a 'tree' and 'free' is the sound t/f. We derive meaning by its sound and consequently by way it appears when written.

The second principle is Saussure's la langue and parole. For him, 'langue is something that is at once social—langue is the possession of the community of speakers—and constraining, langue is something fixed; parole is the realm of freedom' (Jackson, 42). The langue (that is, as language) is the system where all significations rest. Parallel with this, we can say that Filipino as a language is typically the Saussurean langue and the outgrowth of this with its present jargon, slang, neologism, and attachment with the English language is where the realm of parole stands. Jonathan Culler has something to say about this:

> 'A language is thus conceived as a system of differences, and this leads to the development of the distinctions on which structuralism and semiotics have relied: between a language as a system of differences (langue) and the speech events which the system makes possible (parole)...and between the two constituents of the sign, signifier and the signified (1982: 98).'

Saussure hence accentuates the primary defense or strength of his project that "in the linguistic system there are only differences, without positive terms(Saussure, 166)". Here is where Derrida enters because for him this claim for linguistic difference or differentiation is problematic. He also articulates the valorising appropriated by Saussure to sound, phoneme or speech at the expense of writing. It is said that because Derrida has left a destructive imprint on Saussure's works in particular and in structuralism in general, critics have typed-cast Derrida as a post-structuralist. Without much attention with this typecasting, he only proceeds with his framework.

Derrida's attack on Saussure's concept of difference, phonemes and privileging of speech shall be discussed after a treatment of a framework used as a critique, and even far more violent as a critique. This framework—which has captivated modern thinkers and until now, has been a subject of intellectual debate among philosophers, scholars, literary theorists, teachers, students and many others—is known as deconstruction. In a philosophical discourse the apparent division and opposition had been very prevalent to pair terms like soul/body, being/non-being, mind/matter, good/bad, essence/existence and so on. All of these hierarchies according to Derrida, which in some degree, venerated as something that has reached a certain truth or value must be consistently transformed. To quote him,

> I believe that every conceptual breakthrough amount to transforming, that is, to deforming, an accredited, authorised relationship between a word and a concept, between a trope and what one had every interest to consider to be an unshiftable primary sense, a proper, literal or current usage...All of this is grouped together under the title of deconstruction (Montefiore, 40-41)...'

In this process of transforming and deforming any relationship of opposition, 'the deconstructor proceeds then by reversing the hierarchy, not perversely, but by discerning a chink in the discourse which allows their reversal (Selden, 89)'.

Derrida makes his attack or criticism by reading the philosophies of past thinkers. His approach needs the examination of what has been written before (the text). In this particular textual discourse, he looks for inconstancies, intricacies, ironies...etc. that may serve to start any attack. 'Deconstruction is the critical procedure by which this supposed other is unearthed and shown to be an operative if invisible in an ongoing scheme of meaning (Fay, 130)'. In relation with this, reversal happens within the structure or content it wants to deconstruct. It works internally and further scrutinises the hierarchy that maintains that conformity. Derrida is adamantly against a metaphysics of conformity and presence. But 'the point is not simply to invert the values of a common place hierarchical distinction but to push the enquiry much further back and ask what presuppositions are concealed by the structural difference in question' (Norris, 215). This is very important in the next point of deconstruction, which is displacement.

Displacement happens in order to demystify a so called return to hierarchy after a reversal of oppositions. In this sense, a deconstructor eliminates the possibility of conforming to valorise the reversed of the opposition (e.g., matter/mind). The chain of hierarchies is therefore shattered by assuming that no equilibrium shall forge again. In other words, displacement destroys conformity. Raman Selden puts this by saying that:

> The newly asserted hierarchy is itself displaced and is not allowed to install a new 'truth' or structural fixity. The rule of indeterminacy prevails. While structuralists had treated binary oppositions as stable terms in a formal structure, Derrida sees them as organised in unstable disequilibrium (1989: 89).

Truth here refers to conformity or acceptance of an edifying structure of meanings and values imposed universally just like the privileging of soul over body and so on. The rule of indeterminacy implies here the resistance to closure; otherwise a possible conformity will rise again. Because of this there is no fixed meaning as for language that has no universal claim for structuring. Language is indeterminate, interminable and thus man cannot exhaust within and beyond the possibilities of meanings.

Following this argument, deconstruction manifests the 'un-closure' of discourse whether textual, cultural, political, etc. Philosophy also as inferred must remain un-closed to be able to disclose at the same time the endless possibilities of interpretation, understanding and criticism. "Deconstructionists seek indeterminacy, self-subversion, transgression, vertigo and aphoria, and find them anywhere..."(Harwood, 180). Hence in can be surmised that there is no finality in deconstruction. Any attempt to reach a verdict of truth or truth-claims applying deconstruction is only a beginning, an end or whatever, because such claim to truth is furthered to an endless scrutiny, to an aphoria of deconstruction. "Argument by deferral and complication is the characteristic of Derridarean mode, 'interminable'...haunted by infinite regress and yet insisting on the ethical imperative to proceed in no other way" (Harwood, 164). Entering into deconstruction is like an endless labyrinth with no entrance and exit. If indeed there is, outside the labyrinth is another endless one. Here re-deconstruction persists to an infinite, interminable task, again and again.

The pragmatic epistemology does not give a clear answer to the question where knowledge or models come from. There is an implicit assumption that models are built from parts of other models and empirical data on the basis of trial and error complemented with some heuristics or intuition. A more radical point of departure is offered by constructivism. It assumes that all knowledge is built up from scratch by the subject of knowledge. There are no 'givens', neither objective empirical data or facts, nor inborn categories or cognitive structures. The idea of a correspondence or reflection of external reality is rejected. Because of this lacking connection between models and the things they represent, the danger with constructivism is that it may lead to relativism, to the idea that any model constructed by a subject is as good as any other and that there is no way to distinguish adequate. A most recent, and perhaps most radical approach, extends this evolutionary view in order to make knowledge actively pursue goals of its own. This approach, which as yet has not had the time to develop a proper epistemology, may be called mimetic. It notes that knowledge can be transmitted from one subject to another, and thereby loses its dependence on any single individual. A piece of knowledge that can be transmitted or replicated in such a way is called a 'meme'. The death of an individual carrying a certain meme now no longer implies the elimination of that piece of knowledge, as evolutionary epistemology would assume. As long as a meme spreads more quickly to new carriers, than that its carriers die, the meme will proliferate, even though the knowledge it induces in any individual carrier may be wholly inadequate and even dangerous to survival. In this view a piece of knowledge may be successful (in the sense that it is common or has many carriers) even though its predictions may be totally wrong, as long as it is sufficiently 'convincing' to new carriers. Here we see a picture where even the subject of knowledge has lost its primacy, and knowledge becomes a force of its own with proper goals and ways of developing itself. That this is realistic can be illustrated by the many superstitions, fads, and irrational beliefs that have spread over the globe, sometimes with a frightening speed. It is better to quote Aristotle here:

> The gods love wisdom or desire to become wise, for they are wise already — nor if someone else is wise, none of the gods love wisdom or desire to become wise, for they are wise already — nor if someone else is wise, do they love wisdom. Neither do the ignorant love wisdom or desire to become wise; for this is the grievous thing about ignorance, that those who are neither good nor beautiful nor sensible think they are good enough, and do not desire that which they do not think they are lacking.
>
> *Plato, Symposium 203E-204A*

Works Cited

Butler, Gillian, Ph.D. and Hope, Tony, M.D. (1996). *Managing Your Mind.* New York: Oxford University Press.

Mehrabian, Albert and Morton Wiener, 1967, "Decoding of inconsistent communications", *Journal of Personality and Social Psychology* 6:109-114

Mehrabian, Albert and Susan R. Ferris, 1967, "Inference of attitudes from nonverbal communication in two channels," *Journal of Consulting Psychology* 31:248-252.

Pearson, J. (1983). *Interpersonal Communication.* Glenview, Illinois: Scott, Foreman and Company.

Pinker, Steven (1997). *How the Minds Works.* New York: W. W. Norton & Company

Littlejohn, S. W. *Theories of human communication.* 7th edition, Belmont, CA: Wadsworth, 2002.

Emory A Griffin, *A first look at communication theory.* 3rd edition, New York: McGraw-Hill, 1997.

Miller, K., *Communication Theories: Perspectives, processes, and contexts.* 2nd edition. New York: McGraw-Hill, 2005.

Werner, E., "Cooperating Agents: A Unified Theory of Communication and Social Structure", *Distributed Artificial Intelligence,* Vol. 2, L. Gasser and M. Huhns, eds., Morgan Kaufmann and Pitman Press, 1989.

Sense, Reference, and Philosophy, Jerrold J. Katz, Oxford, 2004 [25.5K].

Meaning and Naming in Michael Devitt and Kim Sterelny's *Language and Reality,* MIT Press, 1999 [23.2K].

Words and Rules, The Ingredients of Language, Steven Pinker, Basic Books, 1999 [13.0K].

Evidence and Inquiry, Towards Reconstruction in Epistemology, Susan Haack, Blackwell, 1993 [14.5K].

Beyond Objectivism and Relativism: Science, Hermeneutics, and Praxis, Richard J. Bernstein, University of Pennsylvania Press, 1983 [25.7K].

Culler, Jonathan, 1982, *On Deconstruction,* (Cornell University Press).

Derrida, Jacques, 1967, 'Speech and Phenomenon' in Kamuf Peggy (ed.) 1991, *A Derrida Reader* (London: Harvester Wheatsheaf).

______________ . 1967 (trans. Gayatri Spivak 1974) 'Of Grammatology'

______________ . 1967 'Writing and Difference'.

______________ . 1972 (trans. Alan Bass 1982) 'Margins of Philosophy'

______________ . 1972 (trans. B. Johnson 1981) 'Dissemination'

Empiricus, Sextus (trans., R. G. Bury 1933) *Outlines of Pyrrhonism* (Cambridge: Harvard University Press).

Fay, Brian, 1996, *Contemporary Philosophy of Social Science* (New York: Blackwell Publishers).

Index